Theda Bara

ALSO BY ROY LIEBMAN
AND FROM McFARLAND

*The Ritz Brothers: The Films, Television Shows and Other
Career Highlights of the Famous Comedy Trio* (2021)

Broadway Actors in Films, 1894–2015 (2017)

Musical Groups in the Movies, 1929–1970 (2009)

*Vitaphone Films: A Catalogue of the Features
and Shorts* (2003; paperback 2010)

*The Wampas Baby Stars: A Biographical Dictionary,
1922–1934* (2000; paperback 2009)

*From Silents to Sound: A Biographical Encyclopedia of Performers
Who Made the Transition to Talking Pictures* (1998; paperback 2009)

*Silent Film Performers: An Annotated Bibliography of Published,
Unpublished and Archival Sources for More Than 350
Actors and Actresses* (1996; paperback 2012)

Theda Bara
Her Career, Life and Legend

Roy Liebman

McFarland & Company, Inc., Publishers
Jefferson, North Carolina

All illustrations are courtesy Phillip Dye.

ISBN (print) 978-1-4766-8725-4
ISBN (ebook) 978-1-4766-5002-9

LIBRARY OF CONGRESS AND BRITISH LIBRARY
CATALOGUING DATA ARE AVAILABLE

Library of Congress Control Number 2023028491

© 2023 Roy Liebman. All rights reserved

No part of this book may be reproduced or transmitted in any form or by any means, electronic or mechanical, including photocopying or recording, or by any information storage and retrieval system, without permission in writing from the publisher.

Front cover image: A striking example of Fox poster art for *The She-Devil*, a 1918 film. Bara thought this was her first comedy; the Fox studio had different ideas (courtesy of Phillip Dye).

Printed in the United States of America

McFarland & Company, Inc., Publishers
Box 611, Jefferson, North Carolina 28640
www.mcfarlandpub.com

To my family:
Janine Liebman, Marissa Foss, Hannah Tragesser,
and Russell Foss. And to my four-legged family member, Honey,
and the undying memories of her predecessors, Twinkie and Coco.

Acknowledgments

Theda Bara did actually exist beyond all the stills and photographs, but she had been almost forgotten as a flesh-and-blood person for many decades. That this ultimately did not stand is due to the work of film historians such as Phillip Dye, Hugh Neely, and Eve Golden who brought her back from obscurity. I am happy to stand with them in extending what we know about this once world-famous star.

Kudos to the television and movie documentarians who included her in their work. And kudos to those who have developed websites which help researchers like me to uncover more interesting facts about the subject of this book. Primary sources have become available on sites such as the invaluable Media History Project. Future researchers can now build, as I have, on the work of their predecessors.

Table of Contents

Acknowledgments   vi
Preface   1
Introduction   3

Theda Bara: The Life and Legend   7
The Feature Films   28
The Short Subjects   165
Archival Appearances: Film and Television   170
Onstage   186
Miscellany   194

Appendix: Film Censorship in the Mid-1910s   203
Bibliography   205
Index   209

Preface

In a way, this book is the happy culmination of an idea I first had 60 years ago. In 1963 I began extensive research with the goal of writing the first full-length book about silent film star Theda Bara. Accessing her memorabilia housed at the old Theater Collection of the New York Public Library was my starting point. By a circuitous route I had become interested in an actress I had never heard of until, as a college student on vacation, I entered the grand lobby of the Library of Congress. Staring hypnotically at me was a huge photographic blow-up of an exotic woman with dark-rimmed eyes. It was my first glimpse of Theda Bara. Upon her death the following year I learned about her fabled but brief career as a silent superstar.

Silent movies then were something I only knew about from local television shows which ruthlessly cut them, sped them up, and satirized them with supposedly humorous voiceovers. (See *Flicker Flashbacks #2* in the *Archival Appearances* section.) As an art form, silent films seemed to be largely overlooked in the 1960s. I had no interest in film history of any kind then, but fortunately the Silent Movie Theatre in Los Angeles was still true to its name. It was there that I really began to appreciate the art of the silent cinema.

One of the films screened was the apparently original uncut version of Bara's last film performance, the 1926 Hal Roach comedy *Madame Mystery*. Then a work colleague casually mentioned that she had been a next-door neighbor of Mrs. Charles Brabin, née Theodosia Goodman/Theda Bara, in Beverly Hills. I was gradually becoming "hooked" and made the decision to go back to my hometown, New York. During that visit I arranged to see the 1915 film that made her an instant star, *A Fool There Was*, at the Museum of Modern Art (MOMA).

At a time when the average movie ticket cost 85 cents, I gladly paid $10 to sit alone in MOMA's plush auditorium. While there, I obtained contact information for Frank Powell, the film's director, and received in return a postcard written in the spidery handwriting of a very old man. He was surprised that anyone was still interested in him or Theda Bara. He advised me to apply to the Library of Congress for information, an ironic suggestion considering that is where I first "saw" her.

My manuscript was completed in the mid–1960s and was submitted to a publisher that had done several *Films of…* books. I was eventually informed that although they had liked the manuscript, there was *absolutely no interest in silent films*. Gradually, this benign neglect came to be redressed, and the reputation of Theda Bara along with it. A 1968 *Films in Review* article and many film books had some kind of account of her career. In 1971 another of her films, *East Lynne*, was rediscovered. There was a 1972 master's thesis titled *Theda Bara and the Vamp Phenomenon*. Although not everything that was written was completely accurate, it was a start.

Her name had not completely fallen into total obscurity, but with almost all of her films apparently lost, little more of note was done for the next 20 years. The 1996 publication of two full-length biographies by Ronald Genini and Eve Golden attempted to bring some clarity to the life, legend, and career of Theda Bara. In her own time the actress had been the object of one of the first extreme public relations blitzes in cinema history.

I added to the Theda Bara store of knowledge that same year of 1996 with an extensive bibliography in *Silent Film Performers*, my guide for silent film researchers. It was a busy year for resuscitating Bara; the film nostalgia magazine *Classic Images* also ran an article. Although she had died more than 40 years earlier, Theda Bara was getting noticed again. Some 15 years later I authored the entry on Theda Bara for the reference book series *Great Lives from History: Jewish Americans*. A few years after that I chose a fictionalized version of Bara's career as the basis of a full-length play, *The Vamp*. Its protagonist, Zelma La Tour, came to life in various readings, and a well-received performance was given by professional actors in a Hollywood theater.

This book is not another biography, although I have included an overview of her life and many anecdotes for those who might be unfamiliar with her. It complements earlier works by largely concentrating on her individual films, totaling more than 40 in number. All but four are still considered lost; however, a few minutes of the lost film *Salome* have been rediscovered recently. Some new or updated information has undoubtedly emerged since the earlier books were published.

Joining the books and other Bara-related productions are a 2006 documentary called *The Woman with the Hungry Eyes*; a 2016 memoir by Joan Craig, who was a young friend of the long-retired Theda Bara; and a documentary and book called *Lost Cleopatra* by Phillip Dye. The documentary is a painstaking reconstruction of Bara's most famous film, the lost 1917 blockbuster *Cleopatra*. The University of Cincinnati, which houses Theda Bara's fragile 1920s memoir, has again announced plans to someday publish it. Thus, the "vamp" lives on. Numerous additional Theda Bara-related information can be found in this book's *Bibliography*, *Miscellany*, and *Archival Appearances* sections.

All portions of this book are organized chronologically except for the *Miscellany* section. The *Feature Films* section encompasses all of her *oeuvre*, from her first-known brief film appearance in 1914 to her final cinema effort in 1926. The *Archival Appearances* section describes the several movie and television archival productions in which film clips of hers were included. These extend into the 21st century, proving that her reputation still has considerable cachet.

Along with comprehensive information about the films, each film's entry includes numerous contemporaneous reviews or critiques both from professional reviewers and from movie theater managers. In those days, every small and rural town had its movie theater, often the center of the town's life. Many of these communities no longer even exist. In their comments will be seen the rise and fall of Theda Bara. Information about her directors and co-stars and her Broadway and vaudeville careers is also provided.

In 2022 I was the invited expert for a silent film website Q&A relating to Theda Bara's last extant feature, *The Unchastened Woman*. Perhaps more of her films will be rediscovered in time, providing the chance to further evaluate her storied career. In her prime she was the equal of Charlie Chaplin and Mary Pickford as a superstar. Hopefully, this book will serve as a further reminder that Theda Bara's place in film history should, equally, not be forgotten.

Introduction

In any comprehensive history of the American cinema, there will be at least one film still or publicity photograph of a raven-haired woman with dark, kohl-rimmed eyes. She will be gazing at you with expressions that range from malevolent to demure. She might be sharing the picture with a skeleton, or a raven, or a skull. She may be scantily-clad, with only a few beads and bangles covering her incipient plumpness. Inevitably, the word "vamp" or "vampire" will be found in the accompanying text. You are looking at Theda Bara (1885–1955), a major film star of more than a century ago.

It is an unfortunate irony that there are hundreds, maybe thousands, of such images, but nearly every one of her 40 starring features is considered lost. Yet she is still emblematic when nearly all her contemporaries are forgotten. How many would now recognize the names of her once very popular contemporaries such as Earle Williams, June Caprice, Anita Stewart, Harold Lockwood, or J. Warren Kerrigan?

Many leading silent film players lost their entire body of work, and Theda Bara came perilously close to it. It is said that, later in life, she learned about the dire fate of nearly all her films. "All my work is gone! This is karma," she is said to have cried out in anguish. By then she knew that a disastrous vault fire in 1937 had destroyed almost all remaining negatives of her pictures for Fox. She thought her own copies were safely stored in her home, but they too were discovered to be nothing but unpreserved crumbling memories.

Film historians and buffs are always happy when a "lost" film is finally found. Often, they are fragmentary or incomplete and/or severely damaged. But the truth is that many of these turn out to be minor efforts, not the masterpieces that may have been hoped for. It is estimated that the vast majority of silent films will never again be available to view. However, lightning may strike at unexpected times. In late 2021 it did: A few scenes of Theda Bara's final big hit, 1918's *Salome* with Spanish intertitles, were found in a Spanish archive.

Having a fragment from one of her relatively late Fox dramas makes it possible to judge her acting style. After more than three years in front of the camera, Bara had not achieved the more nuanced style of some of her contemporaries. Her penchant for 19th-century melodramatic gesturing and grimacing is obvious. Nevertheless, among those lost films that are most sought after is Theda Bara's 1917 epic *Cleopatra*, of which only a few seconds are known to exist. Film historian Phillip Dye's documentary, *Lost Cleopatra*, has painstakingly reconstructed the film from stills, and that reminds us how much we want to see the film itself.

Why has Theda Bara been remembered whereas so many of her once very popular peers have been almost totally forgotten? It is surely because of the memorable "vampire" image captured in all those stills and photographs. She was not the petite virginal heroine so popular in the mid–1910s; rather, she was its antithesis. Theda Bara literally made the Fox studio in 1915, and for a considerable while she was its biggest attraction. She was not the first to play the seductive vampire; America and Europe had seen her like before. But audiences came to see her as the arch-symbol of forbidden sex. To quote what was said of Lord Byron: She was "mad, bad, and dangerous to know." After all, her name was an anagram of Arab Death!

Perhaps another reason that she is remembered was the fantastical public relations campaign that Fox launched for Theda Bara. Her instant stardom was pretty much an anomaly, given that she was almost 30 (officially 24) and a total unknown. She had not, like her fellow superstars Mary Pickford and Charlie Chaplin, come up slowly from one-reelers, gradually becoming audience favorites.

She was actually an obscure theater actress stage-named Theodosia De Coppet or De Cappet, born Theodosia Goodman in Cincinnati, Ohio. According to Fox, she was the daughter of an Italian sculptor and a French actress, born in the Sahara Desert in the very shadow of the Sphinx. Bara had come to the American screen from a distinguished theater career in Paris—or so claimed the shameless publicity machine.

Once Theda Bara assumed the role of heartless vampire, censorship sometimes threatened to eviscerate an entire Bara film. If it was not because of her immoral characters, it was for her often-sketchy costuming. Bara could and did play "good girl" roles, but those did not make her reputation. For three years or so, her audiences kept flocking to her films, good, bad, or indifferent. Fox put her in film after film, sometimes 10 in one year. Quality did not seem to always be Fox's first consideration; the studio overexposed her, sometimes literally. Ultimately, Fox, which had launched her to stardom, destroyed her career in five short years.

An examination of contemporaneous reviews indicates that, over time, her *oeuvre* was a very mixed one indeed. This is indicated by the reviews from newspaper and periodical critics as well as from terse evaluations from theater managers. Those reviews from small towns or rural areas are especially useful because of the immediate feedback from audiences. Every town had a theater, and good patronage made the difference between success and failure.

In recapping reviews, I have generally reproduced them exactly, with deletions noted and with some clarifying punctuation. This includes retention of some very awkward sentences that give an idea of the colorful way in which some of them were written. Feedback from the theater managers was published in periodicals such as *Motography* and *The Motion Picture Herald*. Such feedback was usually found in a column headed "What the Picture Did for Me."

Besides her first Fox film, *A Fool There Was*, the only other complete film extant from Theda Bara's period of Fox stardom is 1916's *East Lynne*, a remake of a once very popular novel and stage play. Rediscovered in 1971, it was an old-fashioned warhorse melodrama even in the early 20th century. It is, as many film historians have opined, probably one of the very least of Bara's films we cared to see survive. Theda Bara plays a grieving mother, not a soulless vampire. Atypical or not, any surviving film of a major silent star is a gift to cinema history. Also surviving are her 1925 Chadwick film, *The Unchastened Woman*, and the now seemingly incomplete *Madame Mystery*, a Hal Roach comedy of 1926.

The diminishing artistic and monetary value of her films led to the parting of ways in 1919 from Fox and a rapid decline into near-oblivion. Her growing star ego and the demands that it generated also contributed to her fall. She might have "made" Fox in 1915, but by 1919 the studio had many other assets. She at least had her considerable earnings to console her, if they indeed were sufficient consolation. A seemingly happy marriage to director Charles Brabin provided her with a firm place in Beverly Hills society.

There remain unanswered questions. If, as Theda Bara averred, she eventually disliked being portrayed as a vampire, why did she continue to acquiesce to that image? She said she secretly laughed at the *outré* publicity put out by the Fox public relations people. But she herself continued to willingly project an eccentric image. It did seem that she really was not in control of her career, like Pickford and Chaplin were of theirs. Perhaps because she was from a stable lower-middle-class family, she simply lacked the driving ambition that poverty had bred into her fellow superstars. Or perhaps she was simply so grateful to Fox that she practically never exerted her star power until the very end.

Soon after her Fox days ended, Bara was already regarded as hopelessly old-fashioned. This was probably because she was regarded as a "type," not a fully well-rounded talent. And that type was ultimately so unbelievable that it could never be sustained. The heedless vampire, who destroyed lives just because she could, was replaced by newer generations of women who had psychological reasons for acting as they did.

Whatever the questions about her actual acting ability, and despite the paucity of her films, Theda Bara has an important place in cinema history. Her coral, black, and brass star is set into the speckled black terrazzo sidewalk in front of 6307 Hollywood Boulevard on the Hollywood Walk of Fame. The ceremony unveiling her star was held on February 8, 1960, the first official year of the Walk. Almost all the millions of tourists who come to gawk at the stars that are laid in the cracked, grimy sidewalk will walk right past hers. Only a handful may stop. To those in the know, she is not forgotten. First, she was a star, then she became a legend!

Theda Bara:
The Life and Legend

A Star There Was, and her name was Theda Bara. By the time of this writing (2022), the actual facts of her life would seem to be known with certainty, except for what I have dubbed her Striving Years from 1908 to 1914. Since the mid–1990s, assiduous researchers have gone far in separating fact from legend. For those not very knowledgeable about Theda Bara, basic biographical facts are provided in this section, enriched with what I hope is interesting anecdotal material. Detailed information about her career is to be found in the individual entries for her 40-plus films and in the *Onstage*, *Short Subjects*, *Archival Appearances*, and *Miscellany* sections. Taken together, they should present a reasonably comprehensive picture of the famous silent star.

Over the years, Theda Bara continued to publicize her own memoirs, usually advertised to be published under the title *What Women Never Tell*. Supposedly written in the early 1920s, the book was relentlessly publicized as being imminent; it never appeared. The poorly-typed, fragile, and apparently unfinished manuscript was said to have at one time been owned by a rare book dealer. At the time of this writing, it still resides in manuscript form at the University of Cincinnati, Bara's alma mater.

1885–1908: The Family Years

Theodosia Burr Goodman was born in Cincinnati, Ohio, on July 29, 1885, the eldest of the three children who would eventually complete the family. She was, for some reason, named for Aaron Burr's daughter and within the family was called Teddy or Theda, pronounced Thay-da. During the overheated 1915 Fox publicity campaign around Theda's supposed birthplace in Egypt, a columnist would humorously ponder: "If her mother has the gift of bi-location, [was] she born both in the Sahara and in Cincinnati?"

The only boy, Marque (1888–1954), came second. He is listed as Mark J.N. Goodman in the 1900 United States census records, but he was always known as the French-sounding Marque. Census takers of that era often misspelled names. When his sister Theodosia later fudged her age by five or more years, he suddenly found himself designated as the eldest child. At the time of his death, he was described as a former East Coast movie director and an Oklahoma oilman.

The youngest Goodman was late arrival Esther (1897–1965). She was nicknamed Lori or Loro. Pretty blonde Esther would strive to be a movie actress like her sister, but she would not make her mark. She had a bit more luck as a scenario writer. None of the Goodman offspring would survive past their 60s—Theda came very close—and none had children.

Their father, Bernard Goodman (1853–1936), was an immigrant from Poland. His original surname was believed to have been Gutterman (literally Goodman in Yiddish). He became a fairly prosperous tailor who was able to bring his family into what now might be called the lower rungs of the middle class. There was enough money in the family to support the employment at times of two servants. In 1900 the servants were listed in census records as Ida and Anna.

Their mother, Pauline Louise Francoise Decoppet (1861–1957), of La Chaux de Fonds, Switzerland, was a wigmaker. According to an 1888 article in the *Cincinnati Enquirer*, Pauline had been born a Lutheran but converted to Judaism upon marriage because "she was a devoted wife who wanted to avoid any discord on account of religion." She was eight years younger than her husband, whom she married in 1882. In late 1920 it was reported that Theda Bara regularly attended synagogue with "Ma and Pa Goodman."

Pauline's Christianity may have been a factor in at least two of the children's later attraction to that religion, Theda being one of them. She was to use a version of her mother's surname, spelling it De Coppet or De Cappet, as the stage name she adopted during her early unsuccessful theatrical career. Theda would often be labeled "a nice Jewish girl" during her career. In her youth she did go through the Jewish ritual of a *bat mitzvah* ceremony in 1898.

Theda had the advantage of a high school education, something that was not all that common for girls of the time. Even less common for girls was her completion of two years of college at the University of Cincinnati in 1905. The date of her graduation from Walnut Hills High School in 1903 formed the basis for establishing her true birth year after she became famous. Not then believed to have a discoverable birth certificate, Theda Bara usually gave 1890 (and sometimes anywhere from 1891 to 1893) as her birth year once she was in show business. In late 1920, when she was actually 35, her age was given as 27.

Family photographs show the dark-eyed adolescent Theodosia to be a shapely but not conventionally pretty young lady. During her starring years, she was often described as being beautiful. More frank descriptions included an overbite, a bulbous nose, and a squint. (The latter could be attributed to her nearsightedness.) Other descriptions included "a broad flat face," "asymmetrical features," "heavy-jawed," "thick-waisted and chubby-legged," and "large, bosomy, and heavy-thighed." She herself claimed to have a Bourbon nose. In her starring days she was carefully photographed to avoid showing her less attractive features. Whatever those might have been, Theda Bara's looks could truthfully be described as exotic, even fascinating. In her ghostwritten article, "My Theda Bara," Mrs. Pauline Bara described Theda in infancy as having blonde ringlets and violet eyes. "She loved bananas, which she called 'nanas,'" she cooed proudly. Mother Bara was also not above a little embellishment of her own life. She claimed to be of French birth. Her uncle, she said, was court surgeon to the French emperor and Bara was actually an old family name.

In maturity, Theda's height was usually given as five feet, six inches, although a few accounts were five feet, five inches. She was somewhat taller than the average movie actress of her generation, especially the often-petite leading ladies favored at that time.

Her weight was invariably given as 135 pounds; sometimes she tended toward plumpness. During her starring career, certain techniques were utilized to make her appear taller. Among them were slightly scaled-down sets, including the doors, and many of her costumes had high collars and long trains.

1908–1914: *The Striving Years*

The acting bug had presumably bitten young Theodosia early in life, and she supposedly acted in local theatrical productions. She is said to have enrolled in a Chicago acting school around 1906. While in that Midwest metropolis, she may have seen her idol, Sarah Bernhardt, on the stage. Her ambition was such that she moved to New York City in 1908, no doubt financially supported by a doting father. Luck seemingly favored her at first; she was cast that year in a very small role on Broadway in a play called *The Devil*. She did not join the touring company of that play, but a small number of roles in touring productions would come along later.

These are the years during which some mystery remains. What did she do to survive all those years in New York City? Did she work, as rumored, in the Yiddish theater? Did she wait on tables, as at least one source claims? How did she continue to support herself—and in 1910 afford a trip to Europe? Again, it was probably courtesy of Papa Goodman and any small sums she might have earned. In 1911 and 1912 Bara did tour briefly with a couple of shows after their Broadway runs. There could have been others which have not definitively come to light.

The 1910 census reveals that Theodosia De Coppet returned from her European jaunt on the liner *Teutonic*. She was then resident on West 139th Street in Manhattan. If the census records are correct, this would now be in the Hamilton Heights area of the Harlem neighborhood. At that time, Harlem was not quite yet at the center of African American life in New York City.

In 1914 Theodosia Goodman was cast as a movie extra, playing a nun in director Frank Powell's *The Stain*. Although she is often said to have played a gun moll, this was not the case. She is even supposed to have sewn her own costumes. For years she denied ever being an extra, claiming she always was a star. Not only did she eventually admit to this tiny role, but other extra jobs were also rumored over the years. In 1919 movie leading man Creighton Hale recalled a time when he was an extra in a Virginia Pearson film (probably *The Stain*). Bara was also an extra, he recalled, "and she was queer even then." In 1918 *Photoplay* magazine had also revealed that she had done extra work.

For whatever reason, probably her physical appearance, she was literally plucked from obscurity at the age of 29 in 1914. She was a willing blank slate upon which could be written anything—and it would not be the "nice Jewish girl," Theodosia Goodman from Cincinnati, Ohio. In *A Fool There Was* and in many other films to follow, she would be the archetypal vampire, a woman who figuratively sucks the life essence from her victims, leaving them penniless and broken and sometimes even deceased.

1915–1919: *The Starring Years*

The screen vampire did not originate with Theda Bara, although what might be called the Bara "Creation Myth" might have it so. Vitagraph's Helen Gardner could certainly claim some credit for it with her 1912 *Cleopatra* and other roles. Danish cinema also had its vampiric ladies. The official Fox Pictures version of "Mlle" Bara's selection for *A Fool There Was* stated that director Frank Powell recalled an actress he had seen at the Theatre Antoine in Paris. Although she was a leading stage favorite, she accepted the role (presumably with haughty reluctance).

One version, told by Bara herself (there were other stories over time), was that after a great deal of theatrical experience, including Shakespeare, she was temporarily at liberty. A stranger approached her on a New York City street, offering $175 weekly if she would consent to appear in films. At first preferring starvation rather than appearing in the "flickers," she changed her mind after seeing Frank Powell direct a film.

Photoplay, looking back a decade in 1924, had its own version of the sudden rise of Theda Bara. According to that source, Virginia Pearson had declined the vampire role in *A Fool There Was*, whereupon Edward Jose, the film's male star, stepped up. He asked William Fox if he had to have a big name. "No," Fox is said to have replied. "We'll make [it one]."

Jose remembered an extra who had appeared in *The Stain* in a scene shot on Lake Ronkonkoma, New York. He had only seen her for a moment and did not know her name. The casting director studied his address book and found Pearson lookalike Miss Theodosia De Coppet. Jose contacted William Fox, who saw her for the briefest moment and nodded his head. She would do. No matter which of the many versions was closest to the truth, Theda Bara would always claim "I started out as a star and remained a star."

Offered about $100 a week to play the leading role in *A Fool There Was*, she got an extra $50 for buying her own costumes. After *A Fool There Was* was completed, Edward Jose, the nominal star, was unhappy with it, so the publicity all went to *The Vampire*. In a rather snide conclusion to its 1924 article, *Photoplay*, long no friend of Theda Bara, wrote that the verb "to vamp" might prove to be the only lasting contribution of the "Fox-Theda barrage." It also concluded that "the Theda Bara myth became so pungent that it defeated itself."

It is generally accepted that the name Theda Bara was devised by Frank Powell from her childhood nickname for Theodosia and from a version of Barranger, supposedly the surname of relatives of hers. The derivation of her new surname would occasionally change in the telling, but "Theodosia De Cappet" was presumably gone forever. Was it just a coincidence that the new name just happened to form an anagram of "Arab Death"? As late as 1917 some articles were still claiming that Theda Bara was her actual birth name, and as late as the mid–1930s she herself said that the aristocratic-sounding De Bara had been her actual surname.

In January 1915 it was announced that Theda Bara had been made a permanent member of the William Fox stock company. *A Fool There Was* became a major hit for Fox and a triumph for Theda Bara. It can be fairly said that she had elevated the fledging studio almost singlehandedly. She was rushed into her second film, *The Kreutzer Sonata*, nominally starring stage diva Nance O'Neil, but widely publicized as being a Theda Bara film. It was her final supporting role.

Because Theda Bara's past was unknown to the public, Fox publicists Al Selig and John Goldfrap launched their fevered campaign. The Vampire had been born in Egypt, in the Sahara Desert, and in the very shadow of the Sphinx no less. She was the daughter of the French actress Theda De Lysle or possibly an Arabian princess, and Giuseppe Bara, an Italian sculptor. Further "clarification" said she was born in the Sahara because her parents were on an archeological exploration. "A half–Arabian embodiment of wicked delight," she was taught many languages and wrote poetry. She was the toast of the Theatre Antoine in Paris.

Of course, not everyone out there was buying it. A 1916 letter to a film magazine inquired whether Theda Bara was "a Jewess." The response came that she was not, she having had a French mother and an Italian father. Her "aunt in Paris" had found a photo, it was breathlessly reported, of six-year-old Theda astride a camel in a Sahara oasis, her birthplace.

According to his own publicity, Goldfrap had been a rancher, an advance man, a reporter, a rewrite man, a writer of juvenile fiction, a scenarist, and a magazine article scribe. In response to all this, a clearly unbelieving wag said: "Theda Bara claims to be a reincarnation of Hoo-Sis, a Pharaoh's daughter. It looks like she may be able get away with it, because no-one can prove she isn't." Another wrote: "Theda Bara has colored blood in her veins. Hey hold on, we mean blue blood. She's a descendant of an Egyptian queen."

However she was presented to an often-gullible public, Theda Bara's popularity by fall 1915 "accounts for the work that is being piled upon her." She was to have 10 films released in that year alone. Her burdensome filming schedule would not significantly decrease over the course of her career. Fox seemed determined to wring everything it could out of her.

Theda Bara's 1915 films were *A Fool There Was*, *The Kreutzer Sonata*, *The Clemenceau Case* (her first starring film), *The Devil's Daughter*, *Lady Audley's Secret*, *The Two Orphans*, *Sin*, *Carmen*, *The Galley Slave*, and *Destruction*. In five of them she was a deep-dyed villainess, the persona that launched her career. Two others had elements of vampirism. For the first time, one of her films, Fox's version of *Carmen*, opened head-to-head with another version of the same story.

In "My Strange Life," a *Picture-Play* article of February 1916, Bara persisted in the myth of her Sahara childhood. A supposed "burning love epistle" from an Australian fan read: "I have gone insane over dreams of you, my Egyptian queen, soul of my soul!" Also in February 1916, the *New York Times* published an article lengthily headlined "Some 500,000 Spectators Follow Her Every Day: This is the Amazing Public Assembled in a Year by Theda Bara, the Flaming Comet of the Cinema Firmament." Unusually gushing for the staid *Times*, the article pointed out that there were 40 prints of each film (of which there were 11 by that time) in circulation every day. It speculated that her annual audience might amount to a mind-bending 182,000,000 souls.

Theda Bara's 1916 films were *The Serpent*, *Gold and the Woman*, *The Eternal Sapho*, *East Lynne*, *Under Two Flags*, *Her Double Life*, *Romeo and Juliet*, and *The Vixen*. This time, only one of the films, *Gold and the Woman*, featured her as an unredeemable bad woman. In some others she was no saint but found some measure of redemption or at least comeuppance. For the second time, a film of hers, *Romeo and Juliet*, opened in competition with the same story from another studio.

When Bara was asked about her enigmatic past, she replied: "And what, pray, has that to do with my art? What does it matter who I am and whence I came? Is it not enough that I am here with a certain gift, perhaps, for expressing my feelings through the new pantomimic art of the cinema, without knowing about my antecedents?" (This was an early example of the stilted language often used by Theda Bara in interviews.) She went on to hint about her supposed antecedents, saying that her mother was descended from the royal French Bourbons. "Some say Bara is Arab spelled backwards, but what's in a name? ... There has always been an air of mystery around me."

She did not add that the mystery was self-created with the help of Fox publicity. Again, she certainly did not fool everyone. In late 1915 the "Screen Gossip" column half-correctly dubbed her "the famous vampire from Gay Paree and Cincinnati." In an interview 10 years later, at the time of her brief comeback, Bara claimed that she had gone into films "when shortly out of school." She also claimed to have "lived much on the other side."

Somehow, that invented background caused her to pose with ravens, snakes, skulls, and skeletons. Since Theda Bara had been cast as the heartless vampire in her first few films, it had to be true that the real Theda Bara was also evil personified. She was called "Purgatory's Ivory Angel," "Destiny's Dark Angel," "The Wickedest Woman in the World," "The Devil's Handmaiden (or Maidservant)," "The Priestess of Sin," and the most amusing, "The Arch-Torpedo of Domesticity." Children supposedly feared her, wives kept their husbands close lest Theda Bara swoop upon them—or so said Fox publicity.

The story went on: She, like her mother, became famous in the Paris theater. She was no mere lucky extra; rather, she was a famous actress who was deigning to bestow her vast talent on the "flickers." As the years went by, it was increasingly clear that Bara herself was the originator of at least some of the fantasy. Describing her "wicked" face, she said her eyes had the "cruel cunning of Borgia"; her mouth like "the sinister scheming Delilah"; her hair like "the serpent locks of Medusa"; etc. Her hands she described as "being like the talons of a Circe, or the blood-bathing [child murderess] Elizabeth Bathory." She claimed to wear poison-bearing rings and bracelets. Men killed themselves for her love.

There also were interviews in which she decried such descriptions. In April 1916 she expressed her dislike of being called a love pirate and a vampire. She claimed "vampiring" was the hardest kind of work, that it left her completely exhausted. Bara claimed she felt heartbroken whenever she was called a vampire woman. She said it was impossible to accustom herself to the hate-filled letters in which she was dubbed a menace to the human race, and worse. And yet she continued to play the vampire, justifying her portrayals as "a great moral lesson."

At about the time Theda Bara's film *Sin* was released, an article (greatly helped by Fox publicity) gushed: "This remarkable young woman possesses a type of beauty which is described by artists and sculptors to be of an absolutely unique character. [She] has become a literally international figure since she first burst upon us from the Theatre Antoine.... While Mlle Bara declares emphatically that her true nature is very far from being a heartless vampire, her reputation for splendid and artistic work in such roles led to her casting as the evil genius whose beauty is as fatal as the deadliest poison."

The unnamed "New York artists and sculptors" went on describe Bara as having "the most wicked and seductively beautiful face in the world." Readers were told that "Mlle Bara has probably a bigger personal following than any other actress on the screen. Her serpent-like beauty and compellingly alluring methods have made her name known from coast to coast." This supposed avalanche of praise from "artists and sculptors" may have given Bara or Fox Pictures the idea to have her appear as an artist's model in several films.

It was not until sometime later that "ancient Egyptian inscriptions" would deem her a good and virtuous woman. By that time, she had played some virtuous heroines, but so ingrained was her vampire image that audiences, for the most part, did not respond at the box office. In time she publicly foreswore the image that had been so carefully built up. She was really just a nice woman giving a performance. It saddened her when she was shunned on the street, etc. The 1916 Fox *Studio Directory* said Bara's hobbies were such normal things as riding, dancing, sculpture, and drawing in crayon.

Still, the mythmaking would not abate. Bara admittedly was not a reincarnated Egyptian princess, but she was allegedly possessed of mystical powers. In 1917 she was "discovered as the original daughter of Seti, the High Priest of the Pharaohs. The immortal remains of her maternal ancestress Umslopagaas have been sandwiched from her sarcophagus in the pyramid of Chephren and haunt the mummy room of the Metropolitan Museum, New York." In a different version, the symbol for Theta on the stone walls of a tomb near Thebes had foretold the coming of a woman who would lead men to destruction by her wiles.

This time there were few willing takers among the press. One article demanded: "When do we see the last of this Sahara Desert stuff that her press agent thinks is good publicity? That last bunch of stuff about the hieroglyphics affected me like a red rag affects a bull. Cincinnatians love to say that Theda Bara is nothing but a Cincinnati kike, in which statement there is more truth than elegance.... Mister Press Agent won't you please tie the cans to the Sahara stuff and give us a little human interest?" The casual use of the offensive word "kike" to describe a Jewish person was a sign of the casual racism of the day. Theda Bara herself was not above exhibiting it. (*See below.*)

Bara claimed she always had a good laugh at all the perfervid Fox publicity, but her own public pronouncements only added to her eccentric reputation. She said that she was "self-hypnotized" when playing vamp roles and had learned to vamp by studying birds. She said that "a mystery is the most attractive thing in the world, and if you are a mystery to yourself, you are a mystery to everyone." She was a believer in spiritualism, and informed the public that the Moon had a tremendous fascination for her: "Its cold rays seem to harmonize with my very soul."

Theda Bara also was reported to believe that each letter of the alphabet has its own vibrations for good or evil. When the right letters were combined, the ensuing vibrations make for the success of the person. Apparently, younger sister Esther Goodman had a name that would not achieve harmony; hence the change to Lori Bara or Loro Bara.

In a 1916 interview, Bara said she possessed two three-inch-tall miniature gods named Daikoku and Abesu, whom she consulted each morning when she awakened. They were made of the mysterious (i.e., nonexistent) substance plajumtrin. Daikoku held a hammer, with which he could knock either sorrow or joy into a person's life. Abesu had a smile which emitted sunshine and happiness. Bara said she refused to work on those days when these gods' predictions did not augur well.

Her perfumer, a Mme. Haviland, wrote: "The very first impression you get of Miss Bara is one of eeriness. She seems to glide into the room like a vapor.... In departing she leaves that same weird feeling." Bara told of a dream in which a woman would be the person who fostered peace in the Great War. *Film Fun* wondered if the woman whom Theda Bara saw in her dream had a name that began with a "T" and ended with an "A." Eeriness (or plain weirdness) would indeed continue to be a characteristic ascribed to Theda Bara. She herself would continue to foster her otherworldliness, and it was ripe for parody.

In a 1917 *Film Fun* article called "Spring Styles in Vamping," the author supposedly comes upon Bara gazing into a crystal ball. She recounts her supposed colloquy: "I cannot tell you anything about anything, for I am a mystery even to myself. Never understand yourself, for if you do not, no-one will be able to understand you either. There is nothing in this world that attracts as mystery does. I am always wondering about myself; consequently I always have something to think about and I am happy. To prevent the contingency of my ever understanding myself, I have hired an excellent corps of mystery writers. They turn out new stories about me every day. I am a reincarnation of Cleopatra, the Serpent of the Old Nile.... It is fascinating not to understand oneself."

During this period, Bara acquired the sobriquet "Sarah Bernhardt of the Screen." The renowned French actress was an idol of Bara's, and the title was very possibly a self-proclaimed one. (At some point she had also dubbed Italian diva Eleanora Duse her ideal.) Bernhardt was "The Divine Sarah"; Bara would come to be known as "The Divine Theda." It would also be a reminder to the world of her supposed triumphs in the Paris theater. When she later starred in the play *The Blue Flame*, Bara claimed that she came to the stage already a star, as she had already claimed with her film career.

Theda Bara also was a budding filmmaker, it seemed. In 1916 it was reported that she was making a split-reel movie featuring her cat Tweedle-Dee, now apparently another "lost" film. By this time her fame was worldwide. In May 1916 *Variety* reported: "Theda Bara has made the biggest film hit in Australia since the rise of Charlie Chaplin. Mary Pickford still draws but is considered a dimming light." Perhaps as another sign that Bara had made it, she was parodied by comedienne Fannie Brice in the *Ziegfeld Follies of 1916*.

By this time, Bara's signature heavy eye and mouth makeup (described by a critic as the "shoe blacking and the jam pot") and the Delsartian facial grimaces, were easy prey for broad parody. One reviewer dubbed her grimaces "the ability to make hideous faces."

Describing herself, perhaps as a provocation aimed at William Fox, as "an actress who has become celebrated through *her own efforts*," in 1917 Theodosia Goodman petitioned the New York Supreme Court to legally change her name to Theda Bara. In November of that year, a Supreme Court justice granted the petition. Her parents and siblings also assumed the legal surname of Bara. There were fans who thought differently. One letter writer insisted Bara's name was actually Edna Goodrich; another, that she was born in Pottstown, Pennsylvania.

Theda Bara's 1917 films were *The Darling of Paris, The Tiger Woman, Her Greatest Love, Heart and Soul, Camille, Cleopatra, The Rose of Blood,* and *Du Barry* (aka *Madame Du Barry*). Only in one of these films, *The Tiger Woman*, was she again the irredeemable murderous vampire. In it she hit a high-water mark in villainy, stacking up several victims in only five or six reels.

In 1917, after having churned out 23 starring films, Bara made the epochal *Cleopatra*. Running 11 reels, it was a major success and was still playing in theaters two years later. It is for that lost film that she has become legendary. It was shot in California, to which Theda Bara would finally move and establish residence. A press conference held in Chicago on the way to the West Coast is recounted in Louella Parsons book *The Gay Illiterate*.

According to that gossip columnist, the press waited in an anteroom of Bara's hotel suite. It was a day that Parsons described as "hotter than the proverbial hinges of the proverbial hot spot." Finally, Theda Bara emerged swathed in furs. A press agent confided that the star was cold because she had been born in the Sahara, where it was always hot. When the press conference was over, Bara flung off her furs and threw open the window, gasping for air. This story has been often recounted, although Parsons was not above a bit of colorful exaggeration.

In July 1917 *Variety* quoted "a man close to Triangle [Pictures] that the concern has a contract with Theda Bara." The press conference had possibly been part of a negotiating ploy. Her contract with Fox came up for renewal in the spring of 1917. While the actual hardheaded details were being hammered out, Fox publicity put forth some supposed contract clauses that only seem to have existed in the imaginations of press agents. Among them were restrictions on Bara's private life, including no marriage, no non-studio public appearances unless heavily veiled, no unofficial photographs, and—heaven forbid—no transport in public vehicles, where she might have to rub shoulders with the *hoi polloi*. Often stated over the years to be genuine, these supposed stipulations were only intended to feed into the Bara myth.

A lawsuit was filed against her by a Fox lawyer, claiming she owed him $15,000 for drawing up her new contract. The suit claimed she would be earning $354,000 over the two-year period, which is the 2022 equivalent of some $8.5 million.

From that splendid *Cleopatra* peak, Theda Bara could now only descend—or totter there precariously. She always said *Cleopatra* was her favorite film, until her handpicked misfire *Kathleen Mavourneen* in 1919. Her decline would be rapid and was sometimes cruelly noted by critics, except for the brief reprieve of *Salome* in 1918. That year, in the "Movie Dictionary" feature of *Motion Picture Magazine*, the definition of "X" was given as "an unknown quantity.... Also stands for has-beens such as Theda Bara, ex-champion vampire of the world."

In most of her films, she had not been a deep-dyed vampire, and she often said she was tired of playing one. In July 1918 she announced that she would definitely "vamp no more." However, like it or not, that would be her legacy. A 1919 article summarized Bara's screen persona: "She has slain men's hearts by the dozen. She has triumphed as snake-like women whose charm and allurement are like draughts of poison, whose love is deadlier than hatred."

In an October 1919 interview, Theda Bara said: "I went out on strike and I stayed struck until I had my way. I refused to vamp another single solitary second unless I was given the opportunity to be good as easily as I was bad." (Had she forgotten that she had been "good" many times?) The so-called strike was to force Fox into allowing her to film *Kathleen Mavourneen*, a film in which she was miscast and which literally caused mini-riots in some cities. Also, her story judgment, as in the case of *The Soul of Buddha*, did not prove to be sound.

More than three years earlier, in August 1916, Fox publicity had announced: "Theda Bara has been forced to bow to the demands of the public that their 'vampire lady' be returned to them. Bara has just started work on her third picture in which she is cast in a sympathetic role. This will be her last, for William Fox has said Miss Bara will return to a role more vampirish than ever [presumably *The Vixen*]." Probably to assuage the star, the statement continued: "William Fox has proved to the world's satisfaction, and Miss Bara to her own [satisfaction], that the peerless vampire could be just as peerless in a sugar-coated role."

In July 1918 it was announced that Theda Bara was working on her 32nd film: "A record that is looked upon with pride by Miss Bara and Fox Film Corporation.... Miss

Bara's record is one of consistent excellence, tireless industry, and constant study for betterment. After a vacation of two weeks, Miss Bara will begin work [again]."

Theda Bara's 1918 films were *The Forbidden Path, The Soul of Buddha, Under the Yoke, Salome, When a Woman Sins,* and *The She-Devil.* She claimed to have written the story for *The Soul of Buddha* on the train going from California back to New York. She also claimed that an enthusiastic William Fox gave the personal green light to turn this highly improbable melodrama into a film scenario. It would be Bara's final real vampire role.

A 1918 article made it appear that she was very much involved in all the films she made. "No matter where Theda Bara is, the second she gets a new idea about her picture, she rings up her continuity writer. Her ideas come in such rapid succession, according to reports from the Fox scenario department, that the aforementioned continuity writer's day is just one telephone call after another."

In 1918 it was reported: "Theda Bara announces that she does not believe in marriage for screen stars. 'One cannot serve two masters.... When a player goes home after a nerve-wracking day of hard work in the studio, tired and cross, she isn't any kind of a comfort to her husband. After the day is over I'm a nervous wreck myself and don't want to talk to anybody.... Frankly, I need a business manager, not a husband, nor do I mean to have one. I am wedded to my career.'" This may have been intended to quell the rumor that she was engaged to one Russell (or Arthur) Palmer. An article in *Moving Picture World* of August 31, 1918, reported that "filmdom is thrilled to its innermost core" at the news of the supposed engagement.

Theda Bara did find the time to raise millions of dollars from personal appearances to sell Liberty Bonds for the war effort. She was proud to be made godmother to the 158th Infantry Regiment stationed at Camp Kearney. The 346th Infantry Company, shipping out of Fort Lewis, Washington, for France, sent their company mascot, a black bear, to Bara. They were not allowed to take it overseas, and it was donated to the zoo.

In May 1918 Bara sat for an interview with *Photoplay*. In the article that followed, "Does Theda Bara Believe Her Own Press Agent?" columnist Delight Evans observed: "I think Theda Bara is ridiculous, clever, pathetic, impossible, a remarkable woman." She noted the accent that Bara had cultivated: "She talked with a carefully cultured and rather painful accent." Evans quotes Bara as saying: "I try so hard to show the soul of the character I am to portray. Sometimes I study for days and days, and nothing comes to me. Then something—it may be a rag lying about the studio—gives me my thought." Evans went on: "I don't know if she expected me to believe that, but I think she half believes it herself."

Theda Bara went on to say that she now only worked two and a half hours a day and that she never saw any films but her own. *Photoplay* had been one of her more severe critics for some time, panning most of her films. This article upset her by implying that she was pretentious. An angry Bara wrote to *Photoplay*, fulminating that "there is one [God?] who avenges all lies, insults, and betrayals." It would not be the last time the periodical held her up to an unflattering light.

Approaching the end of her Fox years in 1919, she seemed to be able to poke a little fun at herself. She told *Motion Picture Classic* that *Cleopatra* was her favorite film, and with the casual racism of the time, she said: "Do you know what my Jap [sic] said of me [in *Cleopatra*]? You fat on the screen, Miss Bara, but not a bit fat off. I think the boy was disappointed." The "Jap" and "boy" referred to was her house servant.

By 1918, when she began receiving $4,000 per week plus a percentage of film rentals, Theda Bara was making star demands. She would not arrive on set until one in the afternoon, and then she complained about the noise and delays caused by the crew. Although she had some justice on her side, given the punishing work schedule she had endured for years, the demands only hardened William Fox against her.

Over the years, Theda Bara was described in many ways, almost all of them based on no evidence at all. It was said that she lisped; was cross-eyed, deaf, blind, lame, friendless; was married to this lucky man or that one; was the mother of two "very adorable" children; and was even dead. She reportedly rode around the streets of Los Angeles in "a motor car, crushed-strawberry in color, herself wrapped up in crushed-strawberry veils." It was also reported that in spite of her playing vampire roles: "Offstage she was a sweet and wholesome woman, and a worker for the French Red Cross."

She received thousands of letters. Many were offers of marriage; others were more bizarre; some may have been the product of Fox publicity. A letter from a Texas fan promised to kill a mountain lion for her and send the pelt to be made into a kimono. "I have never heard of a kimono made from a lion's skin, but I think such a garment should be very useful. You can wear the kimono about the house. When you go outdoors it will be unnecessary for you to change, for the garment will be plenty warm. Please send me a picture of the kimono after it is made."

The belief that Bara was blind was a literal one on some naïve moviegoer's part, but she was extremely shortsighted. She tried to make a pseudo-poetical statement about it in 1917. "You know, I cannot see—at least I cannot see as other people see. To me, the world is just a misty blend of beautiful colors. I see everything as [the painter] Whistler saw it, or at least as he loved to have us see it. No outline is distinct, and I am happier, for I cannot see the defects." In practical terms, she was so nearsighted that she used a lorgnette to navigate around movie sets when the camera was not running, and she had to memorize the position of possible impediments.

Some of the misconceptions about Bara were the genuine befuddlement of fans; some, misguided publicity. When Bara was reported as having died, her career was in swift decline. This ploy had been used some nine years earlier when IMP star Florence Lawrence was supposed to have been killed in a streetcar accident. Her "miraculous" reappearance was worth a few headlines. In late 1918 hundreds of thousands of people were actually dying from the so-called Spanish influenza. The pandemic caused a shutdown of the studios and numerous movie theaters for several weeks.

In January 1919, Bara issued a sworn affidavit that indeed she still lived. It is written in the exaggeratedly "proper" style that she had adopted, and read in part: "There is current a grossly exaggerated, mournfully inadequate report that I have died, said report doing me a grave injustice.... I expect to return to Los Angeles soon to live and die the hosts of death which I hope still await me in my career." She mentioned her upcoming film, *A Woman There Was*, in which she indeed did die—so did the much ridiculed film, one which hastened the actual demise of her career.

Theda Bara's 1919 films were *The Light, When Men Desire, The Siren's Song, A Woman There Was, Kathleen Mavourneen, La Belle Russe*, and *Lure of Ambition*. *Kathleen Mavourneen* was the film that Bara seemed to believe would salvage her career, but her starring days were moving toward their end.

Another 1919 example of the stilted Bara writing style was published by the new *Shadowland* magazine as a testimonial. Stars such as Douglas Fairbanks and Norma

Talmadge had sent in their informally worded testimonials. Theda Bara's read: "Allow me to tender my subscription. The name pleases me. It would be splendid always to have the shadow of one's possibilities, or the field in which one is striving, stretching on ahead of one. Though one walked beyond it, surmounted certain difficulties, the game would not be worth playing if there were not new issues to contend with, new shadows to pass over."

She frequently talked about reading ponderous tomes, sometimes in their original foreign languages. In 1918 a letter writer was assured: "Theda Bara is a very charming young woman of the screen and a very learned one too. There is scarcely a subject concerning past or present times on which she can't talk intelligently." In an interview the year before, the interviewer had described her as speaking (supposedly knowledgably) about "Esoteric Buddhism, English literature, and bungalow plumbing." Her voice was characterized as being "soft and low, very even, and very oddly colorful."

Years later in September 1925, she was still presenting herself as an intellectual. In a *Picture-Play* interview, she averred that she read French literature from Balzac to Anatole France, studied the philosophy of Hegel, liked the humor of Mark Twain and Rabelais, "and of course there is always Shakespeare." As for poetry she enjoyed Keats, Swinburne, Oscar Wilde, and Walt Whitman. She also reeled off contemporary authors such as Carl Van Vechten, Havelock Ellis, Ronald Firbank, Fannie Hurst, and Sherwood Anderson.

When, in 1919, Fox declined to give Bara a new contract, it was rumored that a possible successor would be actress Fontine (sometimes Fontaine) LaRue. Bara's departure from Fox was not a dignified affair; squabbling was carried out in public. In August 1919 *Variety* reported that Theda Bara had been "dickering with Paramount. Miss Bara wants a salary of $5,000 a week [about $81,000 in 2022 terms]. She has been receiving $4,000 a week, but Fox refused to renew its contract at that price. In the middle of her last feature, Miss Bara suddenly quit work and refused to continue unless she got $4,000 a week; she had been getting $1,500.… Those close to the star say she might organize her own company. She frequently complained because Fox gave her only vamp parts."

However, there followed a seeming effort to save face, on Theda Bara's part, or Fox's, or both. In July 1919 an announcement was made that Bara would continue with Fox "for the upcoming season but she will not have vamp roles. Vamps apparently are out of order. At all events she will not portray them for Fox." Another announcement read: "In speaking of the expiration of Theda Bara's contract with Fox it was stated that if she were put into other productions which did not necessitate the exercise of her well known vamping ability, and would give her more opportunity to portray the emotional roles for which she is fitted, she would make a wonderful success.… This is exactly what Miss Bara is going to do, with types of productions that will eminently, profitably, and splendidly be adapted to this star's talents." This did not happen, at least not at Fox.

Understandably, she did not bring herself to admit her time in the limelight was over, but she was already being regarded as a spent force. To quote from my book *From Silents to Sound*: "In Hollywood—then as now—perception was frequently the reality. Once performers were perceived to be through, they *were* through. If they did not acknowledge this and still attempted to continue their careers, they were invariably referred to as 'former stars' or as 'attempting a comeback.'" This reality almost immediately faced Theda Bara.

The press was already beginning to pounce. Some elements of it almost seemed to relish knocking her when she was down. *Picture-Play Magazine* published a snarky note: "Theda Bara has been missing for several months. William Fox is overcome with grief. It is reported he will start a special exploitation campaign to win her back." *Photoplay* said: "Theda Bara is pondering an adventure into the two-a-day [vaudeville]. Theda probably figures that the fans who enjoyed her for two-bits will all flock to see her for two and three times that admission price. Maybe."

In October 1919, Theda Bara still spoke as if she were continuing her film career. "I will not slink and writhe and wriggle my eyes day in and day out. I demand to bob my curls, and climb trees, and love for love's own sake. I want to be natural." Before too many more months had passed, she was playing a murderous vampire again onstage in *The Blue Flame*.

In 1919, *Photoplay* had reported (in somewhat tortuous prose): "Theda Bara is said to be planning a return to the stage.... Mr. Fox is said to not be averse to Miss Bara's designs on the realm of the footlights. The acknowledged depreciation in the famous vampire's photodramatic efforts of late is alleged to be due to the famous vampire's insistence on directing her director J. Gordon Edwards. He finally jumped the job and is now directing William Farnum." Another Fox employee who switched his talents to Farnum at this time was Al Selig, one of the publicists who had dreamed up Bara's mysterious Saharan antecedents.

There was the rest of her life to consider. Officially not yet even 30 (she was 34), she was wealthy but not yet ready to be an ex-star. Continuing her pattern of blaming others for many of her career problems, Bara said: "My health was bad and I needed a rest. I had been getting wretched stories. Studio life was beginning to get on my nerves. The inefficiency is appalling." She went on to blame studio workmen and their hammering, William Fox, and her directors, except for J. Gordon Edwards—and, of course, not Charles Brabin.

Theda Bara had not, like her fellow superstars Mary Pickford and Charlie Chaplin, built her career deliberate step by deliberate step. Her stardom had burst on the public like a supernova, and like that celestial phenomenon it had dazzled briefly and then burned out.

The Persisting Years, 1920–1929

Theda Bara's appearance in the 1920 stage melodrama *The Blue Flame* brought her added riches by touring in cities from Boston to Kansas City. Her former movie audiences clamored to see and hear the live star, and they probably were not overly fussy about the quality of the play. She insisted on bringing the play to New York, but harshly critical scorn led to a short run there. (See the *Onstage* section.) It can be conjectured that both the play and the subsequent vaudeville tour were undertaken to keep her name before the public. Returning to films seems to have remained her goal, and she continued to single-mindedly pursue it.

Her subsequent vaudeville tour added to the Bara coffers as well. However, her hopes for a return to films were frustrated; it seemed the time for yet another report of her death. In late 1920 the rumor spread that she had died in California, and that her lookalike sister Esther had consented to step into her shoes. According to the rumor, Fox had earlier tried to recruit Esther for films but "found she didn't measure up to

Theda's standards—such as they were." The folderol was scotched when the sisters were seen together, and the opinion was that Esther did not look enough like Theda to fool the public.

In 1920, *Photoplay* continued its negative drumbeat: "She was ridiculous—a sacrifice to the Great God Bunk on the altar of publicity. When she was offered a contract, she had to make her choice. She might have money and notoriety; she might have all the chances she wanted to act. She might have the position of star and the deference that comes to a celebrity. In return for this, she must allow herself to be exploited as the strangest sort of freak."

The *Exhibitors Herald* in December 1920 huffed: "Theda Bara has just announced she had quit pictures. Fox Pictures wasn't a minute too soon in making its announcement to that effect last year." The public also seemed to have adjusted rapidly to the fall of its once-revered star. In the *Motion Picture Classics* annual popularity poll for female stars in 1920, Mary Pickford retained her lead by a wide margin. Theda Bara came in at number 11 between Mary Miles Minter and Dorothy Gish.

She seems to have found happiness in her July 2, 1921, marriage to the divorced British director Charles Brabin (1882–1957). He had directed her in two of her final 1919 films for Fox, the ill-fated *Kathleen Mavourneen* and *La Belle Russe*. They honeymooned in Nova Scotia and later purchased an extensive property there. In 1927 it was rumored that she was to become a mother, but the Brabins never had children.

In February 1920 the *Los Angeles Times* had announced that Theda Bara had been married in New York to an unnamed man who was "formerly the manager of Frank Moran, the pugilist." According to the article, the marriage had taken place in a Catholic church "into which faith Miss Bara was born." It went on to say that her husband was now the stage manager of a musical comedy in which Bara was part owner. It had previously been rumored that she was engaged to an evangelist.

Presumably as a tongue-in-cheek joke, in 1921 a rumor sprang up to the effect that Theda Bara had gone back to her birthplace in Egypt and was living in a tent at the base of the Sphinx.

In September 1921, Theda Bara began a 12-week vaudeville tour. "Covering the principal cities of the United States, Miss Bara will be seen in the most prominent [Loew's] picture theaters. She will be introduced by a new two-reel picture made especially for this tour.... The purpose is to stimulate interest in the forthcoming screenplays in which Miss Bara will star. The pictures are due to be made, one in Northern Italy and one in the South of France." The title of the two-reeler, a kind of home movie, was *A Day with Theda Bara*.

Variety reported that Bara would perform a monologue, preceded by the film, that would supposedly reveal something about her private life. She would enter the stage just as the film was concluding. Her filmed face would dissolve, and she would appear in person, making it seem that she had just stepped out of the film. The monologue consisted of stories about her picture experiences. By the time the tour began, the two-reeler seems to have become a single reel.

In Cleveland in October 1921, at a Loew's theater, her take for a week was said to be $5,500. This included noon and midnight performances. Her publicity was said to be of the "circus order." A later article claimed that she was not even a headliner on the bill, but "an also ran."

In November, a St. Louis theater oddly announced that Theda Bara would be appearing in a film called *Pilgrims of the Night* and that she would appear live in conjunction with its showing.

For whatever reasons, professional redemption and star ego possibly being among them, Theda Bara would not abandon hope for a return to the screen—just never call it a comeback! It might have been merest coincidence, but probably not, that yet another report of her death came just at the time she was fruitlessly hunting for movie roles. If previous reports of her death had had some publicity value, then another might be even better. This latest version had a similarity to the one two years earlier.

In 1922 under the headline "Is Theda Bara Alive or Dead?" *Screenland* ghoulishly pondered: "Is Theda Bara preparing to resume her career … or is she sleeping in a quiet grave in a Cincinnati cemetery, while a sister, strangely resembling her, perpetuates the famous name?" The conspiracy theory postulated that the real Theda Bara had perished in the Spanish flu epidemic in 1918. She had passed away in the midst of shooting, and the Fox studio could not afford to scrap the film. Among the "facts" presented were that Theda Bara's real name was Esther Goodman, and that it was her unnamed half-sister who had been impersonating her.

In March 1922 the *San Francisco Chronicle*, long one of Theda Bara's stalwart supporters, said she was attempting a comeback (a no-no word with her). "Like all ex-champions the modern world's greatest vampire will make a mighty effort to regain her lost laurels.… It isn't altogether hopeless for a champion to make a comeback. Most of them fail because they never change their tactics. They repeat the same mistakes for which the public originally deserted them. If the exotic Theda Bara will bear this in mind, she may be able to make the grade. While touring the big cities recently, Miss Bara always asked her audiences how they would like her to come back: as a vampire or a good girl? Everywhere she was greeted with shouts of "Vampire!"

The tour seemed to augur well. A June 1922 article read: "That personal appearances will revive the popularity of some stars who have come out of retirement is testified to in the fact that Theda Bara, long absent from the movies, will next Fall star in several pictures." Since she was back in the news, she was included in an article about the heights of current-day, i.e., 1922, actresses. It noted that most were on the petite side, adding: "Even Theda Bara, *of ancient memory*, was a small woman."

In 1922, Theda Bara was finally preparing to restart her career with Selznick Pictures. The studio head's son, the young David O. Selznick, claimed to be enthusiastic about her. After many roles were considered, the film version of the Broadway sensation *The Easiest Way* was selected for her return. Tests were done, but the studio went into bankruptcy in 1923.

Photoplay continued its needling in one of its "10 Years Ago" columns: "Theda Bara, not yet having discovered that she was born in the Egyptian desert of royal and ancient lineage, was acting in a little theater in New York City's East Side." The source for this assertion is not known, but it could refer to the possibility that Theda Bara had acted in the Yiddish theater.

The 1922 Fox remake of *A Fool There Was* starred Estelle Taylor. A heavy-lidded brunette beauty, Taylor seemed physically right to play The Vampire, and she was ably supported by character actors Lewis Stone and Irene Rich. Although much more slickly produced than the 1915 version, it nevertheless failed to overshadow its cruder predecessor.

In 1922, three years after it was first suggested that Theda Bara might start her own company, husband Charles Brabin announced the formation of a production company. He stated that it would produce four Bara films a year. Production would take place in the East "as soon as a suitable story can be secured." The company was not actually chartered as Theda Bara Productions, Inc., until July 1924 in Dover, Delaware.

It was capitalized at a figure reported as ranging between $30,000 and $500,000. In December 1924 the California State Corporation Commission temporarily suspended the permit granted to the company. The permit had allowed for the sale of stock, but the attorney for the production company stated that no stock had ever been sold.

In a May 1923 *Los Angeles Times* article, Bara recalled her experiences as a member of a traveling outdoor Shakespeare company. "I was the newest member of the company, and I was awkward and always falling over things. The company hated me; I was sort of a fifth wheel. They made it cruelly hard for me, as companies can for an inexperienced player. In one scene in which I was carried out dead, the carriers used to stick pins in me. One night I fell into a little artificial lake and I appeared, all wet and disheveled. Oh, how miserable I was and the director scolded me. My tears finished the job of drenching me."

This episode, if true, could be related to her trip to Europe in 1910 where, she sometimes said, she had worked with a travelling Shakespeare company. It is also possible that this whole story is a fabrication; no actual evidence seems to exist. It also feeds into her continuing feelings of victimization. Then Bara turned her attention to her present attempt to return to the cinema. "I'm really a changed woman. I feel I have a great deal more to bring to the screen than I had when I left. I have a broader sympathy, more understanding of life and people. Everybody used to be more or less a joke to me, except those nearest and dearest."

In 1923 independent producer Whitman Bennett announced a deal to make a film with Theda Bara to be called *A Daughter of Salome*. It was to be distributed through Chadwick Pictures, a so-called Poverty Row company. "Whether or not a series will be made with this once famous vamp," said Whitman, "depends entirely on the way the first picture catches on." Apparently, Bara had decided that playing another vampire was not so bad, but the film was never made. Whitman folded his tent in 1925 after five years as producer.

Many other roles were bruited about for her return, but none came to pass. In October 1923 it was announced that Tod Browning was set to direct Theda Bara in *Beauty Hunger*, to be produced by the assistant head of production at Paramount Pictures. (Recall that she had been "dickering" with that studio four years earlier.) The following year, two more films were announced: *Restless Wives* and *Madam Satan*. The latter was to be directed by Herbert Blache, ex-husband of pioneering female director Alice Guy Blache; neither film was made with Bara. *Restless Wives* was made starring Doris Kenyon in 1924; in 1930 Cecil B. DeMille made a talkie called *Madam Satan*.

Oddly, given the ridicule which had been heaped on the whole Sahara birth fantasy, in 1925 Theda Bara herself took credit for it. In a *Picture-Play Magazine* article she said: "The legend designed to make me mysterious in the public eye were inventions—and my own. I wish they would stop giving the press agents credit for their fabrications."

She then returned to her often stated feeling of victimization. "I have had hours of bitterness when my efforts to return to pictures met snags. The unfair treatment to which I was subjected when I made unwise contractual connections put me into the dumps. As I heard one [mid–1920s flapper] ask 'What's a thedabara? Something that happened in the Dark Ages?' The Bara of yesterday is buried." This last statement was presumably meant to proclaim that there was a *new* Theda Bara.

Finally, in late 1924 Theda Bara's efforts to return to films were realized. She was signed with Chadwick Pictures and in 1925 was seen on the screen again. It was *The Unchastened Woman*, a comedy-drama based on a Broadway success. However, three months prior to its opening, Bara renounced the film. She claimed the producers had re-edited it and rearranged the titling so that the film made no sense. In conjunction with the filming, she once again had trotted out her long-publicized memoir. According to the October 1925 *Pictures and the Picturegoer*: "Theda Bara is going to publish her *Confessions*. She is going to tell all."

In the very same issue, under the heading "Sad Comebacks," the columnist opined: "I think it rather a mistake for film stars who have gradually faded out of public notice and retired to stage comebacks. The results are, as [a] rule, painful to them and disappointing to the public.... [This] applies to Theda Bara. I don't think she'll be able to hold her own amongst the more poised screen vampires of today."

Bara then opted for what she hoped was high comedy in the 1926 Hal Roach two-reeler *Madame Mystery*. It was well-received, but she was merely a straight woman in the midst of some good comic performances. Her husband was said to have put his foot down: "No more!" It was her final live onscreen performance, although there would be many films thereafter which featured her iconic image. (See the *Archival Appearances* section.)

That year also brought a round of retrospective looks (or postmortems) at the once-storied Bara career. In an article headed "Oversold!" *Motion Picture Magazine* noted: "Probably the first fine example of being oversold in filmdom was contributed by Theda Bara. The William Fox exploitation forces oversold the first celluloid vamp as a siren with a mysterious past." In December 1926, *Film Mercury* wrote: "Theda Bara held her own as long as the average life of a star, but had she alternated or perhaps modified her characterization of roles, she no doubt would have lasted much longer."

The *Universal Weekly* quoted one of its divisional managers as opining that a Theda Bara vampire film would now be a joke: "As out of date as a horsehair sofa." However, in its column "Did You Know That...?" *Motion Picture Magazine* reported: "Lillian Walker, Theda Bara, and many other old timers are making large salaries appearing in person in movie theaters."

In 1926 a *Screenland* columnist recalled an interview with Theda Bara years earlier. "Theda Bara was installed in state at midday in a darkened incensed room with dark draperies. But the room wasn't half as incensed as I [was] when she began to pull her line. It was a good line if you liked that sort of thing." The "line" was her Egyptian birth and her time in the Parisian theater.

Film Daily quoted the "chief scenic artist" at Fox as recalling that Theda Bara began as a $35-a-week extra at the studio in Fort Lee, New Jersey. For the 60th birthday of Universal Pictures head Carl Laemmle in 1926, it was announced that an unnamed 1910 film starring Mary Pickford and King Baggot would be screened. Among the promised surprises was that the IMP film would show Theda Bara as an extra.

In the late 1920s an article in *Picture-Play Magazine* read: "Nine out of ten who act in the films received their original training on the stage. Reversing the process, Theda Bara, after having been very popular in the movies, tried her luck in the theater, ill-advisedly starring in a piece called *The Blue Flame*. She failed so dismally that her career was practically ended."

Her husband's foot down notwithstanding, in April 1929 *Variety* reported that

Theda Bara "is negotiating for a return to Fox to work in dialogue pictures." Later that year she went back into vaudeville with an ill-fated sketch called *Serpent of the Neva*. (See the *Onstage* section.) Like other former silent stars who turned to vaudeville, this tour was no doubt undertaken to prove she could "talk."

The Final Performing Years, 1930–1939

As she entered her late forties, Theda Bara still did not seem quite ready to give up her time in the spotlight, although she had said "marriage is the hardest career of all." Perhaps being a Beverly Hills matron and party giver was not as fulfilling as it could have been. Charles Brabin was still directing films, and would be until mid-decade. She was serving tea to her society friends.

The Brabins were known for their slot machine parties. A wag joked that the machines never paid off. Instead, the nickels went down into a concealed slot and lodged beneath the house! When there were so many nickels that the house was actually raised off its foundation, the money was retrieved, and it was time for another slot machine party.

Bara performed in at least two plays during the first half of the decade. She toured in 1931 with the Minneapolis-based Bainbridge Stock Company in the play *Fata Morgana*. In 1934 she played the lead in *Bella Donna* for a few nights in a Beverly Hills theater. She also made at least three, possibly four, appearances on radio, discussing her career and hopeful future plans.

Although definitely considered as *passe*, Theda Bara certainly had not been forgotten like many of her contemporaries. The memories of her were not always flattering. A 1931 article in the film magazine *Close Up* included the line: "One remembers Theda Bara now as a squat, determined woman with quantities of untidy hair."

In a 1933 article titled "The Mystery of the Vanishing Vampire" Bara claimed that she had been offered $50,000 to stay on at Fox, but she had quit because of exhaustion. However, the article concluded that she had not left pictures; rather, pictures had left her. It went to say that Theda Bara was simply washed up. Fox had found her hard to handle because stardom had gone to her head. She could still perform a strong seduction scene, but nobody wanted her to do one.

In June 1934, Theda Bara proffered the *Los Angeles Times* her opinions about some of the screen sirens of the day. During the interview she offered some "alternative facts" about herself: "De Bara was a family name. I merely shortened it when I went into pictures.... It wasn't that I consciously tried to be mysterious. Because I didn't see people, there grew up around me all sorts of fanciful tales. Many people still believe [them]." Now, almost 20 years later, she was again claiming to be an innocent bystander in the creation of the wild Bara legend.

Theda Bara's father, Bernard Bara (formerly Goodman), died at Clementsport, Nova Scotia on August 8, 1936, at about 83 years of age.

In film circles, interest in the vampire phenomenon was still alive, even though the phenomenon itself seemed headed for extinction in the United States. In December 1937 the British publication *World Film and Television Progress* laid out a somewhat florid premise for its demise in an article headed "Who Killed the Vamps?" The final sentence of the article has a particular resonance for the anticlimactic end of Theda Bara's career.

"Full-blooded, sexy, slinky, unscrupulous creatures, compounded half from the bad women of Victorian melodrama and half from the odalisques of naughty French novels. We haven't seen them for many a long year, and their names come down the chromium corridors of film history more as whispered echoes from the past. Theda Bara, Nita Naldi, Lya de Putti…. How the women must have hated them for their luscious contours swathed in black velvet—and particularly Theda Bara for wearing garments made from ropes of pearls."

The article continued: "I don't think it was the censors who killed the vamps; it was the decadence of the post-war generation. So the long decline began, the vamps had no chance. Their successors from Gloria Swanson to Jean Harlow had all the talent, from sex to slapstick. The queen of darkness finally capitulated before the majestic and undeniable onslaught of Mae West. Here was the Apocalypse. Here, in direct negation of the vamp tradition, stood, or rather swayed, the ideal of every stout, middle-aged woman. That swooning, cynical, luscious voice could never issue from the constricted throat of Theda Bara. The untold riches of the vamp have crumbled into dust. The long cigarette holders and the beckoning sinuous arm are the prerogative of Hal Roach."

The Final Years … and Beyond

In 1941 the British Film Institute published a list of 12 stars who had made the greatest contributions to the cinema. Theda Bara was on the list, as were Charlie Chaplin, Mary Pickford, Douglas Fairbanks, Greta Garbo, Rudolph Valentino, Fred Astaire, Spencer Tracy, Tom Mix, Harold Lloyd, Marie Dressler, and Shirley Temple.

In September 1948, speculation arose that Betty Hutton would play Theda Bara in a film produced by Buddy De Sylva to be called *The Great Vampire*. Possibly it was Hutton's portrayal of Pearl White in 1947's *The Perils of Pauline* that gave rise to the idea. In June 1950 the blonde comic actress Marie Wilson was announced as possibly playing Bara, after the deal with Betty Hutton fell through. The "Sarong Girl" Dorothy Lamour was next to be named a possibility. De Sylva's death in July 1950 put an end to the whole idea.

In January 1953, Theda Bara was announced to appear at a gala for Adolph Zukor's 80th birthday. Bob Hope was the M.C. for an expected crowd of 1,000. That same year, Hollywood celebrated its golden anniversary. One of the festivities was a pioneer luncheon honoring such old-time greats as Jesse Lasky, Mack Sennett, Frances Marion, Louise Fazenda, and Theda Bara.

In 1954, Theda Bara's brother Marque Bara (formerly Goodman) died at about the age of 65.

As late as 1955 it was announced that Columbia Pictures would film *The Vamp*, a musical comedy. It too was supposedly based on the novel *The Great Vampire*. *The Vamp* was the title of the 1955 Carol Channing musical which failed on Broadway, and there is no record of a published novel titled *The Great Vampire*.

Either way, the film was never made; both Hutton and Wilson would seem totally the wrong types to play Theda Bara. Other reports said that her unpublished autobiography was the source for the picture to be called *The Vamp*, and that Rita Hayworth was the logical choice for the lead. Although Hayworth might have been an interesting choice, it is unlikely that Bara's poorly written manuscript memoir could be the basis for what might have been an expensive movie.

The first known operation that Theda Bara had for "appendicitis" was performed on June 28, 1954. It was reported as emergency surgery; another surgery followed in August. In March 1955 she fell into a coma. Her age was then given as 62; she was actually 69. According to one obituary, in her final minutes she had called for water, and her last words were "I feel better." The cause of death was given as abdominal cancer. Funeral services were performed by a minister of the Unity Christ Church. She had apparently left much of her Jewish heritage behind, as would sister Loro (Esther).

Upon her death from cancer on April 7, 1955, just a few months shy of her 70th birthday, most major newspapers featured her obituary. She was interred in the Forest Lawn Cemetery in Glendale, California. The bulk of her estate was said to have been left to Esther (Loro). She would have been happy to know that she was not fated to die in obscurity like so many others who had once blazed across the screen.

Theda Bara's husband, Charles Brabin, died two years later at age 75. Her mother, Pauline Decoppet Goodman Bara, also passed away in 1957, having outlived her two elder children and surviving well into her nineties. Theda Bara's sister, Esther Bara (née Goodman), died in 1965, some 10 years after her famous sister, at age 67.

Theda Bara has become iconic of a certain type of persona, an image kept alive by her thousands of extant stills and photos. She has been dubbed the first Goth: "The Goth subculture has modeled its female style after Theda Bara, regarding her as an icon of Goth fashion." Another honor, although it seems apocryphal, was that the curvilinear streets of Beverly Hills, her hometown for decades, were modeled after the shape of Bara's torso. During Bara's stardom, a New York socialite staying at her summer home in Lackawack, New York, named several streets and geographical features after screen stars. Theda Bara had a valley named for her, but that honor did not endure. In 1937 the State of New York buried three small towns under a new reservoir. Of the three, Lackawack was the only one relocated; the Theda Bara Valley was presumably lost.

In 1963 her name still represented the vampire image, although only the first one of her 39 Fox features was then available. An announcement for a television series read:

"There's a world of difference between the passionate posturing of Theda Bara and the child-woman blandishments of Brigitte Bardot." In 1964, UCLA presented a program titled "Vintage Vamps." Included with Theda Bara and some excerpts from *A Fool There Was*, were films of Clara Bow, Louise Brooks, and Mae West.

Theda Bara is still unforgotten in the 21st century. In 2003, invitations printed in silver ink were sent out for a séance to contact Bara at the Velaslavasay Panorama in Hollywood. The séance was a collaboration between the Panorama and the Traveling Wondershow. Conducting the séance were Spirit Medium "Magda Rockmore" and Spirit Facilitator "Cristo Bulan." Since Theda Bara was often accused of being humorless, she no doubt refused to be summoned by these undoubted jokesters.

The real Theda Bara/Theodosia Goodman remains somewhat of an enigma. Unlike her superstar counterparts Mary Pickford and Charlie Chaplin, she did not seem to be in control of her stardom. The little Canadian and the little Englishman had unstoppable drive, perhaps because they both came up from adversity. Bara seemed to drift at the whims of the Fox Studio.

Pickford and Chaplin may have had steel behind their engaging public personas, but they understood how to shape and project them. Of course, Pickford was not really an innocent ingénue, nor was Chaplin a mere clown. Theda Bara's persona was amorphous: the reincarnated Egyptian princess/priestess; the eccentric mystic; the really nice vampire star; the actually evil vampire star; the pseudo-intellectual; the demanding but victimized star.

Yes, she was "a nice Jewish girl" who no doubt loved her family, but was there a "there" there? Was it burning ambition that impelled her toward acting? How did she handle the failure before her improbable success? What did she really feel about her fantastic luck in being plucked from total obscurity and literally made an overnight sensation?

Her unpublished memoir, which she bruited about for years, skims the surface of her life and does not reveal true feelings. She apparently made no effort to update it past 1917, perhaps because that was her most triumphant year. It held so little interest to publishers that up to the date of this writing (2022), it remains an ill-typed and fragile manuscript. Her proposed title *What Women Never Tell* was truthful because she really did *not* tell!

Yet, for a star whose last film was made almost 100 years ago and for whom practically none of her work survives, she remains a potent symbol. To some it is a symbol of old-fashioned, scene-chewing, unintentionally risible moviemaking. To others it is a symbol of the cinema in its unsteady rise to a true art form. If more of her *oeuvre* was available, she might be regarded as even more, or perhaps less, of a major star. The enigmatic stare from her kohl-rimmed eyes still retains the power to fascinate. For now, that is enough to remind us that A Star There Was!

The Feature Films

The Stain (1914)

Background

The Stain was presumably the first film in which Theda Bara appeared, albeit as an extra. She had been styling herself professionally as Theodosia De Coppet or De Cappet, the name she had chosen for her largely stalled stage career. However, she is said to have worked in this film under her real surname of Goodman, possibly because picture work was not then considered a high art. Either way, she was uncredited.

The film was based on the 1913 novel of the same name by William Forrest Halsey (1877–1949), who wrote under the name of Forrest Halsey. He was the author of several other novels, among them *Fate and the Butterfly*, *A Term of Silence*, and the interestingly titled *The Bawlerout*. He was also to be a very prolific scenario writer in the 1920s for such stars as Gloria Swanson, George Arliss, and Rudolph Valentino, as well as for director D.W. Griffith.

Canadian-born director Francis (Frank) Powell was also born in 1877, although accurate biographical information about him seems somewhat elusive. The exact date of his death appears to be unknown, although he was certainly alive in the early 1960s when I received his postcard (see *Preface*). He was directing this film when signed for *A Fool There Was*.

Powell had a distinguished career even prior to this. He was a director for the popular playwright Augustus Thomas, and he worked in Europe with the great star Ellen Terry. In Europe he was with Pathe Freres as a producer of romantic and historical dramas. In America he directed for Biograph and Powers Motion Picture Company. (See the subsection below devoted to *A Fool There Was*.)

The Stain was advertised as "the first of a series of multiple-reel features produced by Eclectic by Pathe Freres." It was filmed at the Pathe Studio in Newark, New Jersey, and at Lake Ronkonoma on Long Island, New York.

The Film

Directed by Frank Powell. Written by Forrest Halsey [and Robert H. Davis?]. Eclectic Film Company; released by Pathe on July 17, 1914. 6 reels.
Cast: Edward Jose (Stevens aka Harding), Eleanor Woodruff (Mrs. Stevens), Virginia Pearson (Louise Stevens aka Gray), Sam Ryan (Boss Dunn), Thurlow Bergen (Norris), Isabel

Evessen (Mrs. Dunn), Mildred Manning (Mary Dunn), Creighton Hale (Clerk), Ada Sherman (Mrs. Brown), M.O. Penn (Gangster), H.S. Chamberlain (Norris's brother), Gertrude Norman (Norris's mother), Margaret Cagney (Dancehall girl), Theodosia Goodman (Nun) (uncredited).

Synopsis: Stevens, a young bank clerk, wants to study law but needs money to do it. He steals a large sum of money from the bank and prepares to flee with his wife and young daughter Louise. Mrs. Stevens refuses to go with him, so he deserts them and assumes a new identity as a Mr. Harding. His wife falls into poverty and puts her daughter in an orphanage.

Eventually he falls in love with Mary Dunn, the daughter of a political boss, but is deterred by the thought of his deserted wife. By a series of coincidences, he comes to believe that his wife has died, and he and Mary are wed. Louise, now grown and known as Louise Gray, works with a young lawyer named Norris, and they fall in love. Unbeknownst to Louise, her father is now a judge in the same city.

Louise is falsely accused of a crime and appears before her unrecognized father. Just as he is about to impose a harsh sentence, his former wife appears in the courtroom to support her daughter. She recognizes the judge as her ex-husband and confronts him with his own guilt. He dies of a heart attack, and mother and daughter are reunited.

Reviews

"This is one of the first pictures, outside of *The Perils of Pauline*, that have been produced by the Eclectic Company in America. The picture has a punch that only a truly American picture can have. There is not a scene that is not realistic, nor a scene that lets the observer's attention lag for a moment. There is no plot that contains more human appeal than this one. Such a story, although it has appeared on the screen more than once, has never been previously produced with such strength as here.... The humor is of a kind that would draw a smile from the severest critic.... That the picture will be a success is a foregone conclusion." *Motion Picture News*, May 30, 1914.

"The story has an interesting holding power that does not relax until after the word *finis*. Respect for realism is shown in the completeness of interior scenes." *Motography*, June 13, 1914.

"So many lines in this that after the fifth reel one wonders how it will be able to finish the remaining reel. With practically no nature scenes, the merits of this picture must stand on the acting of the principals.... The cast fills their parts admirably. Although there are gruesome bits it is bound to hold the attention of the average movie fan." *Variety*, June 1914.

* * *

Although some modern-day cast lists have Theodosia Goodman playing a gun moll, people with personal knowledge of the film state that she plays a nun. Presumably, she appeared in the orphanage scenes. She supposedly made her own costume because the two habits for nuns provided had already been taken by other extras.

The Stain was long believed to be a lost film, but a copy was discovered in Australia in the 1990s and it has now been restored.

For a Bowery scene in the film, Powell was reported to have gathered 150 men and women, gave them a dance and a dinner, and then told them to "muss it up." Chairs and glassware flew; black eyes were common. This was all in the cause of supposed realism.

Belgian-born Edward Jose (1865–1940) became the first leading man to the newly christened Theda Bara in *A Fool There Was*. He was signed for that film while making this one. Irish-born Creighton Hale went on to become a popular leading man of the 1920s, and he was seen onscreen in small roles until the 1950s. He stated that during this film, the future Theda Bara was already behaving "eccentrically."

Virginia Pearson, later to be dubbed "The Girl with the Perfect Back," had a couple of roles on Broadway and was hired by Frank Powell for this film while appearing on stage. She was later considered for the role of the vampire in *A Fool There Was*. Hired by Fox to be a second-string vamp (possibly to keep Theda Bara in line), her career had largely petered out by the end of the silent era. Publicity for this film called her "one of the most popular and beautiful leading women of the stage who has been picked by Frank Powell, the popular Pathe director, to work in pictures."

Sam Ryan played in two-a-day vaudeville with a partner; the act was known as "Lewis and Ryan, the Irish Humorists." He also worked with George M. Cohan on Broadway. Thurlow Bergen was praised as an author, singer, playwright, and songwriter who had performed for President Grover Cleveland at the White House and had written the song "Esther" for Cleveland's first daughter. Eleanor Woodruff worked in stock companies and for the Schubert Organization. She is said to have gone to Europe as a Red Cross nurse at the outbreak of the Great War.

In an act of amateur press agentry, a Hot Springs, Arkansas, theater manager issued "subpoenas," directing people to "witness" a performance of the film. He advised potential patrons to ask lawyer friends for subpoena forms or to have a law stationer print them. They were to substitute their name for that of a judge to "avoid contempt of court." The manager enthused that this publicity worked better than fake telegrams.

A studio plug to theater owners read: "The kind of dramatic soul-stirring photo-play you have always wanted to offer your patrons. A powerful human interest drama, superbly acted." An ad for the film dubbed Edward Jose as "Edouard Hose."

A Fool There Was (1915)

Background

Not many films could boast about being the culmination of a long trail of creative endeavors: a painting to a poem to a play to a book, and finally to the film. And it was a smash hit film, too: 1915's *A Fool There Was*. It put Fox Pictures in the cinema firmament, and it created a brand-new star in Theda Bara. For a few years thereafter, their mutual success was closely linked.

Because success has many fathers, more than one person was to claim the credit for discovering her. Among them were *The Stain*'s leading man, Edward Jose, and director Frank Powell. Jose also claimed he had a hand in directing this film, and he did go on to direct numerous films in the silent era. In a *Cleveland News* article, a man claimed he had discovered Theda Bara in Churchills, a tony Manhattan restaurant, with an implication that she was a waitress there. Upon reading that, a furious Bara demanded a speedy retraction.

In 1918 a Fox executive named Abraham Carlos told a newspaper columnist that it was he who had discovered Bara in a New York cabaret and had hired her for $30 a week. Hearing of this, Bara sent an irate telegram calling the story "scandalous, and the most insulting innuendo I have ever read." She demanded a retraction. Why Carlos waited for so long to tell this story is unknown. By this time, she was making $4,000 a week.

An 1897 painting called "The Vampire" by Philip Burne-Jones (1861–1926), son of the more famous artist Edward Burne-Jones, unwittingly began the saga. It shows a very pale woman, clad in what could almost be a negligee or nightgown, leaning over a supine man. A kind of half-smile plays on her lips, perhaps one of triumph? The famous red-haired actress Mrs. Patrick Campbell was said to have been the model for the mysterious lady. Although photographs exist of it, the current whereabouts of the painting is unknown.

Rudyard Kipling, novelist, poet, jingoist, and a Burne-Jones cousin, was inspired to write a poem based on the painting. (In at least one catalogue of Burne-Jones paintings, the poem is reproduced as the frontispiece.) Also called "The Vampire," the poem is little more than catchy doggerel, but its six stanzas do have an undeniable rhythm. The first reads: "A fool there was, and he made his prayer/ (Even as you or I!)/To a rag and a bone and a hank of hair/(We called her the woman who did not care)/But the fool he called her his lady fair/(Even as you or I!)."

Some of the poem is used in the film's intertitles, the fifth stanza being the final one: "The fool was stripped to his foolish hide/(Even as you or I!)/Which she might have seen when she threw him aside/(But it isn't on record the lady tried)/So some of him lived but the most of him died/(Even as you or I!)."

Enter playwright Porter Emerson Browne (1879–1934), whose first Broadway play this was. Presumably suggested by the Kipling poem, the three-act drama *A Fool There Was* opened on Broadway at the Liberty Theater on March 24, 1909. It starred English actress Katherine Kaelred in her first Broadway appearance as "The Woman"; i.e., the Vampire. Robert Hilliard was the unfortunate husband/victim. (He was not related to future Bara co-star Harry Hilliard.)

The review from the *New York Times* of March 25, 1909, was generally tongue-in-cheek and read in part: "Mr. Porter Emerson Browne is the darling young author who has undertaken to prove Mr. Kipling's poem in seven scenes with slow music…. It is a beautiful sort of story. Taken in installments it would be a fine substitute for the sort of things school girls hide in their geographies. This one may be a bit raw and rough at times, but there is no denying its moral: Beware of sirens who wait on ocean liners to sprinkle rose leaves in your path."

The play ran for a respectable 93 performances, closing in June of 1909. Katherine Kaelred did many more Broadway plays; her last in 1920 served as the basis for her final film in 1921. Browne's final Broadway play *The Bad Man*, a comedy with the redoubtable Holbrook Blinn, also opened in 1920 and was a sensational hit, running for almost 350 performances.

Browne was encouraged enough at the reception for *A Fool There Was* to novelize it in 1911. It may have been this book that brought the story to the attention of what was then called the William Fox Vaudeville Company. Frank Powell and Edward Jose had been signed up for it while still shooting *The Stain*. Virginia Pearson, who was also in *The Stain*, as well as Madlaine Traverse and Valeska Surratt were said to have been considered for The Vampire.

Apparently for financial reasons, William Fox wanted an unknown (i.e., cheaper) actress. Theodosia Goodman, stage-named Theodosia De Coppet/De Cappet, who had played an uncredited nun in *The Stain*, was that unknown. Legend has it that she was brought to Mr. Fox's attention by Frank Powell and, glimpsed for a matter of seconds, she was hired on the basis of a nod. Whatever the actual truth of this encounter, one of the superstars of the 1910s was accidentally created. Most unusual for that era was her age, at almost 30, although she was "officially" 24. Her new name was supposedly crafted by Powell from her first name and a shortened version of a relative's name. (See the *Life and Legend* section.)

Miss Goodman was offered anywhere from $75 to $100 a week to play the female lead (sources differ), plus an additional $50 to buy her own costumes. The scene where the Vampire's ill-fitting nightgown keeps falling from her shoulders has been much commented upon as what we now call a "wardrobe malfunction." It is not only an example of careless costuming, but also of a reluctance to do necessary retakes.

So unknown was she that a December 1914 ad spelled her name as Thedda Barra. She would play the unnamed woman who wreaks destruction on vulnerable and all-too-willing men. There already had been films called *The Vampire*; the first was a now-lost one-reeler with Margarita Fischer. The 1913 three-reeler by that name featured Alice Hollister and the perfervid Vampire Dance, presumably based on the painting. That film is extant.

The Vampire was the working title of *A Fool There Was*. *The Devil's Daughter* would be the only other Bara film directed by Frank Powell. He had a long list of films to his credit going back to 1910, mostly one- and two-reelers, until he began directing features in 1914. He had worked with D.W. Griffith and claimed to be the discoverer of Blanche Sweet. He later had his own studio on Long Island, New York, which ran a contest to discover future stars.

There had also been a 1914 one-reel comedy titled *A Fool There Was*. When publicity for the Bara version began to heat up, the comedy's title was changed to *She Wanted a Car*, a title that pretty much sums up the entire plot.

In November 1914 it was announced that Powell had left for St. Augustine, Florida, with the film company in a chartered yacht. This was where the Italy scenes were to be shot. At that point Edward Jose was the only cast member being publicized. An ad read: "Do you believe in the magic of names? A magnet that never fails to attract the public? One name is Edward Jose in *A Fool There Was*."

The Film

Directed by Frank Powell. Produced [uncredited] by William Fox. Adaptation by Frank Powell. Picturization [i.e., scenario] by Roy McCardell. Photography by George Schneiderman. Released by the William Fox Vaudeville Company; distributed by the Box Office Attraction Company on January 14, 1915. 6 reels.

Cast: Theda Bara (The Vampire), Edward Jose (John Schuyler), Mabel Frenyear (Kate Schuyler), May Allison (Mrs. Schuyler's sister), Runa Hodges (Mrs. Schuyler's daughter), Clifford Bruce (Tom), Victor Benoit (Parmalee), Frank Powell (The doctor), Minna Gale (The doctor's fiancée).

Synopsis: The film is headed by a credit that reads: "A Psychological Drama by Porter Emerson Browne." Stanzas and partial stanzas of the Kipling poem are inserted throughout.

Middle-aged John Schuyler is happily living in a large house in Larchmont, New York, with his wife and small daughter. He is first seen on his yacht. When he is ordered to England on a mission for his country, his family is unable to accompany him because his sister-in-law has been injured. They expect to join him later.

The Vampire seeks revenge for having been socially snubbed by Schuyler's wife. When she reads in the paper about his trip, she decides to book passage on the same ship. Her evil nature is first revealed when she toys with a drunken suitor, one whom she presumably has driven to alcoholism.

On board the ship, a young suitor brandishing a gun begs her to return to him. She laughingly waves him aside, saying "Kiss me, my fool!" thereby giving a generation of young girls a snappy tagline. He shoots himself; she is unconcerned. The scene switches to Italy, where Schuyler is already in the clutches of the Vampire. They return to Schuyler's New York townhouse, where he falls increasingly under her spell, becoming a hopeless alcoholic and drug addict.

His little girl begs him to come home. His wife refuses advice to divorce him and tries to rescue him by going to their townhouse. Just as she is about to persuade her

A Fool There Was. The heartless Vampire strews flowers over her dying victim (Edward Jose). This is the iconic final scene that launched Theda Bara from total obscurity to instant stardom.

husband to leave with her, the Vampire reasserts her control with a passionate kiss. Eventually she leaves Schuyler, but he is still unable to rejoin his family. Now prematurely aged and broken, he dies. Finding him, the Vampire sprinkles rose petals over his body.

* * *

In 1935 the president of 20th Century–Fox presented a copy of *A Fool There Was* to the Museum of Modern Art Film Library. In 2015 the film was selected by the Library of Congress for preservation in the National Film Registry as "culturally, historically, or aesthetically significant."

The version of *A Fool There Was* which is now extant is the 1918 re-release at five reels; it was originally issued at six reels. When it was re-released, it was edited and newly titled by the studio, and that is the version that was deposited in archives. The *Moving Picture World* review (*below*) may give some clue as to what was trimmed for the re-release. It is very probable that the seduction of Schuyler by the Vampire, which in the five-reel version seems very truncated, was among the scenes partly excised.

A January 1915 Fox plug of this film for theater managers read, in part: "Robert Hilliard's Greatest Success"; "Brilliant assemblage of artists"; "$100,000 of women's gowns shown"; "The greatest photoplay production in history"; "Wonderful sets by arrangement with Tiffany, New York"; "Gorgeous Florida outdoor scenery—The Fountain of Youth." Of course, Robert Hilliard was in the play, not in the film. Edward Jose assumed his role.

Publicity claimed that dancer Isadora Duncan had taught Bara how to make her sinuous moves. It was not long before reviewers were noting Bara's exaggerated facial expressions, something that was commented upon during her entire career. It was a result of her earlier stage training in the Delsarte Method of acting.

Fox claimed that the film had grossed $137,000 against a cost of $29,500. (The studio's first $1,000,000 grosser was said to be *A Daughter of the Gods* with Annette Kellermann.) *A Fool There Was* caused a sensation. Fox claimed that it broke all records in Boston, running for 85 times; a third print had to be supplied.

In February 1915 in Kansas City, the film came to the attention of the censors. At the time it began its run, the censors had not yet seen it, but it was drawing complaints from what was described as "a very influential ladies' organization." The censors then asked for five cuts to be made; but under a temporary restraining order brought by the distributor, the film continued to be played. By the time a judge ruled, it had finished its run. The newspaper coverage of the tiff lent the film great publicity, and the theater did an "immense" business. Some thought it was all a press agent stunt. Many of Bara's future films would bring a great deal of attention from the censors.

Perhaps because of the relative novelty of Bara's characterization in this film, during her active career and even afterwards this film was still considered by many to be her strongest besides *Cleopatra*. The reviews for its re-release in 1918 support this, and that was at a time when all of her Fox films were still extant.

Edward Jose was supposed to be the only star of this film. A 1914 article referred to him as the "Richard Mansfield of the movies." This was a considerable compliment; Mansfield was a renowned Victorian-era actor in Shakespeare plays and even in Gilbert and Sullivan operettas.

Besides Theda Bara, the actor who came out of this film with a solid career was pretty May Allison, whose first film this was. She was a frequent co-star of actor Harold

Lockwood in the 1910s in popular romantic dramas, and she continued in films until 1927. She lived on for more than 60 years, dying at age 98 in 1989. Although some cast lists credit the actress who played Kate Schuyler as Mabel Fremyear, the film itself has it as Frenyear. Only one other film is listed in her filmography.

A ballad called "A Fool There Was" was composed and modestly hyped by its publisher as the greatest ballad ever written. Comic actor Charles Parrott (i.e., Charley Chase) did a burlesque of the film, as did vaudevillians Ray and Gordon Dooley for Fun-Art Films' *A Rag, a Bone, and a Hank of Hair*.

Fox did a remake of the film in 1922 with Estelle Taylor, a talented and smolderingly attractive actress. (It was originally to have been cast with Mona Kingsley.) Lewis Stone played Schuyler. Issued only four years after the original's re-release in 1918, the new version was generally criticized for not measuring up to the original. Despite advances in cinematography which made the new version look much less crude, and the more subtle acting styles, it failed.

Some reviews did acknowledge changes for the better. One read, colorfully: "The old drama had little of the art of repression which marks present-day acting for the screen. Emotions were pounded and hammered like a tough steak." Another read: "Not so extreme a vampire story as the former one. The story is entirely a human one, with actions growing out of the characters of the people."

Reviews

"Bold and relentless, filled with passion and tragedy.... Shot through with the lightning bolt of sex." *New York Dramatic Mirror*, January 1915.

"Powerfully absorbing in all its parts.... No six-reel picture witnessed by this writer has surpassed it in its gripping and tenacious qualities.... Exceedingly excellent." *Motion Picture News*, January 1915.

"Miss Bara misses no chance for sensuous appeal in her portrayal. She is a horribly fascinating woman, vicious to the core and cruel. When she says 'Kiss me, my fool' the fool is really ready to obey and enjoy a prolonged moment, irrespective of the less enjoyable ones to follow." *New York Dramatic Mirror*, January 1915.

"Edward Jose gives a performance so fine and finished that none but the highest praise can be accorded him. Equally fine and equally finished is Theda Bara's characterization of The Woman.... The six reels make it one of the best the film market can offer. Plainly there can be no disappointment attendant on this feature.... A full orchestra was directed by S.I. Rothapfel [who would become better known as the impresario Roxy]." *Motography*, January 23, 1915.

"It remains for the film version to penetrate with the baldness of its disgusting truths the depths of the human tide. The film hits its mark squarely, a splendid production.... Reeks with the foulness, the sorrow, and the horrible consequences of a life wasted in the toils of a human vampire. An inimitable interpretation by Theda Bara, leading woman at the Theatre Antoine in Paris.... There are moments in the first and second reels when there seems to be some little tendency toward padding.... A marvelous attention to the smallest human detail.... A successful artistic effort in every way. Sin has been presented in its most revolting aspect." *Moving Picture World*, January 30, 1915.

"Theda Bara plays the Vampire and she proves herself one of the strongest emotional actresses of the screen.... Her eyes are particularly effective." *Los Angeles Daily Times*, February 1915.

"The strong man caught in the meshes of a wicked woman makes an interesting theme. The life of the man and woman during their time in Italy would make any fellow forget about the old home. Miss Bara as The Vampire scores easily. Jose did better when elderly.... The scene in the Vampire's apartment at the ending is rather broad." *Variety*, March 1915.

"Wonderful appeal to the patrons.... So many calls asking that the picture be shown again." Manager, Novelty Theatre, Louisville, Kentucky.

"It drew remarkably well; bad weather and the usual effects of the off day [had] no effect on the attendance." Manager, Alhambra Theatre, Cincinnati, Ohio.

"Broke all records during the run." Manager, Academy of Music, Fall River, Massachusetts.

"Broke all records.... Desired to book it for another week but [the distributor] was unable to accommodate." Modern Theatre, Boston, Massachusetts.

"The equivalent of your average Sharon Stone epic: lurid, melodramatic, and utterly irresistible.... Though [Bara's] style seems to be as remote as the ice age, one can clearly see the strength of her persona. Her appeal to 1915 audiences must have been profound." Modern-day commentator.

The 1918 Re-Release

Taglines for the 1918 re-release included: "A rag, a bone, a hank of hair—and Theda Bara, Empress of Vampires" and "Theda Bara, Empress of Vampires, acclaimed the world's greatest screen queen."

"[The film] is drawing capacity houses at every performance notwithstanding that it's a return engagement." *Los Angeles Times*, February 9, 1918.

"Success should return to it in its freshly edited and condensed form. Certainly there has never been a more vampish vampire and Miss Bara derives the utmost from the part. The film, despite the passing of the years, is still a good picture of its kind. The story is absorbing and powerful and grips with an iron-like grip from beginning to end." *Motion Picture News*, June 22, 1918.

"Gives Theda Bara her greatest vampire role.... It is an unpleasant but remarkably directed and acted picture." *Moving Picture World*, June 22, 1918.

"Played the film to capacity business. This in spite of extremely hot weather and unusually keen competition." Manager, Little Theatre, Seattle, Washington.

"Played to good business. Good picture of the kind, but that kind doesn't go here." Kentland Theatre, Kentland, Indiana.

"Have just finished playing the film at advanced prices to the biggest business of any week so far this summer. The public remembers the good ones." Manager, Princess Theatre, Oil City, Pennsylvania.

"Like all other reissues the public didn't want it. In my opinion reissues are detrimental to the game, for you are bound to play to some people who have seen them and forgotten the title. A wonderful picture in itself." Manager, Alcazar theatre, Chicago, Illinois.

The 1922 Remake

"If the former picture [i.e., the Bara version] was crude it had at least the flame-like Theda Bara with her voluptuous freedom of action, her sweeping passion, her vividness. I longed for one audacious bedeviling look out of Theda's bold eyes. She was a fast work, was Theda! You didn't forget her." *Los Angeles Times*, June 19, 1922.

"Very much minus Theda, this production is exceedingly feeble; lurid stuff diluted to pass the censor boards." *Los Angeles Times*, July 23, 1922.

It is ironic that Bara was being so praised in 1922, at a time when she was trying for a comeback that did not materialize (unsuccessfully) until three years later. In fact, she was virtually being called a has-been, counted among the "old timers."

The Kreutzer Sonata (1915)

Background

Like the previous Theda Bara film, *A Fool There Was*, this film had more than one creative "father." The original one was Ludwig van Beethoven's 1803 piece of that name, the *Sonata no. 9 for Violin and Piano in A Major, opus 47*. Today it is considered one of his greatest sonatas for those instruments. It was only named for Rodolphe Kreutzer after Beethoven and the original dedicatee fell out. Ironically, Herr Kreutzer did not care for it, calling it "outrageously unintelligible."

Leo Tolstoy's 1889 novella takes its name from the sonata, which plays a part in the plot. The story's basic theme is the rejection of carnal love as a central part of life, even between spouses. (Tolstoy's wife unhappily believed it was autobiographical.) The book was initially banned in Russia and the United States as obscene. An American judge ruled: "It may contain very foolish and absurd views of marriage. It may shock our ideas about the sanctity and nobility of that institution, but cannot on that account be called an obscene libel."

A 1901 painting with the same title by the French artist Rene Prinet followed, showing a richly clad couple passionately embracing by a piano.

A 1906 Broadway play of the same name was based on the Tolstoy story and was originally written in Yiddish by Jacob Gordin. Translated into English, it had a brief Broadway run. Acclaimed tragedienne Bertha Kalich played Miriam Friedlander. Among the supporting cast was Jessie Ralph, who went on to do many Broadway plays and numerous Hollywood movie character parts. It is this play, not the novella, on which the film is based.

William Fox obviously wanted to provide some "class" to his films, which is why several of Theda Bara's earlier films were based on classical sources. Probably he was influenced by Adolph Zukor's "Famous Players in Famous Stories," of which Sarah Bernhardt was the first. It is likely that much of Fox's audience could not even pronounce "Kreutzer."

After a couple of Russian films based on the story, there came the Theda Bara version in 1915—except it was not supposed to be a *Bara* version at all. Directed by Irishman Herbert Brenon (born Alexander Herbert Reginald St. John Brenon), it was supposed to be a Nance O'Neil version. The California-born O'Neil (née Gertrude Lamson, 1874–1965) was a movie tyro (this was her second film), but she had been a Broadway presence since the 1890s.

She actually became a star on tour in England and Australia, and then on Broadway in plays like *Magda* and *Hedda Gabler*. Regally statuesque, she took her stage name from those of two old-time actresses, Anne (Nance) Oldfield and Eliza O'Neil. A theater critic said of her: "She has all the natural endowments for the stage.... She is a graceful leopard-like creature, an artist worthy to stand with the very highest."

Nance O'Neil was to be the star of the film; Theda Bara was to be a supporting player. The problem was that O'Neil's previous film role had been negligible. Bara's previous film had made her an unexpected star, and she had been rushed into this film to take advantage of that. The pre-release publicity featured Nance O'Neil's starring part. However, the average moviegoer of the time did not know about her stage work or care. It was Theda Bara they knew. The reviews often reflected that, and theater managers certainly did.

There were good reviews of Nance O'Neil's work, but she could not have been pleased at reviews like the one in the *Los Angeles Examiner* that read: "Theda Bara is again showing her wonderful art.... She is wonderful and is *ably assisted by Nance O'Neil* and William Shay" (italics mine).

The Kreutzer Sonata. The film's nominal star, theater diva Nance O'Neil, looks on as Theda Bara steals William E. Shay and the film out from under her. It was only Bara's second film, and it was her final supporting role.

The Film

Directed and adapted (scenario) by Herbert Brenon. Story by Count Leo Tolstoy. Play by Jacob Gordin. Produced by William Fox. Photography by Phil Rosen. Released by the William Fox Vaudeville Company on March 1, 1915, 5 reels.

Cast: Nance O'Neil (Miriam Friedlander), Theda Bara (Celia Friedlander), Henry Bergman (Raphael Friedlander), William E. Shay (Gregor Randar), John Daly Murphy (Sam Friedlander), Maude Turner Gordon (Rebecca Friedlander), Sidney Cushing (Belushoff), Anne Sutherland (Olga Belushoff), Mrs. Allen Walker (Natasha), Rhea Van Ole (The maid).

Synopsis: Miriam Friedlander, the daughter of an orthodox Jew, is threatened with disgrace for her affair with a young officer, Count Belushoff. Since they are unable to marry each other because of their religious differences, he shoots himself. He has told her to find someone to say that he (not Count Belushoff) is the father of their unborn child. The elder Friedlander convinces the musician Gregor Randar to do it for a sum of money, and the couple flee to America.

They are followed by her family, including her foster sister Celia. After the child is born, Gregor mistreats both Miriam and the child. Gregor and Celia enter into a secret love affair, and Celia discovers Miriam's guilty secret. She herself has a child out of wedlock whom she places in an orphanage. Miriam feels betrayed by both her husband and sister and confronts them. Her father also denounces the errant pair. When their pleas are unavailing, Miriam shoots them dead and then kills herself.

* * *

In 1923, composer Leos Janacek based his *First String Quartet* on the *Kreutzer Sonata*. Other films, novels, dance pieces including a ballet, and several plays based on the story have been produced in many countries.

Pennsylvania censors wanted to cut so much out of this film that it was tantamount to condemning it. They were overruled by the Philadelphia Court of Common Pleas, but censorship problems for Bara films would continue.

Nance O'Neil made several more films through 1919, and then after a ten-year hiatus she returned to appear in talking pictures. The first was the ill-starred *His Glorious Night* in 1929. It almost ruined leading man John Gilbert's reputation, but it put Nance O'Neil on track to make 15 more films as a character actress until 1932.

The Kreutzer Sonata was the first of four Theda Bara films which Herbert Brenon directed. He had been directing since 1911 and also had been a scenarist and actor. At Fox he had some success with Annette Kellermann films, but his greatest work is considered to have been for Paramount in the 1920s. There he made such hits as *Peter Pan*, *Dancing Mothers*, and the first version of *The Great Gatsby*. He made a transition to talking pictures but was not considered a particularly outstanding director after his silent film days. His final films were made in England.

The film played in San Francisco for three weeks. In an example of early special effects, a Spokane, Washington, theater manager arranged to have the sounds of four gunshots accompany the scene where Miriam kills her faithless husband and sister.

Reviews

"A production with which little fault can be found.... Nance O'Neil does not play her best until the big scene of the production. In this she rises to splendid dramatic heights. Earlier she seems to be working under restraints and a consciousness of the camera. Theda Bara gives a fine portrayal of her role. The sociological significance of the story has been well preserved." *Moving Picture World*, March 27, 1915.

"A wonderful production of the famous Tolstoy novel.... The story is dramatic from start to finish, as is usually the case with productions put on by Herbert Brenon." *Motography*, March 27, 1915.

"Ably upholds the high standards set by recent Fox productions. Nance O'Neil makes her first film appearance [sic] and it is a personal triumph." *Motion Picture Magazine*, April 1915.

"Just closed an eleven day run. We played to 7,000 more paid admissions during the first seven days than ever previously. Eleven days is the longest any feature has ever played." Theater manager, Colonial Theater, Seattle, Washington.

Special Review

Almost two years after the debut of *The Kreutzer Sonata*, a theater in Kansas City brought the film back—and most unusually for that part of the country—advertised it with Hebrew lettering. In its issue of February 17, 1917, *Moving Picture World* reviewed the film again. This time Nance O'Neil was not even mentioned, but the review did allude to the stage performance of Bertha Kalich. "Theda Bara, the famous emotional actress, plays the character with great strength and sinister fascination. In many respects this may be called the drama of the clash of the old order changing, giving place to the new.... It holds the spectator relentlessly in thrall with blood jumping heartward and nerves athrob. This is one of the most remarkable dramas of today."

The Clemenceau Case (1915)

Background

The film is based on the 1866 novel *L'Affaire Clemenceau* by Alexandre Dumas fils (1824–1895), whose most famous novel is *La Dame aux Camellias*. It is said to be partly based on the author's own life. The original publication date of the sequel, which is called *Son of Clemenceau: A Novel of Modern Love and Life*, is uncertain although there is an American edition of 1894. Dumas said about the character of Iza: "I shall never create another such character, though I scribble till Doomsday."

This picture marked the first starring role for Theda Bara. She was once again teamed with William Shay (sometimes billed as William E. Shay), who apparently was born about the same year the Dumas novel was published. They were to be co-stars in two more films.

The film was shot in and around Fort Lee, New Jersey. Publicity claimed that Bara worked with a live python borrowed from the Bronx Zoo. A close look at film stills readily reveals it to be a poor facsimile and the cause of much amused commentary.

The Film

Directed, produced, and scenario by Herbert Brenon. Based on the novel by Alexandre Dumas fils [and a play by Martha Woodrow?] Cinematography by Phil Rosen. Released by Fox Film Corporation on April 12, 1915. 6 reels.
Cast: Theda Bara (Iza), William Shay (Pierre), Stuart Holmes (Ritz), Frank Goldsmith (Sergius), Mrs. Allan Walker (Mme. Clemenceau), Janet (Jane Lee), Mrs. Cecil Raleigh (Iza's mother), Sidney Shields (Mme. Ritz).

Synopsis: Artist's model Iza marries the painter Pierre Clemenceau after he meets her in the Paris studio of his friend Constantin Ritz. Her mother has tried to marry her off to Sergius, a Russian duke. Iza becomes Sergius' mistress anyway and rejects everything decent. She is even responsible for Pierre's mother abandoning him. When Pierre discovers Iza's liaison, he challenges Sergius to a duel and kills him, but Iza has inherited the Duke's fortune.

Pierre leaves Iza and travels to America with Ritz and his family. He is happy with them until Iza arrives, meets Ritz in a café, and vamps him away from his family and a promising career. Pierre is determined to save Ritz from ruin. Pierre pretends to fall back under Iza's spell and arranges for Ritz to find her in his embrace. When she kisses Pierre, he stabs her, telling Ritz, "I have saved you for your wife." Pierre gladly gives himself up, happy to see Ritz back with his loving family.

* * *

The major success of this film proved Theda Bara's drawing power as a rising star. It was the first film in which she would play an artist's model; there would be several more. The use of the adjective "pantherish" began to be seen in reviews. One review stated that the part fit her like the "proverbial wet glove."

Ads were still featuring her as "The Vampire Woman of Theatre Antoine, Paris." That was very tame compared to the fevered ad which practically exploded off the page: "The soul of a siren ruthlessly bared in a unique photodrama of fiery storm-racked emotions that with cyclonic power sweeps straight to a cataclysmic climax."

Following what would have been the fatal excision of 1,800 feet of film by the Ohio Board of Censors, a public uproar ensued. A Cincinnati theater manager (no doubt eager to uphold the reputation of a hometown girl) gave a private showing, at which the audience found nothing objectionable. The Board reconsidered, ordering only minor cuts this time.

The Chicago Board of Censors was a bit more liberal. They did not like a couple of bedroom scenes that showed Iza locking the bedroom door, the scene in which a nightgown falls from her shoulders (shades of *A Fool There Was*), and the scene where Pierre stabs her. How that climactic scene was ultimately presented in Chicago is unknown.

According to her friend Joan Craig (see *Bibliography*), one of Theda Bara's most treasured possessions was her Fox presentation copy of the English translation of *The Clemenceau Case*. It featured Bara's picture on the cover and gold lettering that read: "William Fox Presents Theda Bara in *The Clemenceau Case* by Alexandre Dumas. Pictured and Produced by Herbert Brenon." Possibly one of a kind, Bara's keepsake was sold at auction in 2008.

Stuart Holmes, born Joseph Liebschen (there are variations of that spelling) and usually an arch-villain, played one of his rarer sympathetic roles. He had an amazingly long career in films of at least 55 years, with hundreds of credits to his name.

Fox publicity claimed that after a private showing of this film, a crowd of 500 or 600 women "mobbed Jane Lee, the tiny actress." This was little Jane's first feature appearance after appearing in some short films. She usually was seen as an impossibly angelic little blonde girl. Eventually she and older sister Katherine Lee had a starring series of their own at Fox, in which they demonstrated a mischievous side.

For a few years in the 1910s they were seen as one of Fox's great assets, but like all child stars they began growing up. They were unceremoniously released in 1919 at the exact same time as Theda Bara. As attractive young women, they made their final onscreen appearance together in *Vitaphone Billboard*, a February 1936 one-reel Vitaphone short. They did a comic song lamenting having had to grow up, and a brief dance number.

Another version of this story, the 1917 Italian film *Il Processo Clemenceau*, marked the cinema debut of Vittorio De Sica, who would become one of Italy's greatest film directors and actors. He played the Clemenceau "Bambino."

The Fox film was one of those Fox Pictures rereleased in 1918 under the rubric of "The Big Six." It may have been among the Bara films that were re-edited to five reels and re-titled.

Reviews

"A feature that will live long in the picture world. As a matter of fact it is one of the best released by the Fox Film Corporation. The theme of the story lends itself naturally to screen production, and contains all the elements to go toward making a successful production. No end of thrills, and there are times when the audience waits with bated breath. Theda Bara gives a wonderful performance as the vampire-wife.... Fox has a hit." *Variety*, April 23, 1915.

"Intensely and fiercely dramatic. It contains the sirenic [*sic*] evil which is particularly suited to Miss Bara's remarkable powers in the Vampire type of character. As Iza she created even a greater sensation [than previously]. Few who saw her can ever forget her striking performance. Many of the newspapers throughout the country declared her to be [the] most wickedly beautiful actress in the world. Women besieged the theater demanding to see the fatal end of the siren who wrought such havoc." *Motion Picture News*, May 22, 1915.

"Theda Bara never rose to greater heights than in this production. Her portrayal of the serpent woman who plays havoc with men's hearts is exquisite in every detail." *New York Telegraph*, May 1915.

"Purely Gallic in type, Miss Bara is an ideal selection for the character. She has first-class histrionic equipment, is a genuine artist in pantomime, and gives likelihood to the role which she enacts in every detail." Review, 1915.

"I raised my admission from twenty to twenty-five cents during the run; even then I turned them away. I was sure from my previous experience with *The Kreutzer Sonata* and *A Fool There Was* that this film was going to be something out of the ordinary." Theater manager, Seattle, Washington.

1918 Re-Release

"A work that threshes society with a living whip, as its author Alexandre Dumas described. It shows vividly the lengths to which a woman of pantherish nature will go when her instincts lead her." *Motography*, June 1, 1918.

"William Fox did well to select it as one of his Big Six of 1918. It ranks today with [Bara's] best efforts. She is again the heartless vampire, play[ing] the part of the Dumas lady for its full worth. The interest remains at a high pitch from beginning to end, and there are innumerable powerful situations." *Motion Picture News*, July 13, 1918.

"[It] will undoubtedly meet with its former success with the type of audience who appreciate the Bara style, and the super-melodramatic flavor given the production. The star's ability to vamp is played up as the central pivot of the story to an extent that will be offensive to some…. It has only the charm of melodrama and fails to establish a more serious objective." *Moving Picture World*, July 20, 1918.

"Star always draws, packed them in all night." Manager, Clifton Theatre, Chicago, Illinois.

The Devil's Daughter (1915)

Background

After Theda Bara's success in her three previous films, especially her first starring role in *The Clemenceau Case*, William Fox knew he had struck cinema gold. The titles of those films had been taken directly from the original source materials. It was time to highlight the star rather than obscure "classics" totally unknown to most audiences. To expect crowds to flock to another Bara film, *La Gioconda* was not going to be the lure; *The Devil's Daughter* was. The working title of the film was *The Vampire*, but there had already been films with that name. There had been a 1913 Danish short called *The Devil's Daughter*.

The title *La Gioconda* ("the jovial one" in Italian) has a notable past. It is the official name of the Leonardo Da Vinci masterpiece, commonly known as the "Mona Lisa." It is the title of Ponchielli's 1876 opera, based on an 1835 Victor Hugo work, and now best known for its catchy set piece "Dance of the Hours." This Bara film is based on Gabriele D'Annunzio's 1898/99 play, also titled *La Gioconda*, written for the famous Italian actress Eleanora Duse. Her repertory company had brought it to Broadway in November 1902.

Frank Powell, director of *A Fool There Was*, returned to direct a Bara film for the final time. *The Devil's Daughter* company headed down to St. Augustine, Florida, to shoot some scenes. Publicity touted the "very warm reception" they found in Florida, with the heat hovering near 100 degrees. Fortunately, the owner of the hotel at which the company stayed had placed his 85-foot yacht *Hilda* at their disposal. Scenes were shot at the Villa Flora estate and at the Hotel Ponce de Leon and the Hotel Alcazar. The rest of the film was shot at Fort Lee.

The Film

Directed by Frank Powell. Scenario by Garfield Thompson. Based on the play *La Gioconda* by Gabriele D'Annunzio; translated by Joseph Trant. Cinematography by David Calcagni. Released by the Fox Film Corporation on June 16, 1915. 5 reels.
Cast: Theda Bara (Gioconda Dianti), Paul Doucet (Lucio Settala), Victor Benoit (Cosmo

Dalbo), Robert Wayne (Lorenzo Gaddi), Jane Lee (Beata Settala), Doris Heywood (Silvia Settala), Jane Miller (Francesca Doni), Elaine Evans (La Sirenetta), Edouard Durand (Roffiano).

Synopsis: After her lover steals her jewels and deserts her for flirting with another man, Gioconda Dianti vows to destroy all men. She declares that her heart will be like ice and her passions, consuming fire. It will be up to the men who cross her path to beware. One who does not is the sculptor Lucio Settala, who wants her to pose for him. She seduces him, making him forget about his wife Silvia and his young daughter.

Gioconda taunts Silvia; Lucio, in a fit of conscience, tries to kill himself. His loyal wife nurses him back to health, only to see him go back to Gioconda. Silvia and Gioconda fight, and a statue that Lucio has sculpted falls on Silvia, maiming her for life. Racked with guilt, Lucio loses his sanity. Cast aside by the now demented Lucio, Gioconda, her evil work done, dies.

* * *

The Fox publicity machine really went to work for this ultra-melodramatic film but may have overreached. Not only was it claimed that D'Annunzio himself had written the film's scenario, but he also claimed that he was induced to do so "only after he was assured that this marvelous artiste (Bara) would be assigned to portray his famous vampire character." Considering that Gabriele D'Annunzio (1863–1938) was not only a prolific poet, playwright, and novelist but also a military strategist and politician, these claims seem absurd. He was no doubt better occupied during the war year of 1915 in plotting to get Italy to drop its neutral stance and join the war against Germany and its allies.

Ads touted Theda Bara, in only her fourth film, as "one of the greatest motion picture actresses in the world [and] universally popular ... as a sirenic lady whose chief diversion is wrecking the lives of all men with whom she comes in contact." The picture was called "artistic, clever, unusual, and just the sort of picture-play that reaches across the screen and grabs you and holds you in a vice-like grip until the last scene fades from view." The use of the made-up adjective "sirenic" was also increasing, joining "pantherish" as colorful descriptors.

A perfervid poem called "The Devil's Daughter" was penned by an unknown author and used to advertise the film. Although written especially for this film, it could well serve as the screen vampire's code. There are allusions in it to Theda Bara's publicity ("hollow skulls") and to previous roles.

> Her kiss is death, her love red flame/That scorches like a white-hot brand
> But luring lightning in her eyes/Beckons to that forbidden land
> Where blasted lives, like hollow skulls/Lie whitening on the sun-bit sand
> Her paths are milestoned wickedly/By sunken souls that cry despair
> Hers the glance that breathes delight/The Devil's Daughter, passing fair
> Has wrought her spell and filled her oath/She triumphs to see fools rot there
> The Devil's Daughter takes cruel toll/Her blood-red lips are sugared lies
> That lull her fools in her white arms/And mock them in their parting breath
> And laugh to see their fell work done/As cursing, dupes go down to death.

Censorship threatened to derail the film's showing. The Ohio Board of Censorship went to a private showing at midnight in Cleveland, and they "came, saw, and slashed.

When the snipping of shears had stopped, it was found that 1,800 feet of the film had been put into discard. Every scene in which Theda Bara appeared was eliminated." Regular audience members in attendance, who had expected to be shocked, came away disappointed. They agreed there was nothing terrible about the film and that the censors had struck out again.

Newspapermen in the audience found the film about as vicious as a Punch and Judy show. They theorized that if the film had kept the title of its source material, it would have breezed past the censors. The censors also supposedly complained that since the Devil never had a daughter, the title was wrong! *Variety* commented on the "old-maidenishness" of the Ohio censors.

Fox threatened a court suit; the local police had no problem with the film. An appeal to the Ohio Governor to remove and replace the members of the Censorship Board was considered. A Fox representative voluntarily deleted 300 feet of the film and resubmitted it. The censors reconsidered their decision. The Kansas Board of Censors banned the film.

Some reviews referred to the unfortunate inclination of audiences to laugh at certain places in the film. One such place was a hair-pulling battle between Gioconda and his abandoned wife Silvia, who was played by a rather substantially-built actress. Most reviews continued to remain very favorable to Bara, but some reservations crept in. This may have led to the studio's decision to star her in her first (mostly) non-vampiric role, *Lady Audley's Secret*.

Reviews

"Seems like rather a poor imitation of *A Fool There Was*.... Being all in a lugubrious key, the picture becomes wearisome and occasionally, when comedy was farthest from the intention of the actors, laughable.... Restraint is not recognized as a valuable asset of art in a production that is weak in its dramatic construction and, truth to tell, somewhat negative in the impression it leaves." *Motion Picture World*, June 1915.

"Theda Bara works hard but does not show to as good an advantage as she has in previous productions of this character. This is surely due to the absence of timely close-ups of that wonderful face." *New York Mail*, June 1915.

"In interpreting sensuous roles Miss Bara easily stands in a class by herself. She is a perfect siren of the screen.... Her physical charms and the many scenes chosen for their photographic beauty give the picture considerable artistic value. The plot cannot be taken literally, but the picture is an artistic, dramatic conception, and as a vehicle for Theda Bara is quite sufficient." *Motion Picture News*, June 26, 1915.

"A screen-play of force and powerful appeal. Its central theme is the depiction of an evilly beautiful siren who is half-serpent and half-woman in nature. No actress could have been found, save Theda Bara, who possessed the febrile art and sinister beauty requisite to portray the role of the fascinating and diabolical temptress. Mlle. Bara's striking and beautiful face has been called the wickedest in the world." *San Francisco Chronicle*, June 27, 1915.

"Packed houses greeted the film presentment [*sic*] of Miss Bara's new film play, said to be founded on *La Gioconda*, but the connection seems remote. As the diabolically fascinating temptress Miss Bara is unique." *Los Angeles Times*, June 29, 1915.

Lady Audley's Secret (1915)

Background

The decision to temporarily star Theda Bara in non-vampiric roles was understandable after her last full-on vampire performance in *The Devil's Daughter*. A few reviews had been less than full raves, even though the film was a big hit. It is not known with certainty why *Lady Audley's Secret* was the first vehicle selected. It did meet William Fox's apparent taste for established "classics," but a one-reel version had just been released earlier in 1915. It had already been filmed by Kalem in 1908 and by IMP in 1912, the latter directed by Herbert Brenon. The first known film version came from the UK in 1906.

The 1862 novel was more than 50 years old by 1915 and was regarded as an old chestnut. In its time, though, it had been viewed as almost scandalous, as was its author, M.E. Braddon. That was Mary Elizabeth Braddon, later Maxwell. She was the common law wife of publisher John Maxwell, who had several children by his legal wife, who was still living. Braddon and Maxwell had an additional six children together before she became the legal Mrs. Maxwell after more than a dozen years together.

The novel had originally begun to be serialized, as was then the custom, in a periodical that went bankrupt. Braddon had not yet concluded the book, but the public demand for its completion led her to finish it in another periodical. Beginning in 1863, several stage versions of the novel had been written by George Roberts and others. Because of the novel's initial appearance in serial form, its plot is much more convoluted and has many more characters than the film. This leads to the conjecture that the film may be based on a dramatization of the novel, rather than the novel itself.

For whatever reason, most probably the story's rich melodramatic qualities, Theda Bara was set to play Helen Talboys/Lady Audley. Marshall Farnum, the youngest of three show business brothers, was selected to direct. His two elder brothers were William and Dustin Farnum, both popular leading men in the silent days and frequently on Broadway. William was a particular Fox favorite and was starred in numerous adventure films, losing some favor only when Tom Mix came on the scene. Marshall (called "Ding" by his brothers) had acted on Broadway too and had begun directing films about 1913. He was only 37 when he died in 1917; *Lady Audley's Secret* was one of his final films. It was shot in New Jersey.

The Film

Directed by Marshall Farnum. Adapted by Mary Asquith from the novel by M.E. Braddon. Cinematography by Norton Davis. Released by Fox Film Corporation on August 4, 1915. 5 reels.
Cast: Theda Bara (Helen Talboys/Lady Audley), William Riley Hatch (Luke Martin), Clifford Bruce (George Talboys), Warner Richmond (Sir Michael Audley), Steven Grattan.

Synopsis: Helen Davenant marries George Talboys, primarily to get away from her drunken father. When George leaves to prospect for gold in Australia, he leaves her a note and some money, but her father pockets the money and tears up the note. Because George had ceased to communicate with her, she believes she has either been legally deserted or widowed. She marries Lord Michael Audley.

When she realizes that she has a maid who closely resembles herself, Lady Audley tells everyone that the maid is George's widow. When the maid dies, Helen passes her off as Helen Talboys. In that way she believes she can avoid any possible charges of bigamy should George return. Unfortunately for Helen, her stepson is a friend of her first husband. George does return, having become a rich man from striking gold.

Helen and George meet again at Audley Court. Helen tells him that he never made her happy and begs him to leave so she can live in peace with Lord Audley, whom she does love. He refuses. George Talboys' discovery of her unintended bigamy has triggered Helen's hereditary tendency toward insanity. When a struggle ensues, she pushes George into a well, believing that she has killed him.

George is not dead, having been rescued by a coachman who has seen the incident. Her stepson becomes suspicious. Fearing exposure by him, Helen breaks into his room and steals the key to his London flat. There she retrieves some love letters she had written to George. In an attempt to compromise her stepson, she tells Lord Audley that his son has tried to make love to her.

Helen then learns that she has not killed George after all, that he was rescued from the well. When she actually sees him standing near the well, the shock is so great that she falls dead. George tells the men who know Lady Audley's secret to let it die with her.

There is another version of *Lady Audley's Secret* extant, an "all ends happily" version. Although not used for this film, it is possibly derived from one of the dramatizations. In this version, Lady Audley's sanity is restored, George grants her a divorce, and all ends happily.

* * *

Theda Bara's characters continued to come to bad ends. In her entire body of work through 1919, more often than not her characters failed to survive "The End" title card. Although this film was supposed to be a departure from her deep-dyed vampire villainy, it was not far enough removed for some. The character of Helen Audley, while not trying to destroy all men, was still "smeared with a coat of villainy" as the *Variety* review (below) phrased it. This may well have led to the decision to take her next role even further from her established persona. And there were few roles more removed from it than the one she was to play in *The Two Orphans*.

In some countries of the British Empire, the film was called *Secrets of Society*.

Reviews

"You will enjoy this film because there is an absorbing story and the tempo of the dramatic action is splendid. Theda Bara that 'most wickedly beautiful woman on earth' has done some very fine scenes, and it is chiefly due to her work that the production registers as a success." *New York Mail*, August 1915.

"Does the Fox Company honestly believe that because she is reputed to be 'the most wickedly beautiful woman on earth,' and because she portrayed a number of vampire characters in a fashion that put her in wide demand, the public will be pleased by anything Theda Bara does? I have just seen [the film] and candidly I wish I hadn't. She literally acted all over the place." *Atlanta Constitution*, 1915.

"Dips deep into melodrama.... Smeared from start to finish with a coat of villainy by a woman who stops at nothing to gain her ends. Theda Bara brings some of her facial expressions and ghastly roll of the eyes into play.... A morbid and gruesome affair, and one doesn't leave the theater with a pleasant memory. It's melodrammer of the old-fashioned sort that should be a cyclonic hit in some of the neighborhoods where they dote on this stuff." *Variety*, August 1915.

"The stage success has lost none of its dramatic qualities in the filming. Although decidedly in contrast with the vampire roles, the actress gives the same human touch to her portrayal that has characterized the temptress parts of her other screen successes. Her wickedly beautiful face is equally fascinating, while her work in the mad scene is said to be her greatest bit of acting." *San Francisco Chronicle*, September 6, 1915.

The Two Orphans (1915)

Background

After four torrid vampire roles earlier in 1915 and a follow-up film that had a morally dubious heroine, the Fox studio now decided to go all the way into the light with Theda Bara. They had reached back to 1862 for *Lady Audley's Secret*; for this film they only went back as far as 1874. That year *The Two Orphans* originated as a five-act play in Paris titled *Les Deux Orphelines*.

One of the two playwrights was the extremely prolific Adolphe Philippe d'Ennery (1811–1899); the other was the almost equally prolific Eugene Cormon (1810–1903). Cormon, born Pierre-Etienne Piestre, was primarily a collaborator on plays and opera libretti, one of which was George Bizet's *The Pearl Fishers*.

In December of 1874 an English language version called *The Two Orphans* opened on Broadway, starring two leading actresses, Kate Claxton and Rose Eytinge. It ran to June 1875 for a total of 180 performances. This was considered a long run in those days when most successful plays had limited runs in New York and then went out on tour. Based on their play's success, the authors novelized it in 1877. The play was revived on Broadway at least three more times: 1904, 1926, and 1936.

The Two Orphans was filmed in languages that included Italian, Spanish, Turkish, Arabic, Japanese, and French. In America it appeared as a 1911 three-reeler with the popular Kathlyn Williams, and it had been produced in American one-reel versions previously. Although she would be the nominal star, Theda Bara would be sharing much screen time with the other "orphan," the winsome blonde Jean Sothern. Some reviewers would opine that Bara had been outshone by her petite co-star. However, the strong melodramatic story and action scenes may well have been the actual star.

To demonstrate that this was no mere minor production, Fox had elaborate sets built to emulate France during the time of the French Revolution. The drama inherent in that great uprising provides much of the drama for the story. Seven years later, D.W. Griffith transmuted the story into a near-epic with his *Orphans of the Storm*, starring Lillian and Dorothy Gish.

Publicity claimed—probably to be taken with a large grain of salt—that the prison set cost more than $10,000, requiring 10 tons of masonry, three miles of canvas, a dozen barrels of nails, and four tons of paint. Four open-air sets allegedly cost $15,000 each. Personnel numbered 100 carpenters, 20 painters, 10 stone masons, a score of electricians, and hundreds of extras. One source claimed that some exteriors were shot in Quebec and Montreal, Canada; another, that it was only Quebec; and still another, that it was only Montreal. The remainder was shot in Fort Lee, New Jersey.

This would be the next-to-last film that Herbert Brenon directed for Theda Bara; her next film, *Sin*, would be his last with her. *The Two Orphans* was also almost the last film in which Brenon acted. He portrayed the brave beggar Pierre.

There is a true-life mystery that is almost as interesting as the film. There were two actresses named Jean Sothern, whose biographies have sometimes been mixed up with each other. One died in 1924, the other in 1964. Some sources still seem to be confusing them.

The Jean Sothern who played Louise went on to star in the popular serial *The Mysteries of Myra*. She is apparently the one who passed away in 1924, not even 30 years of age.

The Two Orphans. Theda Bara's first good girl role as one of the two imperiled French orphans; the other orphan was Jean Sothern. Bara (left) is shown with her benefactress, played by Mrs. Cecil Raleigh (Saba Raleigh). Some thought that Bara was outshone by her pretty blonde co-star.

The Film

>Directed and scenario by Herbert Brenon. Based on the play or the novel *Les Deux Orphelines* by Adolphe Philippe d'Ennery and Eugene Cormon. Cinematography by Phil Rosen. Released by the Fox Film Corporation on September 6, 1915. 7 reels.
>**Cast**: Theda Bara (Henriette), Jean Sothern (Louise), William E. Shay (Chevalier de Vaudrey), Herbert Brenon (Pierre), Gertrude Berkeley (Mother Frochard), Frank Goldsmith (Marquis de Presles), E.L. Fernandez (Jacques), Sheridan Block (Count de Liniere), John Daly Murphy (Picard), Mrs. Cecil Raleigh (Countess de Liniere).

Synopsis: Two orphans from Normandy, Henriette and her blind sister Louise, are sent to live with their uncle in Paris. The letter sent to the uncle is intercepted, and Henriette is kidnapped and taken to the libertine Marquis de Presles. Louise, left on her own, is rescued by the hunchback Pierre. His mother, called Mother Frochard, is a beggar, and she forces Louise to become one too. Pierre is forced to kill his good-for-nothing brother to protect Louise.

Henriette is rescued by Chevalier de Vaudrey, who fights a duel for her. He wants to marry her, but his parents object. Henriette reveals that Louise is not her real sister, but is actually the half-sister of the Chevalier, a daughter from his mother's former marriage. Louise is rescued from the beggars, and, her sight restored, she rejoins Pierre.

* * *

The Two Orphans was the first film released by the Fox studio under its "One-a-Week" policy which promised that Fox would supply one new film each and every week. At the time of its re-release in 1918 as one of Fox's "Big Six," the film was "re-titled, re-edited, and revised" and was trimmed to five reels. The studio claimed that 5,000 exhibitors had requested it and that the "Big Six" were the cream of Fox's output since they were first made.

An advertisement for the film boasted: "A stupendous picturization of the world-known and beloved drama. A $500,000 production; hundreds in the picture; massive scenes that involved months of painstaking toil and effort to produce. A true masterwork!" Other sources claimed that the film had cost in the vicinity of $300,000.

To publicize the film, a theater owner in Wichita, Kansas, had a coupon printed that promised: "Entitles holder to a hundred sensations…. Bearer may claim a 10c seat for ten cents." Another ad read: "The story of two waifs whose best friend is Dan Cupid. Kate Claxton's great triumph repeated by Theda Bara. A great melodrama that has moved millions to tears." (It is difficult now to imagine Bara as a "waif.")

In October 1915, Fox was sued by Kate Claxton (then known as Kate Stevenson) to prevent the film from being exhibited. She had played Louise in the 1874 production, and she claimed that she owned the copyright to one translation of the play. She demanded $100,000 in compensation for damages; Fox paid her $2,500.

The Selig Studio announced it would re-release the 1911 three-reel version. Selig claimed to own the rights, not Fox, to make the Claxton version of the play into a film. In 1929 the popular Duncan Sisters, Rosetta and Vivian, floated the idea of starring in a remake of *The Two Orphans*.

Reviews

"Is very apt to draw people back to sit through it a second time…. In it Jean Sothern leaps ahead of Theda Bara in the playing. Miss Bara had comparatively little to look after…. In its sadness and pathetic and sympathetic leanings it's well suited to be among the very few standard films produced so far that will have a long life. There is none other to be made that will resemble it in any way. The feature looks big enough to have stood seven or eight reels for a special show." *Variety*, September 10, 1915.

"Miss Bara is doing some of the best work of her career. It must be confessed that we don't like the idea of her 'reforming,' but she gives a strong and convincing characterization nevertheless…. Miss Bara's versatile genius is quite equal to interpreting a beautiful character. Those who have viewed her in her wicked roles are curious to see how she plays the part of an angelic maiden whose every thought is for others." *Los Angeles Times*, October 15, 1915.

"While Miss Bara has achieved her coveted hope of playing a good girl, it cannot be said that her conversion was altogether a success. As the heroine she was perfectly proper and pasteurizingly nice, but there will be many as likes her bad." *Photoplay*, 1915.

"Again, in this picture, Miss Bara plays the role of the perfectly proper woman. As in *Lady Audley's Secret* Miss Bara seems miscast. Her specialty, the adventuress, appears to suit her personality better than the character of an upright, moral woman." *Chicago Daily News*, 1915.

1918 Re-Release

"It is justly celebrated as a melodrama the world over. In screen form it holds the old-time power, and there are moments when the melodrama rises to the full dignity of drama.... Quite obvious in its heart-appeal, but none the less gripping for that. The big moments of the original play have been carefully brought out and even strengthened in the screen version." *Moving Picture World*, July 27, 1918.

"Theda Bara's reappearance in the 1918 version will be more than welcomed by patrons of the silent drama. This was done when Miss Bara first began to attract an unusual notice on the screen. It is her best straight role. The picture affords real sound entertainment. It carries the same appeal, is just as interesting, and loses none of its attraction and power to give enjoyment." *Motion Picture News*, August 3, 1918.

Sin (1915)

Background

With Theda Bara's "good girl" role in *The Two Orphans* behind her, it was probably felt that she needed to resume her sinning—and what better film to do it in than *Sin* itself. Although it was not strictly speaking a vampire role, her character was hardly morally pure. She was kind of an Italian Lady Audley as measured on the sinning scale.

The genesis of *Sin* was a more recent "classic" than her other features to that date. It was adapted from the three-act 1911 opera *The Jewels of the Madonna* (*I Gioielli della Madonna*), composed by Ermanno Wolf-Ferrari, with libretto by Carlo Zangarini and Enrico Golisciani. The opera premiered in Berlin, where it was called *Der Schmuck der Madonna*. The genesis of the opera itself is said to have been newspaper accounts of an actual event.

The film's working title was *The Jewels of the Madonna*, but such a final title might likely have caused even more trouble with the censors and probably the Catholic Church. *Sin* was the last of Theda Bara's films to be directed by Herbert Brenon, and the last film in which William E. Shay would be her co-star. It was also among the very first film appearances of Swedish actor Warner Oland (born Johan Ohlund), already cast as the villain as he would so often be in silent films.

The Film

> Directed and scenario by Herbert Brenon. Based on the opera *I Gioielli della Madonna* by Ermanno Wolf-Ferrari. Cinematography by Phil Rosen. Released by the Fox Film Corporation on October 3, 1915. 5 reels.
> **Cast**: Theda Bara (Rosa), Warner Oland (Pietro), William E. Shay (Luigi), Louise Briehl (Maria), Henry Leone (Giovanni).

Synopsis: At a village fete, Rosa, an Italian peasant, meets Pietro, a kingpin of the criminal organization Camorra. He has come back to Italy for a visit. He now lives in New York's Little Italy, and he enchants her with stories about America. Leaving her woodcutter fiancé Luigi, Rosa goes with Pietro to New York. The heartbroken Luigi follows, and, determined to win her back, becomes Rosa's protector. He still wants to marry her; Pietro is merely toying with her. Luigi continues to declare his love for her, but she taunts him.

Pietro boastfully tells Rosa that he would even steal the sacred jewels of the Madonna to possess her. She replies that to such a man she would give herself unreservedly. Luigi overhears, and that night breaks into the church and steals the jewels from the church altar. He lays them at Rosa's feet, and she adorns herself with them. An angry mob, hearing of the theft, hunts for the thief.

Overcome with guilt, Luigi returns the jewels and kills himself on the steps of the church. Rosa pushes her way through the Festival of the Madonna to Camorra headquarters to find Pietro. She seeks his protection, but he is shocked by her sacrilege. He denounces her and throws her into the street. Rosa has to be saved by the police from the enraged mob, and she becomes insane.

* * *

The Kansas City, Missouri, censors approved the film without a cut, but the Topeka, Kansas, censors objected to the title and some scenes. The Kansas City manager of Fox Film Corporation offered to change the title, but that was not enough to placate the censors. Despite the general approval of members of several women's clubs, the film was banned outright in Kansas by the state board.

The Ohio Board of Censors snipped 1,800 feet from the film, effectively banning it. Both exhibitors and moviegoers protested that action. Showings were cancelled, and it was announced that a crusade had been launched against Theda Bara's films. A Cleveland theater owner (and would-be orator?) was quoted as saying: "Censorship was conceived in iniquity, was born in sin, and is dying of disgrace." The Ohio censors demanded his arrest (presumably for slander) and a trial date was set.

A private and crowded late-night showing of *Sin* was arranged; the audience found nothing objectionable about the film. A committee of exhibitors went to the state capitol to meet with the censors, and the decision was made to pass *Sin* after all with only a few minor deletions.

Reviews

"The story, while somewhat light in interest, has some excellent emotional scenes. Miss Bara is quite her emotional self and thoroughly at home in the Italian character. It's a feature [that doesn't involve] the usual love affair." *Variety*, October 1915.

"An original and unique photoplay. It is an unusually powerful and convincing story, abounding in strong dramatic climaxes growing out of the clash of elemental human passions." *Los Angeles Times*, October 3, 1915.

"Despite the startling title it is less sensuously frank than several other pictures in which Theda Bara, to put it mildly, depicted women of strong emotional temperament. The film cutter seems to have interrupted a number of promising love passages and left more to the imagination, which is as it should be. As it stands, there is nothing to give offense.... An unusual and quite artistic picture." *Moving Picture World*, October 16, 1915.

"It was time, in the opinion of many, that the vampire crown should be lifted from the brow of Theda Bara and replaced by another, not so gorgeous but set with other jewels. She had worn it so long that her admirers had begun to think that she would have to wear it always. In this picture she is not the lure, but the lured.... Her extraordinary abilities as an emotional actress are therefore somewhat diluted by the very necessities of the part. But when she does have an opportunity, she takes full possession of the screen in the full power of her peculiar genius." *Motion Picture News*, November 14, 1915.

"Personally I have no use for a photoplay of this kind. It is all overdrawn and could never happen in real life. But what is the use of having likes and dislikes when the public wants it? They almost mobbed the theater in their efforts to get inside, and once inside they ate it up." *Chicago Tribune* ("Mae Tinee"), 1915.

"This picture is one of the best seen for some time, and played to good houses. We have rebooked *A Fool There Was*." Manager, Lillian Theatre, Clarksville, Kentucky.

Carmen (1915)

Background

Prosper Merimee's novella *Carmen* was originally published in a Paris magazine in 1845. It was immortalized 30 years later in 1875 as the source of the libretto for the Georges Bizet opera of the same name. Bizet and his librettists, Henri Meilhac and Ludovic Halevy, had produced one of the most popular operas ever composed. Forty years after that, in 1915, the opera singer Geraldine Farrar starred in one of the competing motion picture versions of *Carmen* for the Lasky Picture Play Company; Theda Bara in the other for Fox.

The role of the fiery Merimee/Bizet gypsy Carmen seemed a perfect fit for Theda Bara. It is a role that does not call for much subtlety, and Bara was not known to be a subtle actress. Farrar's portrayal at exactly the same time set up comparisons as to who had better captured the essence of the gypsy cigarette girl. The Fox studio, known for its lavish expenditure on sets, use of extras, and background color did not stint on its version.

Fox was not shy about publicizing (or sometimes greatly exaggerating) that lavishness: "A band of real gypsies were lured from their mountain retreats"; "a noted Spanish artist came from Seville to supervise the technical and architectural details"; "a Spanish army colonel drilled the dragoons"; and even "an Andalusian bull came from Madrid." (Director Raoul Walsh later wrote that the bull had actually come from New Jersey.) Fox also claimed that a 20-acre lot was used to re-create Cordova and Seville.

Theda Bara (or Fox publicity) certainly seemed to believe that her Carmen was a triumph: "I feel I have attained the goal of my artistic ambition. The various types of women which I have created during the last year are more or less akin to the supreme Carmen and may be regarded, I am sure, as having been in some measure a preparation for my greatest achievement."

The Fox publicity machine modestly echoed: "Mlle. Bara has won a position of prominence in filmdom, and the flouting, pouting gypsy flirt is said to be her crowning achievement. Her characterization gives free rein to her marvelous genius." Another Fox advertisement boasted: "Absolutely and indisputably supreme, inimitable, and alone in magnificence of conception, cast, and scenic investiture."

Yet another read: "Theda Bara's life triumph as the haughty and intolerant gypsy beauty in every conceivable way marks an epoch in motion pictures!" Why Fox thought "flouting" and "intolerant" were complimentary words is unknown, but the reviews would not necessarily bear out this orgy of self-congratulation.

The director Raoul Walsh (1887–1980) was at the beginning of a career which would endure for more than 45 years and well over 100 films. Although he was prolific in the silent era, the height of his fame would come with sound, especially in the late 1930s and beyond. With his signature eye patch, he became known as a director who was particularly successful with macho male action stars. He was the older brother of the actor George Walsh, who would appear with Theda Bara in *The Serpent*. In later years Raoul more than hinted about an off-screen fling with Bara, but his tell-all tales were not always reliable.

The rival Carmen, lyric soprano (Alice) Geraldine Farrar, was already a well-known opera diva when she essayed her first movie role in *Carmen* for mogul Jesse Lasky and director Cecil B. De Mille. Unlike many of the hefty female opera singers of that era, she was American, slim, petite (five feet, three inches tall), very attractive, a more than competent actress, and charismatic. Those traits helped her to become a movie star for as long a time as Theda Bara, and she was the first opera singer to have a substantial career in the cinema. She drew a crowd of young women acolytes around her who came to be known as Gerry-Flappers.

Farrar's Don Jose was played by Wallace Reid. He would become one of the most popular leading men in the silent cinema until his tragic early death. Swedish actor Einar Linden played Don Jose in the Fox version and would appear with Theda Bara twice more, in *The Eternal Sapho* and in *Romeo and Juliet*. These roles comprised fully one-third of his entire movie career. Like Geraldine Farrar he was also a singer.

When it seemed that the Farrar version might be the preferred one with critics, the Fox publicity machine became more aggressive in comparing the two versions. "Theda Bara's life triumph, supreme beyond belief. Superbly solitary in conceded pre-eminence. Imitation preposterous and futile." "Theda Bara is not being impeded or restrained by operatic limitations. Here is an original, wild, free, untrammeled version departing from all familiar paths. Stands supremely and resistlessly [sic] alone and unrivalled."

Other Fox ads were similarly over the top: "The wonder of a dazzled moving picture world. Will be everywhere received with spontaneous acclamation and rapturous applause." And alliteration gone wild: "Gorgeously gigantic gypsy gem. A masterpiece of photoplay accomplishment."

What the two actresses may have felt about their supposed cinema rivalry is not known.

There was actually a third actress playing Carmen at roughly the same time, but the placid Edna Purviance would not be a threat to the other two. She was more or less a prop in Charlie Chaplin's two-reel *Burlesque on Carmen*, which came out at the end of 1915. He played Don Hosiery, his comic version of Don Jose. One of the excitements around that film was Chaplin's attempt to stop the Essanay studio from showing the film, to which they had added two extra reels without his permission and in which he did not even appear. The New York Supreme Court denied the injunction. In 1924 *Photoplay* postulated that this Chaplin film was the one which established cinema as a true art form because parodies and burlesques meant the film that was parodied was a work of art.

The Film

Directed and scenario by Raoul Walsh. Based on the novella *Carmen* by Prosper Merimee. Cinematography by Georges Benoit and George Schneiderman. Art direction by Edward Velasquez. New York premiere at the Academy of Music on October 31, 1915. Released by the Fox Film Corporation on November 1, 1915. 5 reels.
Cast: Theda Bara (Carmen), Einar Linden (Don Jose), Carl Harbaugh (Escamillo), James Marcus (Dancaire), Elsie MacLeod (Michaela), Fay Tunis (Carlotta), E. De Varny (Captain Morales).

Synopsis: The young soldier Don Jose goes back to his village to see his mother and his sweetheart Michaela. He later meets and is dazzled by the gypsy cigarette girl Carmen. He allows her to escape after she slashes a fellow worker; for that he is court-martialed and sent to prison. When he is released, he duels and kills the captain who is his rival for Carmen. She helps Don Jose escape to join a band of gypsy outlaws. He is now an outlaw himself, completely in Carmen's thrall.

Carmen. Gypsy girl Carmen realizes she can't outrun fate, as the cards foretell her death. Opera diva Geraldine Farrar starred in a rival version.

Unable to be faithful to any one man, Carmen leaves Don Jose and falls in love with the dashing bullfighter Escamillo. After returning home to see his dying mother, Don Jose pursues Carmen to Seville. In a fit of jealousy, he stabs her; she has already foretold her own death. In reaction to his fatal deed, Don Jose rides his horse over a cliff to his death. (This stunt was performed by a circus horse and the stunt rider Art Jarvis. It was reported that he was injured; the horse was not.)

* * *

The Farrar *Carmen* still survives in its reissued, re-edited version of 1918. Any contemporary comparison of the two *Carmens* is impossible because the Bara version is lost.

It was reported that "the Fox *Carmen* drew immense crowds. The fact that both productions were showing the same week seemed an incentive to bring out crowds to compare the productions."

In its review of the rival versions, the *Moving Picture World*'s headline of November 20, 1915, read: "Miss Bara, a Cincinnati Girl." The review read in part: "Theda Bara is a Queen City [i.e., Cincinnati] girl despite the creepy-crawly stories about her mysterious birth in the far Sahara, etc." Even at that early date, the Fox press agentry was being ridiculed.

The Farrar version came to Cleveland first and ran into censor trouble. A local paper editorialized: "The uncensored version as portrayed by Geraldine Farrar seems to be perfectly acceptable to theatergoers.... No little interest has been stirred up through the attempt of the Ohio Board of Censors to expurgate the film. This illustrates not only the uselessness but also the large nuisance value of the Board. It is a sore and needless irritation to the public. The time is not far distant when the censorship nonsense will be abolished. It is recrudescence of Puritanism wholly out of harmony with the times."

Another response to Ohio's censorship of the Farrar *Carmen* came from an official of the Moving Picture Operators Union. "The censorship of moving pictures will prevent the great mass of people who cannot afford to pay the admission price to legitimate theaters from ever seeing the plays which are now reproduced in motion pictures. They are looked upon as being objectionable when shown on the screen, although on the stage they are given full-hearted popular approbation."

For the Bara version, the Ohio censors ordered these cuts: women smoking; girls fighting and rolling around on the floor; a drunken man hugging a post; a wounded bull; and Don Jose riding the horse over a cliff. Since the latter was the dramatic means of Don Jose's death, it is unclear how the film was supposed to end, at least in Ohio.

Boston critics were generally impressed by Farrar's performance. Reflecting this, a headline in an October 1915 *Motion Picture News* read: "Geraldine Farrar scores triumph. Noted prima donna astonishes with her acting on the screen, superior to her roles on the operatic stage." Since most reviewers had never seen her opera performances, this read more like a Lasky publicity plant.

For a dueling Bara/Farrar showing in Seattle, press agents tried to outdo each other. One got out a brass band and "lighted up the principal block in the city with red fire." His rival attached a big Holstein bull to a cart, which bore the sign "See How the Bull Is Thrown at the Liberty." The Liberty was the theater in which the rival production was playing.

A review reported: "There was not a dissenting opinion among the dramatic critics of the New York daily newspapers. In almost every instance they drew comparisons with the Fox production, which was held to be inferior in the handling of the story and the characterization provided by Theda Bara." There may have been some amount of New York snobbery in their reviews. Farrar was a longtime darling of Metropolitan Opera goers; Bara, a failed Midwestern stage actress. By this time, sophisticated reviewers knew well the stories of Bara's past, including her supposed Paris stardom, were puffery.

However, when both versions were shown in Toronto in late 1915, bigger crowds attended the Fox version. This was because Great Britain was at war with Germany, and Geraldine Farrar had gained a reputation for harboring pro–German sympathies. For perhaps the same reason, the Ontario Board of Censors rejected the Farrar version in its entirety. The decision was appealed and the film was accepted. The Bara film also ran into problems after it had already been playing for a while in Toronto. A government official ordered cuts, leading to a controversy about the legal loophole that had allowed him to take the action.

The perception of Farrar's pro–German sympathies undoubtedly sprang from the fact that she had won a three-year contract with the Berlin Hofoper beginning in 1900, when she was only 18. It was rumored that the German Crown Prince was infatuated with the young beauty. In the throes of the Great War in 1915, it was perhaps unsurprising that some Canadians believed Farrar was pro–German. At the time, many of their fellow Canadians were fighting with the British in Europe.

When the Bara version played in Sydney, Australia, the theater's box seats were festooned with roses. An artificial garden in front of the stage featured illuminated fountains. This was to re-create the atmosphere of Seville.

Reviews

"The *Carmen* of Fox is not as good as the Lasky picture because it is not nearly so coherent. Theda Bara fails in this work to equal the work of Geraldine Farrar." *New York Tribune*, 1915.

"At first glance one would arrive at the conclusion that Miss Bara would make an ideal Carmen. Somehow she doesn't quite carry out the impersonation. She seems to lack the physical allurement of the fiery Spanish cigarette girl. The enticement she should exude is not projected upon the screen by Miss Bara.... The production, despite any fault-finding, can be classed as one of the best features ever filmed. It just misses being a masterpiece." *Variety*, November 1915.

"The Fox *Carmen* is an example of excellent motion picture photography but its scenario is loose and vague. Miss Bara seems very mechanically seductive when compared, as she must be, with Geraldine Farrar. The Fox *Carmen* has none of the elements which make the Lasky version remarkable and none, it should be added, of the elements which make the Fox picture objectionable. Let it be said that among movie actresses, Farrar is one of the best. There is every indication that new millions will soon be calling her 'our Geraldine.'" *New York Times*, November 1, 1915.

"Perhaps the most sensational of all players of [Carmen] has been found by the eye of the camera in the person of Theda Bara. She is adept at picture posing. That is her profession, and she is recognized as the most fascinating of all.... There is evil in her conception of the role, but that is rendered into fascination by the beauty of her face, the grace of her person, and the vivacity of her manner. To beauty she adds allurement, coquetry, charm, abandon, fiery deviltry, and the quality of the vampire." *San Francisco Chronicle*, November 1, 1915.

"With all the elements that make for the success of a picture this production is fully endowed. Never has Theda Bara's strange charm been seen to better advantage than in her interpretation.... The story is in spots a little incoherent. The *Carmen* of Theda Bara is a full-blooded, vibrant, wayward Spanish gypsy with just a touch of the vampire. She has all the vampire's fierceness when aroused, but a depth of willpower and of mystery that a vampire could never have." *Motion Picture News*, November 13, 1915.

"There is one quite apparent merit in this production. This version does not require any previous knowledge of the story. No attempt is made to follow either Merimee or Bizet. Through an excess of practice perhaps, the vampiring of this lady is becoming somewhat tame. Surely there was not a single chord she has not frequently struck before. [She] is in her favorite role as a home destroyer and does not show any new wrinkles. The settings reach a high standard, the support of Theda Bara is just about fair. The errors of direction are greatly overshadowed by its merits." *Moving Picture World*, November 13, 1915.

"Too many of the opening scenes were of local color interest only. The fact that they were themselves highly interesting did not justify their lavish inclusion because after a while the spectator sensed that they bore no real relation to the action. What would have scored in a travel picture was padding in Carmen." *The Writer's Monthly*, early 1916.

1918 Farrar Version Re-Release

"Picture good in every respect; better than those made in other countries. Stick to American produced pictures." Manager, Monroe Theater, Key West, Florida.

The Galley Slave (1915)

Background

The Galley Slave was based on the 1879 melodrama of the same name by Bartley Campbell. The film would also mark the first time that a Bara film was directed by J(ames) Gordon Edwards, with whom she would have a long and generally fruitful relationship. She came to call him the kindest director she ever had. Over time he apparently had learned to cope calmly with the actress's growing ego and star demands. The Canadian-born, saturnine-looking Edwards (1867–1925) was a former stage actor and director who came to films in 1914. He was the grandfather of director Blake Edwards.

Edwards would direct more than half of Bara's Fox output, including the triumph that was *Cleopatra* and the disaster that was *A Woman There Was*, the last of his Theda Bara films in 1919. There would be one more notable production in his *oeuvre*, 1921's *The Queen of Sheba*. Unfortunately, most of his work suffered the same fate as that of Theda Bara. Little of it remains; most were victims of the same Fox storage vault fire that decimated her work and much of Fox's silent film productions.

Bartley Campbell's play had drawn some good reviews from the New York press. "The pathos, passion, and humor of the piece were effectually rendered, and the performance was admirable throughout," said the *New York Herald*. "The play bristles with good dialogue…. It has the merit of several well-conceived and powerfully presented situations," the *New York World* reported. "The play has made such a brilliant opening here that it can hardly fail [to have] a successful week," the *New York Tribune* agreed. *The Galley Slave* apparently did not have a Broadway run and was probably on tour, playing in what might now be considered an Off-Broadway theater.

The Fox studio ran into a problem with the estate of Bartley Campbell. Robert Campbell, who claimed to own the rights to the play, applied for an injunction to prevent release of the film. He contended that he was supposed to receive 10 percent of the gross receipts if Fox did not produce the film before July 15, 1915. If the studio did meet that deadline, Campbell was to receive $500. Fox announced the picture's release in November 1915, but Campbell said he had gotten no money. He claimed the contract stipulated that the rights and title would then revert back to him. Fox denied all charges and claimed he had gotten the royalties due to him.

According to *Variety*, it was evident that Fox believed that the original source material did not contain enough drama and it "turned out two plays in one." The publication speculated that the studio had interpolated some elements of the plot from the successful 1908 drama *Paid in Full*. That play ran for more than 160 performances.

There was a well-publicized kerfuffle on the set when little child actress Jane Lee brought in an aggressive cat that attacked Theda Bara's prized wolfhound. Bara, a well-known dog lover and owner of many over the years, was said to be very upset. She was later quoted as saying that she apparently was a jinx to dogs because so many of hers had come to bad ends.

The Film

Directed by J. Gordon Edwards. Produced by William Fox. Scenario by Clara S. Beranger. Based on the play by Bartley Campbell. New York and Washington premieres on November 28, 1915; released by the Fox Film Corporation on November 29, 1915. 5 reels.
Cast: Theda Bara (Francesca Brabaut), Claire Whitney (Cecily Blaine), Lillian Lawrence (Mrs. Blaine), Ben Hendricks (Mr. Blaine), Stuart Holmes (Antoine Brabaut), Jane Lee (Dolores Brabaut), Hardee Kirkland (Baron le Bois).

Synopsis: Francesca marries Antoine, a young artist, against her father's wishes. Unable to sell his paintings and always needing money, Antoine sends his wife to ask for money from his wealthy and lecherous uncle. The uncle says he will change his will if Francesca will have sex with him; she refuses. He is repentant and decides to provide for Francesca and her young daughter. However, he dies before the plan can be carried out, and the artist then inherits his noble title and a castle.

Antoine deserts his family and plans to marry an heiress. In Florence, Francesca becomes an American artist's model; her husband continues to scheme about landing the heiress. Francesca meets the heiress while posing and threatens Antoine with exposure. He convinces the gullible heiress that Francesca is actually married to the American artist, and she finally consents to marry him.

To avenge himself against his wife for almost spoiling his plans, Antoine contrives to accuse the American artist and Francesca of theft. They are sentenced to the galleys. Antoine is finally exposed as the cad he is, and freedom comes to the wrongly accused. When Antoine threatens to kidnap their child, Francesca shoots him. The heiress and the American artist find love together.

* * *

Reviews

"Theda Bara's performance in the latest Fox success made a tremendous impression on the big afternoon and evening performances. This celebrated drama of thrills and action affords her a role exceedingly well suited to her talents. This magnificent creature has unlimited opportunities to display her wonderful powers of histrionic interpretation.... The production is in every way a noteworthy one." *Los Angeles Times*, November 30, 1915.

"A new type of character for Theda Bara. Odd as it may seem, Miss Bara appears not as a beautiful vampire [but] rather as a suffering mother whose misfortunes are in no way the result of her own misdeeds.... A satisfactory production for a quite sensational melodrama developed along old-fashioned lines." *Moving Picture World*, December 11, 1915.

"Theda Bara has a role unusual for her. The situations built into such a story are tense enough to please the most exacting devotee of refined melodrama. Miss Bara, dominating the action throughout, gives an impersonation that is strong evidence of her ability in parts resembling not at all the vampire.... It is endowed with a theme that could not fail to interest. It gains its strength of appeal from the care and ability with which it is acted. It is essentially not a dramatic narrative, but a play of situations whose home is the speaking stage. But it is convincing because its presentation is in the hands of Theda Bara and her associates." *Motion Picture News*, December 11, 1915.

"The film contains all the elements to appeal to audiences. Theda Bara has unlimited opportunities to emote and she makes the most of them." *Variety*, December 1915.

"Fox occupies a place in melodrama all its own. Consider for a moment the ultra-tropic *Galley Slave* in which Theda Bara emotes to the edge of glory.... There are speed, pathos, power and passion—it gets you. Bara, the sullen, sultry, heavy-jawed beauty is undeniably superior to anyone in this sort of thing." *Photoplay*, late 1915?

Destruction (1915)

Background

Destruction marked Theda Bara's 10th and final release in the year of 1915. Because it was released so late in the year, it is sometimes seen listed as a 1916 film. It was her first full-on vampire role since *The Devil's Daughter*. In the interim she had essayed virtuous women and morally compromised women with varying degrees of public approbation. Presumably, Fox thought it was time for her to return to the type of role that had made her so wildly popular. The reviewers would be divided on how effective a return to total vampirism this was.

Judging by Fox publicity, Theda Bara seemed to be accident prone and suffered a few injuries while shooting her films. In Pennsylvania for this film, she was in a foundry while "an automatic ladle was pouring molten metal into a rubbing bed." The ladle apparently blew, showering liquid fire in all directions. Bara was burned on her hand and shoulder, and she was under a physician's care for a week, causing a delay in the shooting schedule.

Kingston Manor, one of Pennsylvania's most historic mansions, had accidentally burned down at the same time that *Destruction* was filming. A major tourist site, it had been visited by 87,000 people during the previous decade. Director Will Davis utilized the burning house for the fatal fire scene. The exterior of the Manor had served as the Froment mansion in the film. Besides using Pennsylvania locations, scenes from the film were shot in Vermont.

The scenario was supposedly loosely based on Emile Zola's 1901 novel *Travail*. The title could be translated either as work or labor. Zola would not have recognized his next-to-last novel in this feverish adaptation, and it may not have actually been the source. *Variety* reported that the novel had previously been filmed in a three-reel version by Alice Guy-Blache's Solax studio. A search of the Solax database did not definitely confirm this. Zola novel was also the source of a French film in 1920. Zola novels and short stories are said to have been the source material for more than 80 films.

For the first and only time, Theda Bara would be directed by William S. Davis. Usually credited as Will S. Davis (1880?–1920), he had been a Broadway actor and was directing films by 1913. He was the second of Bara's directors, after Marshall Farnum, to have passed away at a relatively young age.

The Film

Directed by Will S. Davis. Produced by William Fox. Scenario by Will S. Davis and [Nixola Daniels?] [Based on a play by Bernard Chapin?]. [Based on the novel *Travail* by Emile Zola?] Released by the Fox Film Corporation on December 26, 1915. 5 reels.
Cast: Theda Bara (Ferdinande Martin), James Furey (John Froment, Sr.), Warner Oland (Deleveau), J. Herbert Frank (Dave Walker), Carleton Macy (John Froment, Jr.), Gaston Bell (John Froment III), Frank Evans (Bonner), Esther Hoier (Josine), Master Tansey [i.e., James Sheridan] (Jimmie), Arthur Morrison (Lang), J. (Johnnie) Walker (Mill worker).

Synopsis: Ferdinande Martin, a woman with the heart of a vampire, sets out to ensnare a wealthy factory owner. The man's son is present when Ferdinande runs her own mother down with a car. She denies knowing the old woman; the young man believes her and comes to her aid. When he sees his father again, the old man has been ensnared by the vampire and has married her. Ferdinande grows suspicious that her stepson is now hostile toward her, and she sets out to ruin him. She convinces her husband that his son is jealous because he had wanted to marry her himself. Eventually the factory owner orders his son out of the house and changes his will to favor Ferdinande.

The vampire schemes to murder her wealthy husband, who has a weak heart, by giving him a fatal shock. She plans to do it by getting the plant manager, who is infatuated with her, to reduce workers' wages. This incites a strike at the factory, but her stepson convinces his father to settle. Ferdinande poisons her husband instead. Unbeknownst to the vampire, her husband, angry at her extravagance, has changed his will so she will not inherit any of his fortune. She continues to plot against her stepson, encouraging a drunken factory employee to think his wife is involved with the young man. The man goes insane, rapes Ferdinande, and sets fire to his own home, the factory, and the mill owner's mansion. He and Ferdinande are trapped in the fire and burn to death.

* * *

A Fox ad bragged: "The famous vampire in her most daring role brings ruin and disaster to thousands!" It might seem odd to modern eyes that a studio would consider this a great selling point—especially when the Great War was doing exactly the same thing overseas.

In Minneapolis, the censors, composed of three men and two women, banned the film outright for being "too cruel and without any redeeming feature." Perhaps with a bit of political grandstanding, the Mayor ordered it to "get out of town." Because there was only one night left in its run, it was allowed to go on.

Reviews

"If it were not for the acting of several members of the supporting company, this picture would be a particularly bad one. Miss Bara is far from being at her best. She seems to employ but three tricks of expression, and these are much overworked. There is not the slightest attempt at continuity. Things happen without any rhyme or reason, and the audience is forced to figure it all out for themselves." *Variety*, December 1915.

"In a vehicle excellently adapted to her, Theda Bara shows the full power and force of her methods. The vampire type has been developed to the extreme, and the potency of such a woman for the wrecking of life and property, and working her own destruction, is well brought out. There are some scenes which are almost tremendous and thrills are plentiful…. The acting of Miss Bara is not always pleasant, but it is of her usual style and is wonderfully effective." *Motion Picture News*, January 1916.

"Theda Bara, famed vampire woman, seldom has appeared to more striking advantage. She does telling work. She has a role peculiarly suited to her fascinating personality, and does some of the best acting of her entire career." *Los Angeles Times*, January 3, 1916.

"The horrors of this melodrama are piled on so heavily, and the vampire played by Theda Bara is so outrageously evil, that an audience finds several of the scenes rather amusing. The attempt to startle and terrify, because it is so overdone, fails to carry conviction…. At a New York theater the audience followed the first two reels patiently, and after that revealed its good sense by laughing at the preposterous wickedness of the character portrayed by Miss Bara in her most forceful manner."

"For a time it appeared as if the melodrama were destined to become a farce. There could be no better indication that Fox has about reached the limit in abnormal photoplays, likewise that Miss Bara is ceasing to touch the emotions by depictions of erotic women. Having provided a diet of horrors for many months, Fox evidently thought the time had come to increase the dose and present something more horrible than usual…. Miss Bara is not to be blamed for the picture's failure, for she acts precisely as in the past." *Moving Picture World*, January 8, 1916.

"A melodrama of the most pronounced type, there are thrilling situations aplenty, one or two of which attain enormous dramatic effect…. Theda Bara improves an excellent opportunity to manifest her rare talents for a part of this kind. She here lives with her usual powers of fascination and wicked beauty." *Motography*, January 15, 1916.

The Serpent (1916)

Background

This was Theda Bara's first film release of 1916. Raoul Walsh directed Bara for the second and final time. Also in the film was his ruggedly handsome younger brother George Walsh, making his only appearance in a Bara film. George was a popular leading man in silent films, but his career petered out by the mid–1930s. He had been the original choice to play the title role of Ben Hur in the 1925 epic, but he was replaced, something that probably tarnished his career.

This film was Theda Bara's first one that was not based on a previously produced or published novel, play, or other creative work. Its genesis was apparently an unpublished short story called "The Wolf's Claw" written by Philip Bartholomae. He was a talented writer, lyricist, and director who contributed to many Broadway plays from the teens to the late 1920s. In the 1930s he became a screenwriter for MGM.

"The Wolf's Claw" may have specifically been written to provide the story for the film. *The Serpent* was also the first, but not the last, Bara film in which the entire melodramatic story turns out to have been a dream. A possible reason for this ending may have been the mixed reviews for her previous film, *Destruction*. The vampire's scenery chewing in that film was so over the top, and sometimes laughter provoking, that it was believed that a dream ending in this film might soften a repeat reaction. *The New York Times* review (*below*) alludes to this.

The film also repeats the often-used plot point of Bara's being deserted by a lover or husband as the trigger for her vampire rampage. (It might be wondered why that would keep happening if she were so irresistible to men.) Fox publicity taglines for *The Serpent* certainly did not soften Bara's vampiric actions: "Theda Bara beckons again to those who dote on vampire photoplays" and "Theda Bara vamps the Russian army in avenging women's wrongs." In *Destruction* she only vamps a Pennsylvania mill town; now she takes on the entire Russian army!

Some reviews referred to the comic element of the film, and the intertitles were written in rhyme. In its "Questions and Answers" feature, *Photoplay* responded to the question: "Why are the captions written poetically [in *The Serpent*]?" The anonymous feature writer replied flippantly: "The Film Muse winged its way across that screen in very wobbly planes."

In 1915 a film of the same title was released by the Italia Film Company of America.

The Film

> Directed by Raoul Walsh. Produced by William Fox. Scenario by Raoul Walsh and Philip Bartholomae. Based on the story "The Wolf's Claw" by Philip Bartholomae. Cinematography by Georges Benoit. Released by the Fox Film Corporation on January 23, 1916. 5–6 reels. [The film was copyrighted at six reels, but reviews referred to it as a five-reel feature. The synopsis does make it seem like there was some padding in the film. Deletion of some unnecessary "business" may have reduced it by a reel, about 10 minutes.]
> **Cast**: Theda Bara (Vania Lazar), Lillian Hathaway (Martza Lazar), James A. Marcus (Ivan Lazar), Charles Craig (Grand Duke Valonoff), Carl Harbaugh (Leo, the Duke's son), George Walsh (Andrey Sobi), Nan Carter (Erna Lachno), Marcel Morhange (Gregoire). [The American Film Institute notes that there was some confusion in reviews about which roles were played by Charles Craig and Carl Harbaugh.]

Synopsis: Vania, the daughter of crude Russian peasants, is being courted by a young man of her own station. The Grand Duke, who has been hunting in the area, enters her hut. When he leaves his cigarette case, Vania is sent to his castle to return it so the family is not accused of theft. The drunken Duke attacks her; when her sweetheart rushes to the castle, he is shot dead by the Duke's guards. The Duke buys her silence, and she is sent to London. There two brothers fight over her, one breaking a wine bottle over the other's head. Vania then becomes a famous star of the London theater.

The Serpent. Vania, the Russian peasant girl, will soon exchange those rags for the luxurious raiment of a duchess. But it would all prove to be a dream.

The Duke sees Vania perform, not realizing that she is the peasant girl he violated. They become intimate. While in her apartment, the Duke receives a message that his son has been badly wounded in battle. He confides to Vania that if his son should die, he will also wish to die. She becomes an army nurse and meets the Duke's son, who has lost an arm. She asks him to describe the battle of Agincourt, which then is shown on the screen.

Vania and the Duke's son marry. She goes to the Duke, having arranged for her husband to discover her in his father's embrace. The young man shoots himself, and Vania reveals her true identity to the Duke. She tells him that she has waited three years to avenge herself on him for causing her peasant sweetheart's death. At that dramatic point, she falls out of bed in her hut, realizing it has all been a bad dream. She thereupon confronts her father, getting him to consent to her marriage to Andrey, her still-living sweetheart.

* * *

Among the possible comic elements described in some reviews is the scene of Vania's father trying to pull on a boot. After tugging on it for a while, he discovers a mouse in it. When the mouse is dislodged, the family cat chases it all around the hut.

If there indeed were comic elements to the film, it was not evident in the usual hyperbolic Fox publicity. One of their ads read: "The greatest multi-reel feature ever produced by William Fox; greater than *Carmen*. This picture will make history throughout the world for its producer [who happened to be William Fox], its star, and its director." An announcement to herald the opening of the film featured the tagline: "And still she writhes!"

Some of the reviews mentioned that it was all a dream. Apparently, there was no fear that this "reveal" would harm the box office. Some reviewers began to allude to Theda Bara's exaggerated facial expressions, a holdover from the Delsarte method of acting.

The Serpent was serialized with illustrations from the film in *Picture-Play Magazine* concurrently with its release to theaters. The film was re-released in the United States in January 1919. In the UK it was titled *Fires of Hate*.

The film was approved by the censors in Ohio, Kansas, Chicago, and Boston, but it was banned by the Pennsylvania Board of Censors. Reacting to this ban, a Philadelphia theater re-ran Theda Bara's *Carmen*. Fox reacted aggressively, as it usually did with adverse censorship decisions, and took the Board to court.

Reviews

"A vampire story with plenty of comedy, and having a comedy finish. Practically all the captions are in verse, and not such good lyricizing at that.... It takes the curse of the vampire stuff off Miss Bara, and incidentally shows that she is capable of the lightest kind of ingénue work. A very effective picture, even for a William Fox output." *Variety*, January 1916.

"Whoever wrote the scenario should be praised for having furnished this actress with a stirring story. Little touches go to make the film above the average for its kind.... The problem of having Miss Bara play the part of a vampire, and still retain the sympathy of the audience, is solved by making her evil deeds the figments of a dream.... Thus is art and virtue served and the sympathies of the audience preserved with no sacrifice of thrills.... Miss Bara is a clever actress with a high sense of screen values. Hers is a marvelously mobile and expressive face that can express deeper scorn by a curl of the lip, or greater sorrow through an expression of her eyes, than the average screen player can denote with exaggerated heavings and writhings." *New York Times*, January 24, 1916.

"Undoubtedly the best thing Theda Bara has done. She has a face when she lets it alone. If she can be encouraged to stop over-expressing, the one thing that everyone but high school graduates turn away from, this woman can count." *Moving Picture World*, February 1916?

"Horror has been piled on horror so heavily that the whole story becomes almost farcical. It has taken a step from tragic toward the ridiculous, and as a result has fallen between the two. The effect of the story is confused to say the least.... After we have been harrowed to the limit, we are told it has all been a dream. The effect on the spectator is one of disappointment, a sense of being tricked. It was all a dream!" *Motography*, February 5, 1916.

"A vampire picture with Theda Bara. That it is well made cannot be denied; but it is an unwholesome offering and a vulgar one." *New York Review*, February 12, 1916.

Gold and the Woman (1916)

Background

After the dark deeds in *The Serpent* were negated by the revelation that it was all a dream, *Gold and the Woman* was all vamping all the time. Obviously believing that Theda Bara's diehard fans wanted no more wishy-washy endings, Fox opted for the full-on evil Bara last seen in the previous year's *Destruction*. The film was directed by James Vincent (1882–1957), whose first and only Bara film this would be. He also acted in many movies.

This was the first Theda Bara film written by the English-born scenarist Mary Murillo (née Mary O'Connor). Beginning as musical comedy performer, she had come to the cinema in 1914. She would go on to write or adapt four other stories for Bara pictures in the next couple of years, eventually becoming a highly paid writer. She would also produce scenarios for European films, including in England and France.

According to the 1931 edition of the *Catalogue of Stories and Plays Owned by Fox Film Corporation*, the scenario of this film was based on Daniel Roosevelt's unpublished story called "Retribution."

Some sources, including the 1916 *Motion Picture Studio Directory and Trade Annual*, list George Walsh as being in the cast. He presumably was to play Lee Duskara, a leading role. However, it appears that this role was actually played by stage actor Harry Hilliard in one of his earliest films. He was to co-star with Theda Bara three more times, notably in *Romeo and Juliet*.

Bara and Hilliard had both appeared on Broadway in the less successful of the two competing productions of 1908's *The Devil*. At that time, she was still calling herself

Theodosia De Cappet (or De Coppet). By the time Hilliard came on board to replace another cast member, Theda Bara was no longer in the play. It would be her last Broadway appearance until she starred in *The Blue Flame* in 1920.

The Mexican storyline of the film was publicized to take advantage of the furor then being generated by Pancho Villa's rebellion in Mexico. He was not only fighting south of the U.S. border, but he also staged a fatal incursion into Columbus, New Mexico, in March 1916. This coincided neatly with the opening of *Gold and the Woman*. Fox publicity, with painstaking specificity, noted that "fifty-six Indians worked in various scenes."

During the filming, Bara was said to have had another one of the accidents to which she seemed prone. This time "a hinged picture released by a spring swung back, violently striking Miss Bara. She just escaped serious injury."

The film was shot in New Jersey and in West Virginia's "coal district," as Fox termed it.

Gold and the Woman. **Juliet, the Mexican adventuress, wreaks havoc in her single-minded quest for a fortune. This was one of her most irredeemable vampire roles, as H. Cooper Cliffe is about to discover.**

The Film

Directed by James Vincent. Scenario by Mary Murillo. Based on the unpublished short story "Retribution" by Daniel Roosevelt. Released by the Fox Film Corporation on March 13, 1916. 5 reels. [The film was copyrighted at six reels, but it may have been trimmed for general release.]

Cast: Theda Bara (Juliet De Cordova), Alma Hanlon (Hester Gray), H. Cooper Cliffe (Colonel Ernest Dent), Harry Hilliard (Lee Duskara), Carleton Macy (Dugald Chandos), Chief Black Eagle (Chief Duskara), Julia Hurley (Chandos's squaw), Carter Harkness (Leelo Duskara), Frank Whitson (Montrevor), Pauline Barry (Ethel), Hattie Delaro (Nurse), Frances Ne Moyer (Murray's daughter), Howard Missimer (Finlay), Joseph Hamish (Murray).

Synopsis: Because of the coal riches in the Valley of Shadows, Dugald Chandos, an early English settler, tries to steal its Indian land. Not being able to buy it, he blows up the entire tribe and takes the land anyway. The Chief's wife invokes a curse on the killers and their family down the generations: there will be no males born, and all the children will become blind. Hester Gray, a child of the settler's fourth generation, and Lee Duskara, a descendant of the tribe, are in love with each other. Hester wants to restore some of the stolen land to its original owners.

Hester is a rich orphan and the ward of Colonel Dent. His private secretary and paramour is Juliet De Cordova, the daughter of a Mexican aristocrat. Juliet was forced to flee the Mexican revolution. The Colonel is in love with her, but he is being ruined by her extravagance. Duskara is jilted by Hester because she discovers him in a compromising position with Juliet, who convinces Dent to marry Hester himself. When the young woman is stricken with blindness, Juliet schemes to get Dent to trick Hester into deeding her land to him, but the scheme fails.

Hester leaves Dent when she discovers the true relationship between him and Juliet. Hester intends to commit suicide, but Duskara saves her. The Colonel, believing Hester is dead, marries Juliet. His unhappiness with her causes him to drink himself to death. Juliet rains gold coins through her fingers down upon his supine body, as she slowly turns into the Devil himself.

* * *

The similarity between the Vampire in *A Fool There Was* raining rose petals down on the dead John Schuyler, and Juliet's doing the same to Dent with gold coins, would probably not have escaped anyone's notice. The critical reviews for Theda Bara's pure vampire roles began to become more and more divided.

At the completion of this picture, it was announced that Bara would be taking her first vacation of "a few days" after 14 months of nearly nonstop filming. This would be her first announced work break since the beginning of her Fox career; she had already made 12 films.

The Fox publicity machine, having already touted each successive Theda Bara picture as the "Greatest!" had nowhere else to go but to also trumpet *Gold and the Woman* as "the greatest vampire picture William Fox ever produced. A picture that will be one of the screen sensations of 1916!"

In 1920, Universal announced that a "non-star" picture with the same title would be made starring Reaves "Breezy" Eason, Jr. If produced, such a film has not been discovered with that title. A 1925 Buck Jones western was called *Gold and the Girl*.

Reviews

"In many ways it suggests Miss Bara's first and greatest success, *A Fool There Was*.... Too much time is wasted planting the prologue to the story proper; this makes the finish of the film seem rushed to get the entire tale over the allotted five reels. It is a film story built exclusively for the purposes of exploiting Miss Bara's well known vampire qualities and that is about all it does. The story is badly told, and there are times when one cannot make head or tail of it." *Variety*, March 1916.

"Theda Bara shines brightly as the Mexican adventuress in the big William Fox drama. The role is one well suited to Miss Bara's manifold talents, and the story teems with action, suspense, and mystery." *Los Angeles Times*, March 4, 1916.

"Miss Bara was born to possess a certain exotic beauty. By chance she was cast as a vampire woman in her first picture and she has remained one ever since. This film is only another variation of the vampire motif. With its tainted emotion it is not much of a picture. In the absurdity of its incidents, it surpasses the fantastic hallucinations of a lotus eater." *New York Times*, March 13, 1916.

"Theda Bara is called upon to enact her familiar role of vampire. It seems almost superfluous to say that she portrays it with the skill and appeal that have come to be associated with her very name.... The action is rapid and well-sustained, although at times a little choppy." *Motion Picture News*, March 25, 1916.

"A uselessly morbid picture. It starts out well, even ambitiously ... but the last reels descend to very little except vampiring by Theda Bara." *Motion Picture Magazine*, April 1916.

"The peculiar work of Theda Bara dominates this offering. Exhibitors are primarily interested in the popularity of her work rather than its quality. Her ability to make hideous faces that are supposed to show a soul steeped in the deepest dyes of hell, and to show the loggy [sic] passion that stands for emotion carried to the final stress of absolute abandonment, do make a strong appeal to many, many spectators. This actress's work is considered good, but there is none of Cleopatra's infinite variety in her. The story is artificial, shows no real dramatic insight, [and] gets nowhere. It is not without moral value since it does certainly make sin hideous." *Motion Picture World*, April 1, 1916.

The above review was written a year and a half before the release of the Fox-Bara epic *Cleopatra*. The "infinite variety" allusion is from Shakespeare's *Antony and Cleopatra*. The last sentence echoes Theda Bara's disingenuous insistence that her films did not promote sin, but instead provided a moral lesson about the terrible consequences of sinning.

"Theda Bara has thousands of admirers who seem more than willing to fall for the vampire thing week in and week out. [This is] an elementary type of melodrama, better than fair technically, but suffers somewhat from the involved story it seeks to tell. At times the average spectator will have difficulty in following the various ramifications of the plot." *New York Clipper*, April 8, 1916.

The Eternal Sapho (1916)

Background

After the mixed reviews of Theda Bara's return to rampant vampirism in *Gold and the Woman*, Fox no doubt thought it wise for her to undertake a few more sympathetic portrayals. This hiatus from the "bad Bara" would last for several films. The studio also returned to classic literature for the source of the scenario. In this case it was French author Alphonse Daudet's novel *Sapho*.

The novel was written in 1884 and was turned into a play the following year by Daudet and Adolphe Belot. This French version was brought to America by Sarah Bernhardt's repertory company many years later. The American version of the play, written by then-famous playwright Clyde Fitch and starring the English actress Olga Nethersole, opened to considerable controversy in February 1900.

The controversy was about the play's supposed indecency. It was serious enough to force the closure of the play by the police after a small number of performances, and to send Miss Nethersole to the courtroom. She was speedily acquitted, and the play's run was resumed. It opened and closed three times during 1900, and it was occasionally revived thereafter. Miss Nethersole also starred in Broadway productions of *Carmen* and *Camille*, roles that Theda Bara undertook in the movies.

Bara was to have yet another new director for the Fox version of *Sapho*, which was finally to be released as *The Eternal Sapho*. The working title of the film had been *A Modern Sapho*. The director was the prolific Bertram Bracken (1880–1952), whose work was to encompass the entire silent era, beginning about 1913. He also was to helm *East Lynne*, Bara's next film.

The scenario by Mary Murillo was apparently based on the novel rather than on the controversial play, but it did not resemble either one very closely. For the third time, but not for the last time, Bara once again plays an artist's model, as she had in *The Clemenceau Case* and *The Galley Slave*.

Although the ancient Greek poetess Sappho (the accepted spelling) has become symbolic of lesbianism, it seems doubtful that many audience members of 1916 would have made such a connection. The phrase from the *Variety* review (*below*) that reads "coupled with the suggestion of Sapho in the title" may sound to modern-day readers like a possible allusion to it. It may have been referring to the racy 1900 stage production, but that was also something that most moviegoers would not know about.

The picture was filmed in New Jersey and at various New York City locations.

The Film

Directed by Bertram Bracken. Produced by William Fox. Scenario by Mary Murrillo. Based on the novel *Sapho* by Alphonse Daudet. Cinematography by Rial Schellinger. Released by the Fox Film Corporation on May 8, 1916. 5 reels.

Cast: Theda Bara (Laura Gubbins), James Cooley (Billy Malvern), Walter Lewis (Mr. Malvern), Harriet (aka Hattie) Delaro (Mrs. Malvern), Einar Linden (John Drummond), Mary Martin (Mrs. Drummond), Kittens Reichert (Peggy Drummond), George MacQuarrie (Jack McCullough), Warner Oland (H. Coudal), Frank Norcross (Mr. Gubbins), Caroline Harris (Mother Gubbins).

Synopsis: Laura Gubbins is brought up as a sullen, ragged urchin in the slums by a perpetually drunken father and an invalid mother. One night, after hiding from one of her father's drunken rages, she is picked up by some artists and taken to their studio, where lots are cast for her possession. H. Coudal wins, falls in love with her, and uses her to pose for a statue of Sapho. The statue makes both of them famous.

At a reception, she meets John Drummond, whom she initially believes is unmarried. Although Laura discovers that he has a wife and child, she continues to consort with him. Ultimately, she severs connections with him for the sake of his little girl. Another suitor is Billy Malvern, who also is in love with her. He breaks off the relationship, believing Laura was involved in his father's murder. In reality she was only a witness to it.

The besotted Drummond is still in love with her and continues to pursue her. Coudal discovers them together and denounces Laura. She tries to go back to him, but she finds that he has smashed the statue of Sapho and has committed suicide from jealousy. Suffering from profound guilt, she becomes mad and dies beside him.

* * *

An ad for this film described it as "a virile photodrama of the soul."

An article in *Picture-Play Magazine* titled "The High Cost of Vamping" mentions the scene in which Theda Bara's character pulls out a thorn from a man's hand with her teeth. It also (mockingly?) refers to the scene where Einar Linden's character John Drummond gallantly transports Bara: "And she is the temptress supreme when she makes the poor fellow carry her upstairs. The stairs are long, Theda weighs 135 perfectly good pounds, but, boy oh boy, with [that] incentive what one of us would fail?" Being a native of Sweden, and only about 29 or 30 at the time, Linden, it was hoped, was sufficiently big and strong enough for his task. Theda Bara's weight was usually publicized as 135 pounds, but it waxed and waned over the course of her career.

Although by this time it was generally known that the stories about Bara's birth and Paris career were Fox inventions, the studio had not yet quite "gotten the memo." In conjunction with the release of the film, the publicity about her supposed past was again cranked up. A May 1916 article in *Motography* was headed "Theda Bara Gives Up Ambition to Be a Noted Sculptress to Become a Famous Motion Picture Star."

It was claimed that while in Paris, she had met the sculptor Rodin. When back in America, she "devoted the greater part of each day to the art [of sculpting]." Her "meteoric screen success" prevented Bara from pursuing her talent for sculpture. Nevertheless, "she is an accomplished and versatile artist who draws well with crayon and Blaisdell pencil and also in brush work." It was further claimed that after the scene in which the statue of Sapho is destroyed, Bara herself was convulsed with sobs. With her sculptress's instinct she began trying to piece the statue back together, causing delays and retakes.

The reviews were generally an improvement over those for Theda Bara's last pure vampire films. Whatever critics may have felt about Bara's films, it seems the public was still enthusiastic. For instance, in a small West Virginia town, the police reserves were called out to contain the record-breaking crowds wanting to see this film. A standing-room-only sign was put up in front of the theater from one in the afternoon until midnight.

The censors did not feel so kindly, even for Theda Bara, the hometown girl. The Cincinnati manager for the Fox Film Corporation was fined $200 in municipal court because he failed to make the cuts ordered by the censors. The manager of the theater at which the film was playing was literally pulled out of his bed by the police at midnight and placed under arrest. The arrest warrant had been sought by a local minister, who claimed he had the backing of the city's churches. The case against the theater manager was dismissed.

The Minneapolis Board of Censors, consisting of about 50 men and women representing the civic organizations of the city, barred the film after it had already been playing. Among the objections were the length of Bara's skirt, the portrayal of drunkenness, the married man's infidelity, and the hint of "easily earned luxury."

There are at least two things which might be gleaned from the reviews. First, it seems as if Bertram Bracken's fresh direction had something to do with whatever success the picture had. Secondly, Theda Bara's vampirism, whether just pure evil or with some motivation as in this film, was more and more being seen as too familiar. *The New York Times*' allusion to a "rumor" (*below*) that "never again is [she] to play such a role" was very premature, but perhaps it was something that Fox should have considered.

Reviews

"Poor old Al. Daudet could learn a lot about modern literature and picture literature in particular by looking at this picture.... As a feature picture it will be a big moneymaker for the combination of Theda Bara, coupled with the suggestion of Sapho in the title. [It] will prove a box office magnet. Pictorially the feature is all that could be desired, but the action could have been strengthened. Miss Bara was Theda Bara and that is enough. All of her usual tricks that have earned her the title of 'The Woman Who Is the Essence of Passion' were revamped in this picture." *Variety*, May 1916.

"In this film Theda Bara shows flashes of character definition and intense dramatic expression which she has not previously manifested. The piece itself is ponderously negligible, except for those who like their sex drama raw with a paprika plot to hide its vulgarity. As for personality, no woman on the screen has a personality more extraordinarily individual than Theda the Scarlet." *Photoplay*, May (?) 1916.

"Theda is weighed in the balance and once more found wanton. That is, she is still the vampire but this time not a cold deliberate one.... This is a Theda who emotes with the best of them; you will like her." *Cleveland Leader*, May 1916.

"Theda Bara demonstrates for the first time that she is an actress. This is a new Theda who is—and is not—the vampire, the *poseur*, the Theda we have known for so long, and the reason for whose popularity we have never been able to understand." *Cleveland Plain Dealer*, May 1916.

"It would be a waste of time to go into the intricacies of the plot and enumerate the number of homes wrecked and lives blasted by the character Miss Bara portrays. She has been doing this sort of thing in every picture for which she has acted. It is rumored that never again is this clever screen actress to play such a role, and for her own sake it is to be hoped this rumor is true. That Miss Bara is clever is proven by the fact that she burst from obscurity into fame. But she has vampired so much that she has lost her sense of values, and caricatures a type of woman she formerly gave a vivid portrait of. Now, accumulation of detail and overemphasis have spoiled the portrait." *New York Times*, May 8, 1916.

"The excellent fashion of telling the story is one of the noteworthy phases of the film. Theda Bara has a following sufficiently loyal to her to be interested in a picture principally for her sake. Her work is interesting and consistent throughout, and she wins sympathy rather than dislike although, true to form, she breaks up a happy home. The story itself, while it becomes melodramatic, is not offensive and avoids suggestive scenes," *Motography*, May 20, 1916.

"The picture play has been exceedingly well directed, and the dramatic portions of the offering are acted in competent fashion. While Theda Bara's type of vampire is quite familiar by this time, nevertheless there are few who can approach her in roles of this character. First class production of its kind." *New York Clipper*, May 20, 1916.

"Exploits the grip of passion on man and woman. It is not a wholesome story for screen use and we don't commend it as a good offering." *Moving Picture World*, May 27, 1916.

East Lynne (1916)

Background

It was back to the classics again for Theda Bara's next film. In fact, way, way back to Mrs. Henry Wood's popular potboiler *East Lynne*. Originally serialized in a British monthly magazine in 1860 and 1861, it was then published as a three-volume novel. It was an instantaneous success, probably one of the most successful of the 19th century.

Translated into many languages and pirated for many editions by American publishers, it was also a big event as a stage play. "Next week, *East Lynne*!" was a theatrical tradition for touring companies. Its earliest American staging was believed to have been about 1863, and it is estimated that about 20 different versions of the play were produced. It became an almost permanent vehicle for actress Clara Morris, whose chosen version was actually a translation back from a French translation. Nance O'Neil of *The Kreutzer Sonata* also played in it.

Despite the extensive piracy, and therefore there were no royalties from those sources, the British-born Mrs. Wood (née Ellen Price, 1814–1887) certainly was enriched by her writings. At her death she left an estate of 36,000 pounds, the equivalent of more than four million pounds in the third decade of the 21st century. She wrote other successful novels, but none with the lasting impact of this one.

Without adequate copyright protection it seemingly sprang up everywhere. Its theme of mother love made it both a serious story and also one ripe for parody. Lady Isabel's immortal line from the play about the death of her child, "Dead, dead, and never called me mother," brought forth either tears or laughter. It was still being revived somewhere into the 1990s, probably most often as an object of satire. There were film versions, including a three-reel production just one year earlier in 1915 that starred pre-fame character star Alan Hale. One-reelers were said to have been produced as early as 1902.

Bertram Bracken and Mary Murillo, the director/scenarist team from *The Eternal Sapho*, were both back, Bracken for the final time. Also back, film historians and silent movie buffs are thrilled to say, is the film itself. A 16mm print was discovered in 1971 and was preserved by the Museum of Modern Art in New York. This is only the second complete Theda Bara Fox film known to be extant. Although some believe that of all Bara films this was among her least typical, it was still a most exciting rediscovery.

Returning from shooting the train wreck scene in New Jersey, Theda Bara narrowly missed yet another of her accidents. This one was supposedly a near miss. Her car, driven by a chauffeur, skidded on a wet street, made three complete circles, and crashed into a heavily laden truck, throwing her to the floor. Although the driver was slightly injured, Bara emerged completely uninjured "like the Phoenix. She had to call on all her presence of mind and serpentine ability to escape being instantly killed." If this all sounds like an eager Fox press agent's creation, it could well have been.

The question remains about why Fox selected this golden oldie as a Bara vehicle. The recent discovery of a couple of minutes from her 1918 hit *Salome* may provide one possible answer. Victorian melodrama suited her still-Victorian acting style. It was a very popular story; the novel was supposed to have sold a half million copies by the end of the previous century. Probably the main reason was to give the public a rest from Theda Bara's decreasingly popular vamping as well as to show her "real" acting ability. Some of the reviews (*below*) bear this out.

The Film

Directed by Bertram Bracken. Produced by William Fox. Scenario by Mary Murillo. Based on the novel *East Lynne* by Mrs. Henry Wood. Cinematography by Rial Schellinger. Released by the Fox Film Corporation on June 19, 1916. 5 reels.

Cast: Theda Bara (Isabel Mount Severn Carlyle), Ben Deeley (Archibald Carlyle), Stuart Holmes (Francis Levison), Claire Whitney (Barbara Hare), William Tooker (Judge Hare), Eugenie Woodward (Mrs. Hare), Stanhope Wheatcroft (Richard Hare), Loel Stewart (Willie Carlyle), Eldean Stewart (Isabel Carlyle), Frederick Norcross (Frederick Mount Severn), James O'Connor (Hallijohn), Ethel Fleming (Aly Hallijohn), Emily Fitzroy (Cornelia), H. Evans (Mount Severn's brother), Velma Whitman (His wife), H.F. Hoffman (Otway Bethel).

Synopsis: Isabel Mount Severn marries Archibald Carlyle, and they move to Isabel's childhood home, East Lynne. They have two children, Willie and little Isabel. Francis Levison covets Isabel for himself, and he forges a letter that convinces her that Archibald is actually in love with Barbara Hare. She and Levison run away together, leaving Carlyle to swear that Isabel will never again enter their home or see their children. Carlyle hears that Isabel has been killed in a train accident; believing himself a widower, he does marry Barbara.

Isabel discovers Levison's villainy and, longing to see her children again, leaves him. She disguises herself, and unbeknownst to Carlyle, becomes the governess to her own children. When little Willie becomes ill and calls out for his mother, Isabel throws off her disguise. She tends to him with all her motherly love, but he dies in her arms. Carlyle forgives her for having left the family, but she cannot forgive herself. Grieving, she soon follows Willie in death.

* * *

Fox publicity called the film "a masterly modernized American version of this internationally famous stage success." It was reported that the Mary Murillo scenario was the first movie story ever submitted to the newly created Maryland Board of Censors, and it came through unscathed. During the run of the film, the scenario was serialized by journalist Gladys Hall in *Motion Picture Story Magazine* and it was illustrated by scenes from the film.

A newspaper columnist speculated that old-fashioned melodrama would be accepted by modern; i.e., 1916, audiences if it was still effective. Calling this movie a "favorite old sob play of the early days," he thought the film was well-acted and beautifully photographed. He stated that the cumulative advertising of more than 50 years ("Next week, *East Lynne!*") should help; in other words, it had name recognition. A more dubious assertion was that "thousands of the younger generation will welcome an opportunity to [have seen] a play over which their parents wept when younger."

For modern-day audiences, there would probably be little weeping, but a bit of merriment. The scene in which Theda Bara as Lady Isabel dons a curly gray wig and smoked glasses as the only disguise to conceal her identity, brought forth laughter at the showing

I attended. However, audiences and reviewers of the 1910s would have been more in tune with stage and motion picture melodrama.

The film was remade in 1925 with the ultimately tragic Alma Rubens and Edmund Lowe. In 1931 the talkie version, starring Ann Harding, Conrad Nagel, and Clive Brook, was actually nominated for a Best Picture Oscar. Other films have taken inspiration from this weepie. Surely the 1993 Robin Williams comedy *Mrs. Doubtfire* owes something to it. Television productions date back to the 1950s.

Reviews

"Theda Bara, in the sad, sweet character of Isabel, dared to match her prowess with the best traditions of the legitimate stage. It is high praise to state honestly that few of the elder heroines surpassed her in emotional depth." *Detroit Free Press*, mid-1916.

"Played to thousands of highly pleased film fans.... Miss Bara has gained many new friends and admirers by her wonderful work in the famous story of a woman's soul. She assumes a role entirely different from that in which she usually appears, but her admirers declare she was never seen to greater advantage. The crowds would go to see Theda Bara play Little Eva in *Uncle Tom's Cabin*, or the name part in *Charlie's Aunt*." *Los Angeles Times*, June 25, 1916.

"The combined popularity of the story and of the actress assures beyond a doubt the success of this offering. The very large number of people who have read the book will enjoy seeing it picturized in the pleasing fashion in which this company has arranged it. The admirers of Miss Bara will be interested in her work in a sympathetic role.... Theda Bara's acting in the role is entirely satisfactory. The part gives her an opportunity for far more lightness and variety than she usually displays. The restraint shown in depicting the emotional scenes is particularly commendable." *Motography*, July 1, 1916.

"Whether it is quite the proper caper to modernize an old stage success, as Fox has done, is a question open to debate. Should the plan become popular, we might look forward to seeing *Uncle Tom's Cabin* with Eliza crossing the ice in a motorcycle chased by overseers in a Ford taxicab.... Theda Bara shows that she can do something quite different from her popular vamp roles when given the right opportunity." *New York Clipper*, July 1, 1916.

"The story is out of the ordinary, and any Fox version of that wonderfully entertaining tale must arrest a good share of attention. This reviewer has never seen any picture of *East Lynne* that was so pretty as this, and none to get the most of the story's human quality. The picture gives a new interest to the story as a story, for it is not so strong on sincerity of emotion.... The story is not, and cannot be made, an American story. It certainly does not fit the references to Boston and New York that this version makes. But many will pass over so slight a fault since the picture is so filled with excellencies [sic]." *Moving Picture World*, July 8, 1916.

"The motion picture version of the dramatic classic is in many respects a new story. The possibilities of the plot are so amplified and extended, and the action so rapid and continuous, that the film has resumed its popularity at once as a theatrical presentation and has been winning success in its new form. Miss Bara discloses the skill of a great actress and proves herself possessed of splendid versatility." *San Francisco Chronicle*, July 26, 1916.

"A good play, well staged. Enjoyed capacity business, but Theda Bara is out of her place in a role like this." Manager, Dreamland Theatre, Chester, South Carolina.

Under Two Flags (1916)

Background

Based on the 1867 adventure novel by Marie (or Maria) Louise Rame (later glamorized to de la Ramee), known as Ouida, this film would bring Theda Bara some of the best reviews of her career. Ouida, a name derived from the author's childhood pronunciation of Louisa, was a talented writer of stories with straightforward narrative styles. An 1893 play was based on the novel *Under Two Flags: A Romantic Play in Four Acts*. As a five-act drama it played on Broadway to moderate success in 1901 with the famous stage actress Blanche Bates. Marie Dressler also reportedly acted in a version of the play.

Ouida also wrote animal stories for children; *A Dog of Flanders* remains one of the most popular. Her novel *Moths* would be the source of another Bara film, *Her Greatest Love*. For George Hall (born George Edwardes-Hall) this would be the only scenario he would ever write for a Bara film. J. Gordon Edwards was back as director for the first time since *The Galley Slave*. He would remain Theda Bara's most favored director for nearly the entirety of her remaining Fox career.

Two versions of the story had already been filmed as two-reelers, both appearing in 1912. The one produced by the Thanhouser studio starred the popular Florence La Badie and upcoming rugged leading man William Russell. The other from the Gem studio had Vivian Prescott and Herschel Mayall in the leading roles. In 1915 the Biograph studio came out with a three-reel version, starring Louise Vale and Franklin Ritchie.

While working on this film, Bara supposedly had yet another close call in her litany of accidents and perilous occurrences. A horse she was riding as she tried to do "western stuff" tried to buck her off. She valiantly managed to hold on.

The Film

>Directed by J. Gordon Edwards. Scenario by George Hall. Based on the novel *Under Two Flags* by "Ouida." Cinematography by Phillip Rosen. Released by Fox Film Corporation on July 31, 1916. 6 reels, later edited to 5 reels.
>**Cast:** Theda Bara (Cigarette), Herbert Heyes (Bertie Cecil), Stuart Holmes (Chateauroye), Stanhope Wheatcroft (Berkeley Cecil), Joseph Crehan (Rake), Charles Craig (Rockingham), Claire Whitney (Venetia), Violet de Baccari (Girl).

Synopsis: Bertie Cecil, the older son of a viscount, takes the blame for his younger brother Berkeley's crime. Believed to be dead, he flees the country and in Algeria joins the French army as a private under an assumed name. He earns the enmity of the regiment's colonel after helping an emir's wife whom the colonel has abducted. Bertie wins the heart of Cigarette, the Daughter of the Regiment, but he does not regard her seriously. An old friend of Bertie's and his former sweetheart Venetia show up at the fort as part of a touring party and recognize him. His friend urges Bertie to reclaim his estate but he refuses. Cigarette is jealous of Venetia but does not reveal it.

Under Two Flags. **For the first time, Theda Bara essayed a rousing adventure story and scored a rousing success as Cigarette, the Daughter of the Regiment.**

When the colonel insults Venetia, he and Bertie fight. Bertie is then sentenced to a firing squad for attacking a senior officer. In order to save him, Cigarette rides off to obtain a letter from the Marshal of France pardoning Bertie. On the way back she faces a sandstorm and is captured by Arabs. Jumping off a cliff on horseback to escape, she races back to the fort just as the firing squad is taking aim. Jumping in front of Bertie, Cigarette takes the bullets meant for him. The letter reprieves Bertie, and he and Venetia reunite. His disgraced brother rehabilitates himself.

* * *

Together with *The Serpent* and *The Darling of Paris*, Fox reissued this film in January 1919. The studio's publicity stated that they were among the most successful from a box office standpoint when originally released, but in their new form they were further improved. This refers to the film's re-editing, re-titling and reprinting. The studio urged theater managers: "Don't apologize for a reissue such as this; just say you are playing this standard drama again. It may be necessary to explain that this is the Ouida novel, not *Under Four Flags*." The latter film was a documentary about the Allies' fight against Germany.

Perhaps affected by injured colonial feelings, a review of the re-release in India's *Anglo-Indian Fortnightly* carped: "Every man-jack in it is palpably acting, and the mummering [*sic*] in it is crude. Fox people please note." The film was remade in 1922 by Universal with stars Priscilla Dean and James Kirkwood, and was directed by future horror maven Tod Browning. In 1936 the now-merged 20th Century–Fox remade it again with Claudette Colbert and Ronald Colman.

Both Herbert Heyes and Joseph Crehan went on to have long careers going well into the sound film era. Heyes usually had substantial dignified supporting roles, while Crehan, with almost 400 credits to his name, was usually seen in smaller roles.

Under Two Flags was probably the most lauded of all Theda Bara's non-vampire films, excepting her pseudo-historical triumphs. It was praised by most critics and theater managers. An Arkansas City, Kansas, theater manager advertised the film by hoisting a huge kite to a supposed elevation of 3,000 feet into the air. It took three men to raise it. He also boasted that banners advertising attractions with Theda Bara were run up to 500 feet in the air.

Reviews

"This film stands as a personal triumph for Miss Bara. She gives a characterization which will never be forgotten because of the buoyant enthusiasm and vivacious personality which she registers with perfect freedom from anything theatrical." *Wid's*, 1916.

"Here is Theda Bara turned respectable and a very good turn it is, both for herself and her [viewers]. Miss Bara has a haunting, wistful personality on which she can play with distinct effectiveness.... Miss Bara is the life of the film." *Chicago Tribune*, 1916. (If this review was written by "Mae Tinee," it was one of the only complimentary ones that Bara ever received from that source.)

"Theda Bara's timid lovemaking carried as much conviction as though performed by Marguerite Clark." *Photoplay*, 1916.

"Very gripping plot and extremely well directed and acted.... Picturesque locales of the Sahara and Algiers. Does Theda Bara justice as an emotional lead, her vampire acting is entirely omitted." *Motion Picture Magazine*, 1916.

"A corking good program feature, a fine line of action from beginning to end culminating in a dramatic climax. It's strictly a Theda Bara film.... Doubly strengthened by a number of anticlimaxes that border on the sensational.... Cleverly constructed, and the views are as good as the best." *Variety*, August 1916.

"Finely produced and is way above the average of the general run of Fox productions." *New York Clipper*, August 5, 1916.

"The story gives Theda Bara ample opportunity to bear witness to the fact that her powers do not all lie in the direction of the vampire role. We got an entirely new view of this star, one who is illuminated by sparkling gems of acting, both in lighthearted girlish moods and those in which show forth the most stirring emotional moments of a woman's life. The far-famed dramatic actress also provides us with a thrill when she jumps from a cliff, and numerous other thrills." *Motography*, August 12, 1916.

"All the elements which go to make a great production are here. The star, supporting cast, and director all attain an extraordinarily high standard of excellence. Theda Bara has given us the best work of her career. Her wonderful versatility of countenance is irresistible and we venture to predict that this role will become her most popular character portrayal.... The action is swift and exciting.... From the exhibitor's point of view one can recommend this production with utmost confidence. Nine-tenths of the people who see this picture would enjoy seeing it a second time." *Motion Picture News*, August 12, 1916.

"Theda Bara has not heretofore impressed me favorably, either in her personality or vampire methods. She seems to have a sort of wicked expression in all she has essayed. Now here we see a human being with soul and mind, a real flesh and blood woman. This picture will do more to convert theatergoers to Miss Bara than all the publicity that finds its way into print." *Moving Picture World*, September 16, 1916.

"Played this two days and had the same people come back the second day. Bad weather, but did good business just the same." Manager, Chicago Theater, Chicago, Illinois.

"A splendid film for business; held the interest from beginning to end. Patrons were well satisfied." Manager, Lyric Theatre, Clarendon, Texas.

1919 Re-Release

"Very good reissue, broke all Wednesday records." Manager, Grand Theatre, East Palestine, Ohio.

Her Double Life (1916)

Background

This was the first time that child star sisters Jane and Katherine Lee appeared together in a Theda Bara film. Fellow cast member Carey Lee was not a relation.

When this picture was being filmed in New Jersey, the sun was reportedly so hot that the extras were "simmered, smoked, and smothered," but not Theda Bara. She was quoted as saying "I have played vampire roles so long that the clinging warmth of a July day is even a help to me. I feel that I can act my particular parts with decidedly more effect when the weather seems to others insufferable." Fox seemed to think that such statements enhanced her eccentric persona, which Fox seemed to have tolerated if not encouraged. To modern ears it just seems insensitive to the sweltering background players.

When a large armored car was needed for a battle scene, one was built in a little over two hours by the set decorator and the carpenter shop. It looked real, but it was actually made of papier-mâché.

The Film

Directed by J. Gordon Edwards. Scenario by Mary Murillo. Based on her unpublished story *The New Magdalen*. Cinematography by Phil Rosen. Set decoration by William Bach. Released by the Fox Film Corporation on September 11, 1916. 6 reels.

Cast: Theda Bara (Mary Doone), Stuart Holmes (Lloyd Stanley), A.H. Van Buren (Elliott Clifford), Madeleine Le Nard (Ethel Wardley), Walter Law (Mary's foster father), Katherine Lee (Mary's foster sister), Jane Lee (Mischievous child), Franklin Hanna (Doctor), Lucia Moore (Lady Clifford), Carey Lee (Longshoreman's wife).

Synopsis: When still a young girl, Mary Doone runs away from home after her father is killed. She goes to live in a London tenement with her drunken foster father, a longshoreman, and his family. After he tries to molest her, she runs away again, aided by Lloyd Stanley, a young man about town. He uses his knowledge of Mary's past to get her to acquiesce to his base desires. Once again she flees, this time to a church where she is sheltered by the young minister, Elliott Clifford. He allows her to live in the parish house.

At the outbreak of war, Mary becomes a Red Cross nurse. Working at the front, she again meets Stanley who is now a war correspondent and still a dishonorable cad. He tries to renew his unwanted advances, but she is saved when the field hospital is bombed. After the attack she discovers the body of society girl Ethel Wardley, who was on her way to visit her wealthy aunt Lady Clifford. Since Mary knows that Ethel is an orphan and is not known in person by her aunt, Mary assumes Ethel's identity and goes to live among London's nobility.

Mary is shocked when Lloyd Stanley arrives with the very-much-alive Ethel Wardley. Although Mary has assumed that Ethel is dead, Ethel has actually been in a state of suspended animation and has suffered from amnesia. Lady Clifford has grown fond of Mary and refuses to believe that Ethel is truly her niece. Ethel Wardley is accused of being the imposter that Mary really is. Stanley says he will keep silent if Mary is "nice" to him, but she spurns him. When he and Ethel threaten to expose Mary, Mary herself admits her true identity to Elliott and Lady Clifford. Elliott overhears Stanley admitting his dishonesty and forgives Mary for her imposture. They are now free to marry.

* * *

Reviews

"Are you a connoisseur of thrills? If so, how would you like to be the patient when Theda Bara is the Red Cross girl? ... The surprising Miss Bara is excellent. Her work rings with a new note of sincerity." *Cleveland Leader*, 1916.

"Does not reach the high standard of excellence that William Fox has set in the past. The title conveys nothing to the mind as to the real story, which is not by any means strong. The incident on which the title is founded could not have possibly occurred in the manner in which it is portrayed on the screen. Although the plot is laid in England there is an appalling lack of English atmosphere. The battle scenes are effective but not realistic. We know too much of modern warfare to believe that these scenes show anything approaching reality.... Theda Bara is as usual a success. Her portrayal of the young girl is beyond praise, and when she has grown to womanhood, she enacts her role with great sympathy. The action drags at times and is jumpy at others. Will pass muster for the uncritical and will be enjoyed by the audience who likes adventures." *Motion Picture News*, September 23, 1916.

"Miss Bara has a part which is productive of dramatic power, especially at the story's climax. This characterization is among the most effective and genuinely pleasing to be found in Miss Bara's long line of effective portrayals. Having as her vehicle a play which deals with the natural course of things, and not with silly abnormalities, her work is bound to fasten itself upon the sympathies of the spectator. The picture does not grow tiresome due to plenty of story material and the other sustaining graces of a good photoplay." *Motography*, September 23, 1916.

"Those who have been in the habit of seeing Theda Bara do her vamp in the usual Fox release will be sorely disappointed.... What there is about the picture that will either charm or interest is the playing of little Jane Lee, rather than either the star, story, or picture. Of course Theda Bara will serve as the box office card. If the audience is bugs on vamps don't let them know it. Capital may be worked up out of letting them know the truth." *Variety*, September 29, 1916.

"I had never seen Theda Bara. When I found myself witnessing [the film] I fully expected to see a slimy vampire crawl sinuously upon the screen. But the Theda Bara I saw was a finished actress with all the finer and tender attributes of a refined woman. Here is an actress who can tell all the emotions and passions in her soul through the depth and wonder of her eyes." *Motion Picture Magazine*, 1917.

"We played a repeat in spite of the fact that it rained the entire day on which we showed it. We did a bigger business than on the first engagement." Manager, Orpheum Theater, Chicago, Illinois.

"My patrons prefer Miss Bara in vampire roles. I don't agree with them, but they pay the fiddler." Manager, Elite Theater, Hartwell, Georgia.

"It went over so big that we determined to run it again. Made a special trip to Chicago to rebook it." Manager, Majestic Theater, Rock Island, Illinois.

"A really great picture. It gave us the biggest weekday this house has ever had." Manager, Bandbox Theater, Chicago, Illinois.

"This picture is a bit different from anything else Theda Bara has ever done. Incidentally it is the best work she has ever done. We played it [to] capacity houses all day long." Small town theater manager.

Romeo and Juliet (1916)

Background

Once again, a Theda Bara film competed head to head with another version of the same story, William Shakespeare's *Romeo and Juliet*. The rival film, made for short-lived Quality Pictures (under the aegis of Metro), starred real-life lovers Francis X. Bushman and Beverly Bayne. The *Carmen* rivalry had resulted in the Geraldine Farrar version being considered superior to the Bara version. This time the Fox version was ultimately judged the "winner."

The general consensus of the reviews was that both films were worth seeing. The Bushman-Bayne version was more lavishly produced; the Bara-Hilliard version was more attuned to popular tastes. These films, and others produced in 1916 based on the Bard's plays, were released to coincide with the 300th anniversary of William Shakespeare's death.

Harry Hilliard, who had last appeared with Bara in *Gold and the Woman*, was

Romeo in the Fox version. Both he (born 1886) and Bara (born 1885) were at least a decade too old to portray the teenaged lovers. Bushman (born 1883) seemed even more mature than his actual age. Beverly Bayne at a supposed 22 years of age was closer to the mark. Bushman, a former model with a classic chiseled profile, was once dubbed "the handsomest man in the world."

Also in the Bushman version was Fritz Leiber in his first film, essaying the role of Mercutio. He would later play Julius Caesar opposite Theda Bara in *Cleopatra*, and he went on to appear in films through the 1940s. Jane and Katherine Lee, Fox's much vaunted child stars—until they were kicked to the curb along with Bara in 1919—played pages. Einar Linden, who had essayed Don Jose in Bara's *Carmen*, portrayed Paris in this film, his next to last movie role. He was reported to have written a song dedicated to Theda Bara entitled "Those Perilous Eyes."

The Fox scenarist who bravely undertook to depict Shakespeare's romantic tragedy was first-time Bara collaborator Adrian Johnson. He would produce scenarios for her films many more times, including the epic *Cleopatra*, and he worked throughout the silent era.

During the film's production at Fox's Fort Lee, New Jersey, studio, *Moving Picture Magazine* enthused that "the film adheres precisely to the poet's masterly play.... The story has not been sacrificed in any attempt to add extra film footage. It was decided that five reels would make the most effective screen version.... Everything in connection with

Romeo and Juliet. Thirty-one-year-old Theda Bara as the teenage Juliet in Shakespeare's immortal love story, with Harry Hilliard, no teenager himself. Once again there was a rival version, starring the younger Beverly Bayne.

the picture was placed in the hands of experts." Johnson did tweak the play's ending to give Bara more of a final star turn, and the film was released in seven reels, not five.

The number of film and stage versions actually titled *Romeo and Juliet*, as well as those based on the story or borrowing elements of it, are far too numerous to mention. One of the more unusual ones was the one-reel clay animation production made by a sculptress in 1917. The earliest known film bearing the actual title was produced in 1900.

The Film

Directed by J. Gordon Edwards. Produced by William Fox. Scenario by Adrian Johnson. Based on the play *Romeo and Juliet* by William Shakespeare. Cinematography by Phil Rosen. Edited by Alfred DeGaetano. Released by the Fox Film Corporation on October 23, 1916. 7 reels.
Cast: Theda Bara (Juliet), Harry Hilliard (Romeo), Glen White (Mercutio), Walter Law (Friar Laurence), John Webb Dillon (Tybalt), Einar Linden (Paris), Elwin Eaton (Montague), Alice Gale (Nurse), Victory Bateman (Lady Montague), Helen Tracy (Lady Capulet), Edward Holt (Capulet), Jane Lee (Page), Katherine Lee (Page).

Synopsis: Despite the blood feud that exists between their two families, the Capulets and the Montagues, Romeo and Juliet fall passionately in love. They are secretly married by Friar Laurence, who hopes their union will end the feud. Romeo kills Tybalt, a kinsman of Juliet, in a duel and is banished from Verona. Juliet's father, who does not know of her marriage, urges her to marry Paris, her longtime suitor.

To foil her father's plan, Juliet goes to Friar Laurence for a sleeping potion that will make her appear to be dead. After she is placed in an open tomb, her plan is that Romeo will return and they will flee. Romeo does not hear of the plan and thinks Juliet is really dead. In her tomb he takes poison. When Juliet awakens and finds him, she stabs herself with his dagger. They are reunited in death.

* * *

In a February 1917 interview with the *Photoplay Journal*, Theda Bara was described as "a firm believer in the science of eugenics." She claimed that Juliet's "heartbreaking time resulted simply from her parents being illy [*sic*] matched." According to Bara, the play revealed that Juliet's father was at least 60 while her mother was only 28 or 29. Bara continued: "Juliet is a tragic figure because the marriage of her parents was wrong." At the age of 31, Theda Bara would therefore have been older than she claimed her Capulet mother really was.

An article on the Bushman-Bayne version was headed "Spirit of Shakespeare's Immortal Love Story Is Successfully Transferred to the Screen by Bushman and Bayne— Picture Is Destined to Promote Appreciation of the Bard's Classic." At one showing the crowd was said to have been so enthusiastic that a viewer shrieked at Bushman's image: "Why don't you run for President?" Metro claimed that its version had cost $250,000. A theater in New Orleans established midnight matinees from 11:30 p.m. to 1:00 a.m. to accommodate the crowds wanting to see the picture.

A two-page Fox ad with large lettering asked: "What is your verdict? Comparison is now possible between the William Fox production of *Romeo and Juliet* with Theda Bara, and that of another producer *who invited* the parallel. The two productions have been given to exhibitors, and the box office acid test applied to each. Your comment and criticism will be appreciated by Mr. William Fox."

Fox claimed that the Stratford-upon-Avon committee in charge of commemorating Shakespeare's anniversaries had viewed all the movie versions of his plays. They had selected the Bara version of *Romeo and Juliet* as the most excellent. Even though the film had been shot in New Jersey, the accuracy of detail had not been approached by any other picturization of a Shakespeare play. Or so claimed the Fox publicity machine.

Reviews

"Splendid entertainment—if one had never heard of Shakespeare." *New York Tribune*, 1916.

"Theda Bara's surprisingly fine portrayal of Juliet is a remarkable tribute to the versatility of an actress who, for some time, has been classed as a vampire woman. As Juliet, Miss Bara gives further and striking evidence of her ability to play almost any role." *Louisville Post*, 1916.

"The picture is put forward frankly to please [Theda Bara fans], and without any great pretensions to artistic purpose. The whole film is highly flavored with Miss Bara; every artifice is employed to emphasize the star. It does take something from the sincerity of the effort to bring Shakespeare to the people.... It goes without saying that Theda Bara as Juliet is far from orthodox. This version is very likely to strike a popular note that a more serious version might miss. It is good, and in theatrical way it attains its purpose, which presumably is to interest and entertain uncritical audiences." *Variety*, October 1916.

"The two productions now showing are as different in character as noon and twilight. Beverly Bayne is a tender and gentle Juliet; then we have the emotional splendor of Theda Bara. It will catch the popular taste even though it may not be as perfectly cast. In the matter of youth, neither Juliet is quite adequate. Bayne looks her role more than Bara, but does not act it with her power. If you want a popularized conception, see the Bara version. If you want one that is rich in innate beauty, see the Bayne version." *Los Angeles Times*, October 23, 1916.

"Theda Bara in a sympathetic, picturesque, and tender performance. This is not only a tremendous success from the point of view of the regular movie fan, but it excites the imagination of Shakespeare students and lovers. It is a visualization such as no stage production could offer of the beautiful romance. It is produced on a scale of magnitude, though no quality of the story is made to suffer." *San Francisco Chronicle*, October 25, 1916.

"Fox has produced a feature extraordinary. The story has been carefully and capably handled, the screen version keeping as close to the text as possible. No expense has been spared.... We have so long associated Theda Bara with vampire roles, it was hard to reconcile her with the sweet, innocent child of Shakespeare's drama. For a while, one expected her to vamp any minute. She has a tendency to roll those big luminous eyes much too much in an endeavor to appear coquettish, but in the stronger love scenes she rose to magnificent heights with compelling force.... The tragic note rather than the love theme predominates. Altogether a very creditable, pleasing screen interpretation." *Billboard*, October 28, 1916.

"A lavish spectacle constructed on lines of splendid magnitude. Photographically, the entire production is a masterpiece. While the story lapses at times into moments approaching tedium, it is in the main interesting. Miss Bara gives an interesting interpretation of Juliet. Her capriciousness in the lighter moments to the emotional heights shows that she possesses ability in directions other than those of the vampire. Indeed it seems a relief to witness her in something alien to vampire roles." *Motion Picture Mail*, October 28, 1916.

"Theda Bara, Fox's leading woman, gives an interpretation of Juliet so far from the vampire type that she has scored a signal triumph in versatility. She is the bewitching, girlish, impulsive Juliet that students of Shakespeare say the real Juliet was.... Of Theda Bara as Juliet opinions may be counted on to widely differ. To those who prefer her exclusively in vampire roles, her Juliet will seem tame. Only in the last scenes is Miss Bara called upon for tremendous emotional expression, such as is her forte. Largely on this point will hang the success of this film. That Miss Bara makes an acceptable Juliet none will gainsay, but does she reach the heights of greatness of her most popular plays? We are sure there will be wide differences of opinion." *Motion Picture News*, November 4, 1916.

"Theda Bara essays her first Shakespearean role, and the success she has had with it will astonish even her admirers. Somehow, though, we can't help feeling that her type is not just what is indicated. However, in view of her great popularity and fine emotional acting, one may forget that she really does not look the part." *Motography*, November 4, 1916.

"It is better to be young and Juliet than to be a Sarah Bernhardt trying to be young, when the cold screen refuses to be deceived. Theda Bara is young, and her long black curls make many a beautiful picture as she enacts in this Fox version.... It is a very worthwhile picture that anyone might be glad to see. If it doesn't reach the heights of beauty that give to the critic who has seen great presentations, it is beautiful enough to inspire many and give delight to them. It tells the story clearly.... It stands as a pretty presentation of the world's sweetest story." *Moving Picture World*, November 11, 1916.

"One year ago, the motion picture public was the jury in the hotly contested case of Bara against Farrar as rival Carmens. Now it is Bara against Bayne as rival Juliets.... Miss Bayne is a beautiful Juliet, but Bara is more than beautiful, she is charming. The scenario used by her has more opportunities for dramatic acting. Her face and movement express every grade of emotion from kittenish vivacity to gravest despair. The world's greatest romantic drama has never been better done." *Motion Picture Magazine*, January 1917.

"A first class production which seemed a trifle over people's heads. The picture undoubtedly is beautiful; the big and artistic sets were really wonderful. I heard many compliments paid to both the stars by people leaving my theater." Small town theater manager.

"People nowadays want snappy, live, and quick fire American dramas and comedies. Pictures like this one are well received by people who like Shakespeare, but there are not enough that like him to fill one's theater." Manager, New Dearborn Theater, Chicago, Illinois.

"A massive production in which Theda Bara shows to wonderful advantage. The scope of roles in which this girl can successfully compare seems to be unlimited." Manager. Boston Theatre, Chicago, Illinois.

"A toss-up as regards the opinion of patrons. There were as many [who] remarked that they were disappointed as said they liked it." Small town theater manager.

"I don't know who is to blame, Theda Bara, Shakespeare, or Fox, but people did not seem to care about this production. Although highly artistic in every way, it is a costume play, and you can't get away from it, people don't want costume plays." Small town theater manager.

"There seemed to be a divided opinion among my patrons. I think if the law of averages were resorted to this picture would get an even break in opinion for and against it." Small town theater manager.

"A massive production in which Theda Bara shows to wonderful advantage. The scope of roles in which this girl can succeed appears to be unlimited." Small town theater manager.

The Vixen (1916)

Background

Earlier in 1916 when she was playing "good girls," as she liked to call them, Theda Bara remarked that she could not wait to get back to vampire roles: "It would be like a homecoming," she said. This film, her eighth and final one of 1916, was the result of that longing to be bad again. Coming as it did on the heels of her well-received, often highly praised *Juliet*, *The Vixen* did not prove a worthy follow-up. Some reviews were not kind.

For scenarist Mary Murillo it was the last of five films she would write or adapt for Theda Bara. Perhaps the negative tone about the film's story in some of the reviews contributed to her decision. According to a 1917 article in *Picture-Play Magazine*, Murillo (1888–1944) came to America from England while still in her teens. She was initially a theater actress and then began selling stories to the movies. As the article stated: "Many of the Theda Bara films emanate from the overworked little head of Miss Murillo, and it is said her income by no means pales into insignificance besides that of the vampirish one [i.e., Theda Bara]."

Originally filmed in six reels, in general release *The Vixen* was only five reels in length. Several of the reviews allude to the picture's unnecessary length at six reels. It is probably due to such critiques that the film was trimmed.

The Film

Directed by J. Gordon Edwards. Scenario by Mary Murillo. Cinematography by Phil Rosen. Released by the Fox Film Corporation on December 4, 1916. 6 reels, edited to 5 reels.
Cast: Theda Bara (Elsie Drummond), A.H. Van Buren (Martin Stevens), Herbert Heyes (Knowles Murray), Mary Martin (Helen Drummond), George Clarke (Admiral Drummond), Carl Gerard (Charlie Drummond), George Odell (Butler).

Synopsis: Elsie Drummond fears that she will spend her life taking care of her drunken father. She sets out to snare a husband at her saintly sister Helen's expense. First, Elsie steals Wall Street businessman Martin Stevens away from Helen, and then she casts him aside after he loses his money. He has been ruined through the criminality of Elsie's shiftless brother. Next, Elsie subverts the love between Helen and Knowles Murray, winning him for herself as he is appointed to a diplomatic post in Paris. Helen is left to take care of their alcoholic father.

Two children are born to Elsie and Murray, and they live happily for a few years. When Murray is stationed back in Washington, Elsie learns that Stevens has regained his fortune. She attempts to seduce Stevens again, narrowly avoiding discovery by Murray while in a compromising position with Stevens. It is Helen who has saved her. Stevens then realizes Elsie's life has been one of deceit. He threatens to expose her to her husband, but the ever-forgiving Helen pleads against it for the children's sake. Helen and Stevens marry; a supposedly chastened Elsie returns to her husband.

* * *

Reviews

"The film is entertaining, but largely as a burlesque of the typical vampire play. Theda Bara is forced to overact and overemphasize her characteristic stage business because of the exaggerated style in which the story is written. The play will appeal to the type of audiences that likes its villainy in chunks." *New York Mirror*, 1916.

"The story is an interesting one and in spite of its length observes the unities, telling a clear, straightforward narrative of two sisters. Miss Bara is at her best." *Variety*, December 1916.

"This film is achieving a tremendous success this week. A shade of difference to the usual run of characterizations of this kind is given by the complex character of the 'heroine.' Her charm and fascination are authentic, but her love of power and desire for position and authority are overmastering impulses in her life." *San Francisco Chronicle*, December 3, 1916.

"Miss Bara wanted to reform but we wouldn't let her, and like all backsliders her last state is worse than her first—she's that wicked! It's a sort of diluted version of the stage play *The Liar*; however, the film lacks everything of the supreme drama of the play. Besides, we who have seen Miss Bara as supremely alluring and wicked, dislike to see her tremendous talent brought to bear on the trivial stuff of which the film is made. When shall we see Miss Bara again in a picture play approximating the cleverness and drama of *A Fool There Was*?" *Los Angeles Times*, December 4, 1916. (Prior to the film's opening, the *Times* had called the production "lavish and beautiful.")

"Theda Bara's return to her vamping has no doubt been awaited eagerly by her many followers. While her wicked ways are expressed not so much physically as temperamentally, the defect is somewhat the same. Miss Bara has the thankless role of a cattish woman. [The film] suffers from the repeating ways of the scenario. When the action begins to let down, put another lie in the vixen's mouth, and so create ten or a dozen more scenes must have been the general plan followed. The result is that [the film] might stop at the end of the fifth reel or at the end of the fourth, just as well as the end of the sixth.... The author has not granted the characters human intelligence." *Motion Picture News*, December 16, 1916.

"While Theda Bara has portrayed many unpleasant female characters, always with the same startling finesse, there was one left, at least which she had not exploited the vileness of. This one will be found in [the film], and it would indeed be difficult to locate a more despicable type of humanity. The type of woman portrayed by Theda Bara is the most despicable that could be imagined, and the play is built around this character in a most obvious fashion. Considerable padding is evident. Six reels are too much for the telling of this story." *Moving Picture World*, December 16, 1916.

"The vamping is overdone in this picture; the patrons did not care for it. It was just the same old story of the vampire ruining three or four men." Manager, Vitagraph Theater, Chicago, Illinois.

"A money loser for us." Manager, Gem Theater, New London, Missouri.

"Poor production, and film in poor condition." Manager, Majestic Theatre, Camden, North Carolina.

"The picture is only fair, and we did not do a very good business. The star draws with some people, but it is not an exceptional puller." Small town theater manager.

The Darling of Paris (1917)

Background

Perhaps it was the relative failure of Theda Bara's return to vamping in *The Vixen* that led to this sympathetic and generally well-received role. Her motion picture career was now into its third and to-be-most-acclaimed year. The proclaimed new Fox policy beginning in 1917 was that Bara and William Fox favorite William Farnum "would appear only in special plays." These would be "super deluxe productions" costing between $100,000 and $300,000 apiece.

Once again, a classic work was the basis of a Theda Bara film, unrecognizable though it was after scenarist Adrian Johnson got through with it. Victor Hugo's magisterial 1831 novel *Notre Dame de Paris* (often titled *The Hunchback of Notre Dame*) was that classic. Hugo was a renowned exponent of French romanticism in his novels and poetry.

Hugo's death in 1882 occurred 35 years before *The Darling of Paris* was released. It obviously received that title to shift the focus to Theda Bara as the star. Among the liberties taken with the original were changing Claude Frollo, the malevolent priest, to a man of science. This was presumably to avoid causing religious problems with Catholic audiences. The real howler was transmuting the novel's deformed bell ringer Quasimodo into a handsome young man of powerful physique. Fox publicity claimed that as many as 1,900 extras were used, and the settings were lavishly up to Fox standards.

As the reviews indicate, most critics were happy with the film. A usual exception was *Photoplay*, which once again took to carping. The acerbic remark that "one of Miss Bara's deficiencies is humor—she hasn't got any" was mostly borne out during her Fox career, at least as far as her characters were concerned. It was not necessarily true for the star herself.

The Film

Directed by J. Gordon Edwards. Produced by William Fox. Scenario by Adrian Johnson. Based on the novel *Notre Dame de Paris* by Victor Hugo. Released by the Fox Film Corporation on January 22, 1917. 6 reels, later edited to 5 reels.

Cast: Theda Bara (Esmeralda), Glen White (Quasimodo), Walter Law (Claude Frollo), Herbert Heyes (Captain Phoebus), Carey Lee (Paquette), Alice Gale (Gypsy queen), John Webb Dillon (Clopin), Louis Dean (Gringouier).

Synopsis: A child is kidnapped by gypsies and grows up to be the alluring Esmeralda. She comes to Paris with her foster mother, and her beauty immediately attracts attention. She becomes part of an Apache band. The scientist Claude Frollo is infatuated and plans to abduct her. She falls in love with the dashing Captain Phoebus, who has saved her from Frollo. Unfortunately, his attentions are not honorable either; she faints away after trying to escape him. While she is unconscious, Frollo kills Phoebus; Esmeralda is then falsely arrested and tortured. She confesses to the crime she did not commit. The handsome Notre Dame Cathedral bell ringer Quasimodo has become her protector. He had previously been cured of his hunchbacked condition by Frollo. Having witnessed the crime, Quasimodo tells the true story and saves Esmeralda from the guillotine. He also has pushed Frollo to his death from the Cathedral's parapets. Quasimodo and his gypsy love are married.

* * *

Fox re-released the re-edited film in February 1919 as part of a package that included some William Farnum films, a Valeska Surratt opus, and the Bara films *The Serpent* and *Under Two Flags*.

The two great versions of *The Hunchback of Notre Dame*, based on—and much more faithful to—the Hugo novel are considered to be the 1923 version with Lon Chaney and the 1939 version starring Charles Laughton. Both their performances as Quasimodo are marked by the elaborately grotesque makeup that the Bara version lacked.

Reviews

"A series of tableaux carrying Miss Theda Bara, empress of vampires, back to Paris of the Middle Ages. Miss Bara throws herself into her delineations with the wholeheartedness for which she is noted, and it is an Esmeralda passably true to novel and period. One of Miss Bara's deficiencies is humor—she hasn't got any, and doubtless is convinced that she has." *Photoplay*, early 1917.

"This is one of the most pretentious [i.e., elaborate] productions ever released by Fox as a mere program photoplay, and as such is entitled to the utmost commendation.... Its main weakness is the casting of Theda Bara in the role of an innocent gypsy girl, with no opportunity to wear modern, alluring costume creations or give her any opportunity to vamp." *Variety*, January 26, 1917.

"Miss Bara adds new laurels to her crown in this splendid work. The role is a complex one, and only an artist of Miss Bara's caliber could make it convincing and true to life. The picture is one of the most lavish ever produced." *Los Angeles Times*, January 28, 1917.

"[Transforming some of the characters] is bound to suit the admirers of Theda Bara, however much it detracts from the strength of the story. The Fox screen version presents a well put together photoplay. An excellent performance is given by Miss Bara. It is doubtful that the star has ever done anything better than her acting in this picture. She looks the character and retains something of the untamed spirit and warmth of passion which must have belonged to a gypsy girl of the Middle Ages." *Moving Picture World*, February 10, 1917.

"As the blithe, winsome French dancer Theda Bara is spontaneous and delightful. She paints the girlish side of the character, as well as the womanly side, with various hues of subtle impersonation. We never saw Miss Bara in a more advantageous role, and it is quite probable she never appeared in one more compatible to her personal as well as dramatic qualifications. There are but a few moments when she is not in the picture, which adds to the importance of the production. It makes a refreshing respite from the stereotypical Bara role.... There is more genuine drama in this picture than in two or three of the mediocre or inferior class. In our estimation it is Theda Bara's best picture." *Motography*, February 17, 1917.

"Theda Bara has several good opportunities to display her wonderful abilities and she takes full advantage.... The close-ups are good, particularly the one where Esmeralda being tortured shows in her facial expressions every vein and sinew affected." *Motion Picture News*, February 17, 1917.

"This is all any audience could ask for, the acme of Miss Bara's career. As a whole it is a fine picture." Manager, Rose Theater, Chicago, Illinois.

"Star draws well; picture great. People unusually well pleased." Manager, Greenland Theater, Greensboro, Georgia.

"Played to good business; picture only fair. Not up to Fox standard." Manager, Busby Theater, McAlester, Oklahoma.

"A splendid picture of its kind. Very well acted by a competent cast. Drew very well for a costume play." Manager, Strand Theatre, Warren, Michigan.

"Poor photography, dark. Lots of grumbling from audience. Lost money on this yesterday, and don't expect anything better today." Manager, Chicago Theatre, Chicago, Illinois.

"Production ordinary. Cannot judge drawing power because the weather was at zero." Manager, Pictorium Theater, Denison, Ohio.

"Beautiful settings, strong characters. Shows evidence of much expense. Good to book as a special; star is big drawing card." Manager, Comique Theater, Montpelier, Vermont.

The Tiger Woman (1917)

Background

Despite the good reviews that Theda Bara had garnered for playing sympathetic roles in films like *The Two Orphans, Under Two Flags, Romeo and Juliet,* and *The Darling of Paris*, it was now back to what Fox seemingly thought was her true (and biggest moneymaking) *métier*. As one reviewer said, she "was a vampire running wild.... She vamped and vamped...." Theda Bara and Fox had seemingly ignored the lessening interest in her vampire portrayals and had concocted an even more bizarre plot than ever before.

In what was left of her career, Theda Bara would nevermore out-vamp the black-hearted Princess Petrovich, the "Tiger Woman." This would almost be the last of such all-in vampire roles, except one she would supposedly write herself in 1918. To an American public watching the cataclysmic Great War about to lap at its own shores, this kind of movie villainy was beginning to seem irrelevant. America would very soon be embroiled in real-life horrors overseas.

Rival vampire Louise Glaum had already done the *Wolf Woman* and would go on to do *The Leopard Woman*. Fellow vamp Olga Petrova would add to the fanged canon with *The Panther Woman*. Her film had tentatively been titled *The Tiger Woman*, but by the time it was released in 1918, the title had been changed for obvious reasons. Seena Owen (Signe Auen) had been *The Fox Woman* in 1915.

Fox publicity touted: "The greatest vampire role by the greatest screen star.... A special super production replete with mystery and thrills." It should perhaps have read "replete with *misery* and thrills," given the widespread swathe of destruction left by the Russian vampire.

Although Theda Bara's characters often wore exotic headdresses, the much-commented-on hat in *The Tiger Woman* seems particularly unique. Consisting of flowers, feathers, and fringes, the hat features a fringed half-veil, above which peer the malevolent eyes of Princess Petrovich. British performance artist Starr adapted it for her 2007 performance art show about Theda Bara.

The Film

Directed by J. Gordon Edwards. Produced by William Fox. Scenario by Adrian Johnson; story by James W. Adams. Cinematography by Phil Rosen. Released by the Fox Film Corporation on February 19, 1917. 6 reels, later edited to 5 reels.
Cast: Theda Bara (Princess Petrovich), Edward Roseman (Prince Petrovich), Louis Dean (Baron Kesingi), Emil DeVarney (Count Zerstof), John Webb Dillon (Steven), Glen White (Edwin Harris), Mary Martin (Mrs. Mark Harris), Herbert Heyes (Mark Harris), Kittens Reichert (Harris child), Edwin Holt (Father Harris), Florence Martin (Marion Harding), Kate Blancke (Marion's mother), George Clarke (Marion's father).

Synopsis: Princess Petrovich lives only for money and jewels. For the love of the count, she turns her husband over to the Russian secret police after first robbing him. She and Count Zerstof take off with half a million rubles she has stolen. In Monte Carlo the Count gambles her money away and begs her to sell some of her jewels. She not only refuses to help him, but she also poisons him when he threatens to leave her. The police are told that he killed himself over his debts. When his valet pursues her, she shoots him.

The Princess heads for America; and while on shipboard, she seduces a millionaire's son. His fiancée breaks off their engagement when she discovers his entanglement with the Princess. Urged to get some money for the Princess, the young man rifles his father's safe. In the process, he kills his father but still gives the money to Petrovich. He is sent to prison and is killed trying to escape.

Next, the Princess goes to work on his elder brother. He leaves his family and installs her in a villa. A former Russian servant tries to blackmail her. She pretends to agree to give him money but has him arrested instead, claiming he tried to rob her. When the servant escapes from prison, the Princess offers him jewels and money, then tries to stab him with a dagger. He turns it on her with fatal results. When her lover appears, the servant tells him about all her evil deeds.

* * *

Not surprisingly, the film ran into censorship problems. Chicago's censorship czar, Major Funkhouser, wanted to ban the film. Surprisingly, the Chicago Censorship Board had voted seven to two to allow the film to be screened. The fanatic Funkhouser was accused of trying to intimidate and overrule the board members, and the Chicago City Council was considering a move—ultimately successful—to strip him of his powers.

In the meantime, Fox got a writ of mandamus in the Superior Court to compel the Chicago Chief of Police to sign the necessary exhibition document. The judge ruled that the censors did not prove the film was anything but "clean and wholesome." The Maryland Board of Censors did ban the film as unfit for public exhibition, calling it "immoral, degrading, and debasing."

A letter to the editor of a movie magazine encapsulated the growing feelings of some Theda Bara fans that her vampire persona had outlived itself. "To say that [*The Tiger Woman*] is extreme is the least I can say. The picture is nothing but a series of ruinations of men. [The plot of the story is] beyond my comprehension. It can't be done in real life, so why should it be done in 'reel' life? I am a sincere admirer of Theda Bara, but why, oh, why is she starred in such pictures? I am afraid to think of her future if she is starred in more pictures like *The Tiger Woman*."

Another letter writer said: "The public is fast becoming weary of the impossible Aladdin-lamp style [of vampire films], and we are glad to welcome the sensible, everyday probable style that can deal with conditions of life." Some reviews, such as that in *Wid's* (*below*), were also beginning to sound cautionary warnings. Such reviewers as "Mae Tinee" of the *Chicago Tribune* had already been sounding them for some time.

The Tiger Woman was also the title of a 1944 serial and a 1945 Republic "B" quickie.

Reviews

"A whaling big chance for Theda Bara in a Russian setting. It will be popular wherever 'vamp' is a household word and Chesterton, Shaw, Dreiser, and such are never heard of. So wide is notoriety and so narrow is fame." *Photoplay*, early 1917.

"If you ever had the slightest regard for the voluptuous Theda's peculiar talent, her exotic charm, and her manner of wearing clothes you'll say the picture is great. If you've never cared for Mam'selle Bara, it's no use trying to convert you by this typical thedabara [sic] film. She's a very tigerish Tiger Woman. Her heart, her soul, her fingertips, her eyelashes, her rounded arms, her heaving buzzum [sic] all vibrate for pearls." *Atlanta Georgian*, early 1917.

"Should clamp on Theda Bara the title of 'Champ Vamp of the Picture World.' The scenario is vamping every minute, and as a vamp Theda is there with ease. The havoc wrought is second only to the European armies. If the Germans are in need of quick aid, they might call on Theda to bust up the armies of the allies.... The film seems somewhat long for a regular weekly release; it's difficult to imagine a better vamp picture.... The 'beware' moral is much more vivid than could be displayed in a stage piece of the same type." *Variety*, February 1917.

"In her newest picturization, Theda Bara met with genuine favor and approval from large audiences. The character that she portrays in this highly overpowering picture outrivals all previous vampire roles that she has attempted. She reaches the height of a siren's art." *San Francisco Chronicle*, February 19, 1917.

"Properly classified, this should come under the heading of 'vampire running wild'... There was an air of artificiality about all this that will keep anyone from regarding it seriously. Miss Bara vamped and vamped all through the offering, and really I'm afraid that this will do a lot toward making people decide they don't care about seeing her anymore. Her efforts never landed at any time." *Wid's*, March 1, 1917.

"A list of crimes committed by the Princess Petrovich reads like the entries for a day on a particularly busy police station blotter. [She is] the delightful heroine of this carnival of crime of treachery, greed, thievery, murder, and adultery on several counts. The picture makes no compromise with vice. The Russian siren is given no touch of softness or womanly feeling, but is shown in all her sordidness and avid love of crime. The contemplation of such a mental monstrosity has been known to afford much entertainment.... The acting of Miss Theda Bara brings out every point at its real value. The role is her most consistent achievement in the [vampire] line." *Moving Picture World*, March 10, 1917.

"Excellent vampire picture, but such stories are losing favor. Good business." Manager, Academy of Music, Selma, Alabama.

Her Greatest Love (1917)

Background

Perhaps Fox hoped to duplicate the success of *Under Two Flags*, its last Ouida (Marie Louise de la Ramee) adaptation. This film is based on her 1880 novel *Moths*, but it is a far different kind of story, and it was to have a far different reaction from many critics and moviegoers. It is considered to have been the author's most popular novel and a prime example of a 19th-century high society novel.

Another probable reason for its production was to distance Theda Bara from the dark and devilish deeds of *The Tiger Woman*, her previous and not entirely successful vampire film. Perhaps to bolster its chances, Bara is reunited with her *Romeo and Juliet* co-star Harry Hilliard. This begins with the 31-year-old Bara gamely trying to pass for an innocent 12-year-old girl in short dresses. The already dicey impersonation does not prevent her from smearing the usual heavy kohl blacking around her eyes and heavy lip black.

The working title of the film was *The Greatest Sacrifice*. Presumably there was never any intention to give the film the same name as the novel. *Photoplay* once more disliked a Bara film, and it was getting increasingly harsh in its reviewing. This time it referred to her supposed lack of humor as "a dreadful desire to be funny." The persistently critical *Chicago Tribune* reviewer "Mae Tinee" dubbed Theda Bara an "unintentional comedienne."

Mae Tinee (i.e., Matinee) was a byline used by several *Tribune* reviewers. Reportedly among them were Frances Kerner, Mrs. Zack Elton, Anna Nangle, Maurine Watkins (later a successful playwright), and Frances Peck Grover, who reviewed under that name from 1911 to 1945.

The Film

Directed by J. Gordon Edwards. Produced by William Fox. Scenario by Adrian Johnson. Based on the novel *Moths* by Ouida. Cinematography by Phil Rosen. Released by the Fox Film Corporation on April 2, 1917. 5 reels.

Cast: Theda Bara (Vera Herbert), Marie Curtis (Lady Dolly), Walter Law (Prince Zuroff), Glen White (Lord Jura), Harry Hilliard (Lucien Correze), Callie Torres (Jeanne de Sonnaz), Alice Gale (Old nurse), Grace Saum (Maid).

Synopsis: Sweet preteen Vera Herbert has remained an innocent English schoolgirl until she goes to stay with her mother. While at the seashore, she meets and falls in love with Lucien Correze, an opera singer who dislikes the fast social set of his patronesses. Her mother is living openly with Lord Jura; Vera in turn is repelled by the social set to which her mother belongs. Vera is tricked into marriage to the degenerate Prince Zuroff because her mother has told her it is to save her father's honor.

Vera, who is leading a wretched life, discovers her husband is harboring his mistress under their roof. By now she also knows her mother has lied to her. After a stormy scene with Zuroff, Vera and her faithful nurse are banished to a Siberian convent. Correze and Lord Jura, now her stepfather, arrive at the convent to entreat Vera to leave with them. Just as they are about to depart, Zuroff appears. He attempts to stop Vera from leaving; he and Jura have a duel in which both are killed. Vera and Lucien are now free to pursue their romance.

* * *

A letter from a moviegoer to a movie magazine complained: "Just survived a performance of *Her Greatest Love*. That director must have had a grudge against Theda Bara. A few more pictures like that one, and Miss Bara (who really is a great artist) will be a has-been. For two interminable reels she was obliged to cavort before the camera as a cute twelve year old. The illusion was far from complete."

The Cincinnati theater running the film raised its admission from 10 to 15 cents, and it still drew full houses for its native daughter.

Reviews

"Theda Bara has had some pretty bad plays, but without any doubt [this] is her worstest [sic] drama. The piece is as saturated with real humanity as Death Valley is saturated with water. Supposed to be the hectic adventure of an innocent in Russia, the play is as Russian as a Russian costume in an amateur masquerade. Miss Bara evinces a dreadful desire to be funny, among other deterrents which this collection of odd shots holds." *Photoplay*, 1917.

"While the story is ancient it is fairly well done and therefore entertaining, but it is hardly up the Bara standard. Imagine a thirty year old face in a twelve year old dress and you will get some idea of how Theda Bara looks in a Mary Pickford or Marguerite Clark part. She made a fairly attractive 'good' woman, but not so attractive as when she plays the 'bad' woman." *Motion Picture Magazine*, 1917. (Because Bara was "officially" only 26 at this time—in reality she would be turning 32 a few months later—the comment about her 30-year-old face is cautionary.)

"A different Theda Bara than we have ever seen before. In this stirring picture the famous star appears in a role fraught with a generous vein of sympathy and deep human appeal. It [enables] the Great Bara to interpret and impersonate a role in sharp contrast to the vampire type. An admirable vehicle in which she proves her unlimited versatility.... Shows a depth of feeling and emotion entirely foreign to one who has made vampire roles famous the world over." *San Francisco Chronicle*, April 2, 1917.

"I believe I have beheld her worst picture. If you ever in your life saw anything funnier than Theda Bara so garbed [in short dresses as a twelve year old], rolling around her be-blackened eyes in horror at the sight of her harridan-like mother lighting a cigarette, or in supposed misery at the sight of a one-piece bathing suit, I miss my guess. Not only is Miss Bara terrible; she is consistently and awfully supported by the rest of the cast. Taking it as burlesque, I may say that as an unintentional comedienne Miss Bara has Charlie Chaplin backed off the boards." *Chicago Tribune* ("Mae Tinee"), April 5, 1917.

"This will go a long way toward squaring Miss Bara with those who object to her vampire roles as too sinister. The play gives Miss Bara every chance that could be desired to show the other side of herself, and she comes out of the demonstration with one hundred percent credit. We have never doubted Miss Bara's powers as a screen star of the first magnitude. This is the first play which made us feel that vampire roles were not necessary to bring out her fullest powers.... The part of the innocent girl seems absolutely real. A really great impersonation; one of the most artistic tragedies ever our pleasure to witness." *Motion Picture News*, April 21, 1917.

"The part does not suit Miss Bara any too well. She is not the right type to begin with. Her assumption of girlish innocence in the earlier scenes is set at naught by the eyes and mouth that have done so much to assure her standing as one of the leading vampires of the screen. She is too good an actress not to have command over the mechanics of the part, but she never suggests the character." *Moving Picture World*, April 21, 1917.

"A classy production. The star made a hit in a role totally different from her customary vampire parts. Audiences anywhere will like this." Manager, McGhie Theater, Columbus, Kansas.

"Fair production, big business. Star is a big favorite." Manager, Temple Theater, Newport, Kentucky.

"For a Fox super-production this is poor. I didn't like to see Miss Bara taking the part of a young and innocent schoolgirl. The story is old. Except for a few changes it has been used thousands of times." Manager, Ideal Theatre, Bloomer, Wisconsin.

"Fair business for two days. Star draws a good crowd, picture fair." Manager, American Theater, Brooklyn, New York.

"A good feature, much better than *The Darling of Paris*." Manager, Gem Theater, Silverton, Colorado.

"No better than an ordinary program picture. Patrons really disappointed; not worth the advanced price the producer asks." Manager, Trio Theater, Bay St. Louis, Mississippi.

"A great picture. The star has an unusual role, really out of her class." Manager, Dreamland Theater, Chester, South Carolina.

"Our patrons were a little disappointed as they want Theda Bara as a vampire." Manager, Metropolitan Theater, Grand Forks, North Dakota.

Heart and Soul (1917)

Background

The genesis of this melodramatic film was probably another effort to reproduce the success of *Under Two Flags*. The two films had similarities, including a sympathetic and athletic role (even a mad gallop on horseback) for Theda Bara, ending with her selfless sacrifice for a loved one. Another possible reason for making this picture was that the United States had just recently joined the Allies fighting in France, and the film carries a patriotic message.

If there was any author who could churn out rousing colonial adventure stories, it was the prolific H(enry) Rider Haggard (1856–1925). Along with Rudyard Kipling he roused the blood of the colonialist Victorian reading public. His most famous novels, among the considerable number that he wrote, were *King Solomon's Mines*, its sequel *Allan Quatermain*, and *She*. Less known but still exciting was the 1887 novel *Jess*, on which this film is based. The locale of the original story is the Transvaal in South Africa, but for the film it was changed to Hawaii.

The working title of this film was *Jess*. The continuity included in the copyright description was titled *The Greater Love*. This might have been a more satisfactory title than the amorphous *Heart and Soul*, but it obviously would have been confused with *Her Greatest Love*.

Although modern-day cast lists spell the name of Harry Hilliard's character as John Neil, the novel spells it as Niel; some reviews spelled it as Niehl. In the absence of the film itself, I have adopted the spelling in the original novel.

The Film

Directed by J. Gordon Edwards. Produced by William Fox. Scenario by Adrian Johnson. Based on the novel *Jess* by H. Rider Haggard. Cinematography by Phil Rosen. Released by the Fox Film Corporation on May 21, 1917. 5 reels.
Cast: Theda Bara (Jess Croft), Edwin Holt (John Croft), Claire Whitney (Bess Croft), Walter Law (Drummond), Harry Hilliard (John Niel), Glen White (Pedro), Alice Gale (Mommy), John Webb Dillon (Sancho), Kittens Reichert (Bess in prologue), Margaret Laird (Jess in prologue).

Synopsis: Jess promises her mother that she will always look after Bess, her younger sister. Just as they are going off to live on their uncle's Hawaiian sugar plantation, their mother dies. When they grow to young womanhood, Bess is wooed by Drummond, a cruel planter and renegade. Bess is in love with John Niel, a young American who has bought an interest in their plantation, but Niel falls in love with Jess and they are engaged.

Bess rejects Drummond's advances and he reacts badly. When Jess finds out that Bess is in love with John, she selflessly leaves the plantation so Bess and John can be together. In order to bring her sister and John together, she has nobly told him that she no longer loves him. Jess is captured by Drummond, who has incited a revolution against the American government. He wants to set up his own island republic; he even puts the governor in front of a firing squad.

Niel rescues Jess but he is wounded. They manage to get back to her uncle's plantation only to find that it is in rebel hands. Jess rides out to a distant fort to bring the militia back and is shot in the fighting when they encounter Drummond's forces. Niel is also about to be shot by the rebels but is rescued just in time. Devoted to the end, the dying Jess tells Niel to always love her sister.

* * *

It was reported that *Heart and Soul* was selected as "the unique medium for entertaining the '400 of Los Angeles'" (i.e., the social crème-de-la-crème of the city). One of the social leaders wished to provide some novel diversion for 500 guests. She hit upon [this film], which was screened in Miller's Theatre."

Possibly because of the military subplot in this film, Theda Bara was chosen in June 1917 to lead a grand military ball given in her honor in Los Angeles.

Reviews

"Another of Theda Bara's 'good woman' parts. [It] has been modernized extensively; admirers of Miss Bara will admire this immensely. Although this writer doesn't care for Miss Bara in 'goody goody' roles, one must admit she does some very clever work. Her riding is especially good." *Motion Picture Magazine*, mid–1917.

"One of Miss Bara's peculiarities seems to be that goodness kills her. She thrives on the vitriol of villainy, but when frozen in virtue, as any of the well-meaning girls in whose personalities she has expired, you may be sure she has but five scant reels to live." *Photoplay*, mid–1917. (Actually, Bara's vampires and historical characters rarely survived their five reels either.)

"Although the picture runs barely an hour, fully three reels are unwound before anything happens. When it does, the action becomes not only rapid but furious.... Plenty of suspense with mob scenes, burning, etc. Good program feature." *Variety*, May 1917.

"Seldom has the famous emotionalist of the screen had a more effective role. It is noteworthy that in this splendidly imaginative story Miss Bara offers a characterization such as her fame is rarely associated with." *San Francisco Chronicle*, May 30, 1917.

"There is excitement all through this, which as a melodrama with thrills and surface action is very passable. The audience, or those members of it who are able to fancy the proceedings as real and logical, will be kept on edge by the very swing of the action. But the story itself fails to register as a thoroughly prepared, logical sequence of dramatic events.... Miss Bara's part as the self-sacrificing sister certainly does not stand out as the featured role. The story would still be intact without her at all. It would make a big hit with those who enjoy theatrical melodrama, but it will be rather empty entertainment for the discriminating. Her fans will be disappointed." *Motography*, June 2, 1917.

"There is plenty of action. The heroic sacrifice made by the heroine is a bit of honest drama which commands the respect and sympathy of everyone. The drama is well acted. Fortunately for Theda Bara she has little lovemaking to do. The gentler passions are not along the line of her best endeavors. She atones for this by the feeling she puts into the rest of her work, and the death scene is thoroughly artistic.... The production is impressive." *Moving Picture World*, June 9, 1917.

"A few more of these wild and wooly melodramas following upon the vampire career of Theda Bara, and that young lady will be laid on the shelf.... Undoubtedly this film cost some money; anybody can see that. But the money didn't save the awful story nor did it help Miss Bara's work." *Wid's*, June 14, 1917.

"Big business in very hot weather. Picture pleased everybody." Manager, Metropolitan Theater, Grand Forks, North Dakota.

"Star draws well; picture great. People unusually well pleased." Manager, Greenland Theater, Greensboro, Georgia.

"A decidedly marvelous patriotic picture which draws well. Pleased and was liked by all; the star is good in this vehicle." Manager, Garfield Theater, Chicago, Illinois.

"One of the best subjects this star has appeared in. Entirely away from the vampire style of acting and altogether pleasing." Manager, Lincoln Theater, Chicago, Illinois.

"Although not a fitting vehicle for Miss Bara, it is a good picture which brought good business. Went over very well." Small town theater manager.

Camille (1917)

Background

It was back to tried-and-true classics for Theda Bara after two melodramas and two vampire films. *Romeo and Juliet* and *The Darling of Paris*, both based on world literature classics, had gotten respectable reviews for Bara. The frequently adapted Alexandre Dumas fils story *La Dame aux Camellias* seemed a good bet to restore some Bara luster as a serious actress. It also had the kind of showy death scene that she seemed to relish.

Once again there was another version of the same story playing against a Bara film. This time, however, the competing version of *Camille* could be largely ignored. It was a co-production by the Hanover studio starring an Italian actress named Helen Hesperia. A reviewer called it "a cheaply gotten up production." Another review said Miss Hesperia's *Camille* was "good if for no other reason than it is different."

Also to become the basis of Giuseppe Verdi's famous opera *La Traviata*, the 1848 novel was adapted as a play by Dumas, staged in Paris in 1852 and on Broadway the following year. Almost all the leading actresses of the 19th century essayed the role of the doomed courtesan, including Laura Keene, Eleanora Duse, Sarah Bernhardt, Helena Modjeska, and Clara Morris. In the 20th century it was undertaken on stage by such stars as Tallulah Bankhead, Ethel Barrymore, Eva LeGallienne, and Lillian Gish.

Bernhardt starred in a French film version in 1912, and Clara Kimball Young starred in a five-reel version in 1915. Other major American film adaptations were to star Norma Talmadge, Alla Nazimova, and Greta Garbo, whose greatest screen performance this was considered. A much later French film starred Isabelle Huppert. There have been more than 20 cinema versions to date.

Theda Bara largely succeeded in garnering good reviews, although there were caveats even in some favorable reviews. *Photoplay* as usual had yet another quotable remark in its snarky, almost tongue-in-cheek review. Bara was supported by actors of the Fox stock company who had been in her previous films, and there was a new addition as her leading man: Albert (later Alan) Roscoe.

A handsome, stalwart-looking actor who was approximately Bara's own actual age, Albert Roscoe was to remain her leading man in several more films. The most important one of these was to be Theda Bara's very next and most famous film: the epochal *Cleopatra*. *Camille* was touted as the first of the Theda Bara super-pictures.

The Film

Directed by J. Gordon Edwards. Scenario by Adrian Johnson. Based on the novel and play *La Dame aux Camellias* by Alexandre Dumas fils. Cinematography by Rial Schellinger.

Camille. Theda Bara as the doomed Dumas courtesan Camille, looking pretty healthy in this modern dress version. With sturdy Albert Roscoe as her love interest, as he would be in several other films.

> Released by the Fox Film Corporation on September 30, 1917. 7 reels, edited down 6, and then to 5 reels.
> **Cast:** Theda Bara (Marguerite Gauthier aka Camille), Albert Roscoe (Armand Duvall), Walter Law (Count de Varville), Alice Gale (Madame Prudence), Claire Whitney (Celeste), Glen White (Gaston Rieux).

Synopsis: Armand Duvall, the scion of a poor but proud aristocratic family, has fallen in love with the notorious courtesan Marguerite Gautier. She is called Camille for her love of camellias. She finds her heart has been awakened by Armand, and they plan to leave Paris and start a new life. Unbeknownst to Armand, his father goes to Camille to ask that she break off her liaison with his son. He tells her that their open connection is destroying his daughter's chance to marry the man she loves. She nobly agrees, but Armand becomes angry at her seeming desertion.

He denounces her in public and is challenged to a duel by Camille's admirer, Count de Varville. Slightly wounded, Armand refuses to see Camille, who then returns to a life of dissipation with de Varville. When the elder Duvall learns that Camille is dying of consumption, he confesses to Armand that he was responsible for their separation. Almost too late, Armand hurries to see Camille and she dies in his arms.

* * *

For much of its run, *Camille* had been trimmed by two reels or about 20 minutes, from seven to five reels. The assumption is that Fox thought that the shorter version would play better in small and rural theaters, where such stories were not as popular as in urban areas.

Fox publicity went to town for *Camille*, which, they boasted, was an "accurate" version of the classic tale. One ad read: "Witness *Camille*, a Theda Bara super-picture that women cannot resist, men want to see it, children too will appreciate it." (That children would want to see a courtesan dying of tuberculosis would seem an odd publicity angle.)

Another even odder ad read: "The Theda Bara wink is scheduled to make its screen debut in *Camille*. There, for the first time in her film career, she indulges in a shy closing of the eye, which means worlds to the man she is looking at. It is estimated that three-quarters of the men in the audience will think that Miss Bara is winking at them."

Yet another advertisement seemed to be aimed at 1917's female liberationists. "The one outstanding heart-story of all literature. It is the story of one woman's revolt against the bounds of convention, of a hopeless fight for freedom. She is the typification of womanhood, vainly trying to cast afar the shackles of restraint."

Exhibitors had mixed reactions: "The seven-reel length makes it difficult to handle crowds"; "The story has been done to death"; "Not a good picture for Bara, women like it though"; "Bara is great, but the picture has small appeal"; "Best production of *Camille* ever offered"; "Great picture, Bara is fine in part"; "Fine picture, well liked. Shows the taste of the people here."

In spite of *Camille*'s wonderful qualities—that is, according to Fox—Chicago censor Major Funkhouser predictably objected to the film. Fox hired an actress and a college professor of history and theology to avow by affidavits that the real message of the film was the Biblical injunction that "the wages of sin is death." Therefore, the film had a moral Christian precept to offer. The Major was not convinced; and as it had done many times before, Fox went to court for an injunction.

Reviews

"The admirers of Theda Bara will find her an excellent Camille. The story has been handled in excellent fashion and should prove seven reels of entertainment.... Since the role of vampire has been a Theda Bara creation, so the role is a perfect fit for Miss Bara." *Exhibitors Herald*, 1917.

"No more fitting star than Theda Bara could have been offered the role. Her portrayal of emotion was vivid." *Philadelphia Telegraph*, 1917.

"Found favor with a good-sized audience. Theda Bara is not the type of actress to put the living soul of emotion into a great drama that capped the Romantic movement. She is thoroughly modern and matter of fact, but the story that she tells certainly interested the spectator. In many ways it is her best work. She is progressing, but she should make every effort to control a mannerism of moistening her lower lip. It is hardly an emotional gesture and is apt to be an anticlimax in an emotional scene.... It is in many ways a very pretty picture, and it will be popular with many." *Motion Picture World*, October 20, 1917.

"We prefer it on the screen because we don't have to listen to the coughing. Personally, we prefer the Theda Bara version to many of the older screen recitals because Miss Bara makes Camille the brazen hussy we believe she was." *Photoplay*, January 1918.

"Business fell down on the second day of a four day run; gradual decrease. Bara is always a drawing card." Manager, Grogg's Theater and Hippodrome, Bakersfield, California.

"Miss Bara never did draw here, but this one got over nicely. A dandy picture, well produced." Manager, Court Theater, Kankakee, Illinois.

"An interesting picture, though not star's best. Drew good business in spite of bad weather." Manager, Realty Theatre, Middletown. Pennsylvania.

Cleopatra (1917)

Background

Many years after her starring career had ended, Theda Bara mused about her greatest success, *Cleopatra*. After the years spent living and performing in New York, she would be traveling to California to film that epic, and to finally reside there as well. In the spring of 1917, she headed west. "The Serpent of the Nile" had been her childhood idol. She was determined that the story of the fabled queen would be told with supreme accuracy and with all the richness that had surrounded the legendary queen. Although critics would come to question the accuracy, Fox Pictures certainly would supply the lavishness.

She was said to have been making a "screen diary" that would be a virtual moving picture of her life. In October 1917, *Photoplay* wrote: "What a treat it would be to behold such a diary of *Cleopatra*. We can get some idea of what a feast some celluloid records are going to be for future generations if Theda Bara succeeds in thus starting a popular fad."

Once shooting had begun, she reported: "Physically the most trying part for me in *Cleopatra* was wearing the costumes." She was to say in a 1919 interview that she had always designed her own costumes "as you must if you want to be a success in the pictures." Since her remark about wearing the Cleopatra costumes (what there was of them) was presumably written in the early 1920s, she must have known that might cause a laugh or two.

In its time, *Cleopatra* received mostly superior reviews. Eventually, after finding that success, it went into comfortable retirement and apparently survived for at least 20 years. At some point, a copy of the film was sought and could not be found, not even by its star. Her own copy had turned to dust.

Other versions of *Cleopatra* had come before it and would come afterwards, but this is likely to be the one most enduringly famous. The 1937 Fox storage vault fire bestowed that dubious fame on this and hundreds, if not thousands, of other films.

This one is legendary mainly because it *has* vanished but has been kept alive by every list of the most sought-after lost films. Were it still viewable, modern-day audiences might be snickering at its photographic crudities, its exaggerated acting, its over-the-top costuming, its historical inaccuracy. But absence has truly made the hearts of film historians and buffs grow fonder. An entire lengthy book and documentary, both titled *Lost Cleopatra*, are devoted to it. Its rediscovery would almost be akin, for aficionados, to finding another inhabited planet.

The Fox studio, knowing that *Cleopatra* was bound to be a success, credited many sources for the scenario, at least six of them. That does not mean that all of them were seriously utilized in the creation of the film. Crediting them gave it a cachet with certain segments of the audience. In the minds of the studio executives, there was surely only one person who should play Cleopatra. Theda Bara, the modern vampire, would become Cleopatra, the historical vampire.

After all, had Bara not been born in the Egyptian desert under the very shadow of the Sphinx? It is true that by 1917 only the most gullible among her fans would still believe that, but Bara would still often maintain that she was the reincarnation of the queen—that was almost as good. Bara finally moved from New York to Los Angeles on a more or less permanent basis to do the film.

Several months of planning went into making this lavish epic. For the first time since D.W. Griffith's *Intolerance*, the inhabitants of Los Angeles and neighboring cities began to see the construction of massive sets. The Sphinx and the pyramids arose in bean fields. The Roman Senate and the palace at Alexandria came to life, as well as a fleet of ancient ships. Uncertainty arose when the United States entered the Great War against the Germans and their allies. William Fox might have worried that his already extravagant expenditures would not result in profits. The Fox publicity machine went into its usual overdrive.

Cleopatra triumphantly premiered at New York's Lyric Theatre on October 14, 1917, running two hours and five minutes, with a five-minute intermission. The opening panorama caused much comment. The camera captured a wide shot of the desert and pyramids outside of Alexandria. Then, moving ever closer to the Sphinx, its ancient face faded, and slowly the face of Theda Bara, eyes closed, was superimposed. She opened her eyes, looking straight at the audience.

With that sensational beginning, the film marched its way through passion, betrayal, sacrifice, and conflict. This was vastly more dramatic than the original opening scene, which just showed Cleopatra pondering in her tent. The spectacular ending set-piece was the naval battle of Actium, filmed at Newport Beach/Balboa Island, complete with flaming ships and fireballs arcing into the night sky.

The subject of Theda Bara's costuming, not unexpectedly, soaked up a large part of the commentary about the film. She claimed her costumes (what there was of them) had been selected by an Egyptologist. "To have ignored the data which have come down through the centuries on the costumes and customs of Cleopatra's time would have made the picture ridiculous and of no historical value." She was said to have spent much time doing research among the mummies and other Egyptian artifacts at New York's Metropolitan Museum of Art.

As one writer put it: "Theda Bara has been hobnobbing with the mummied [sic] dames of ancient fame. She has had her picture taken with Hawara, a mummy who was a high official to the king in the Second Dynasty of the Grecian Period." It was reported that "after a careful study of many books and copies of paintings, the belief was accepted that the queen was entirely of Greek descent, and the Bara interpretation is of a Grecian type of woman rather than an Egyptian one." It was not stated how she might have portrayed that definitive interpretation.

Bara's 50 or so costumes were made from a variety of exotic materials: animal skins, beads, diaphanous veils, and feathers. There were ornate headdresses; everything was glitz and fabulousness. And then there was *the* almost-costume: the thin, silvery snakes with ruby eyes coiled strategically around Theda Bara's ample pale bosom. It was the bra-like accessory that launched a thousand words then and even now, more than 100 years later.

To give her further inspiration for the role, Bara also claimed to be wearing a perfume made by Anne Haviland, "a famous psychic perfumer." It was said to be based on a 2,000-year-old formula. Bara said, "The fragrance is so strong that it would not be strange if it were detected from the screen."

The interest in Bara's scanty apparel continued apace. During shooting, one of her costumes began coming apart, Fox reported, but fortunately: "Miss Bara is followed about by three dressmakers equipped with beads, needles and thread, and a maid armed with a large gray cloak ready to be thrown over the shoulders of the actress." There was no mention of the dressmakers carrying actual material.

In July 1917 it had been announced that: "The real Cleopatra had red hair, as investigators of the Fox Company found out. Theda Bara is now wearing a wig of a titian shade. The change should add wonderfully to Miss Bara's popularity." It is possible that the historical Cleopatra applied henna to her hair, but a titian shade would probably have photographed as dark as black on the screen.

Opulence was piled upon opulence. Whether or not the fantastic wall hangings, furniture, rugs, and costuming came within a country mile of authenticity was probably of little or no interest to the audiences that flooded into theaters. The throne, which was shaped like a lion, looked Egyptian-ish, so who could say whether an actual Pharoah might not have deposited himself on it. And the royal barge certainly looked like it could have floated down the Nile, at least to 1917 eyes.

Some sources aver that the location used to build the streets of Alexandria was a narrow, near-stagnant stream of water close to the southern Los Angeles city of San Pedro. It was openly described as "Nigger Slough" (also to be known as "the Nile of California"). Other sources said that the filming was done at Dominguez Slough near Long Beach. A publicity release said that part of the film was "made on the desert out of Oxnard." That city is nowhere near the desert, being a seaside agricultural community south of Ventura, California. The sunken gardens of a former California governor were used for the Roman scenes.

Because the nearest railroad station was 10 miles away from the Newport Beach/Balboa Island location for the battle of Actium, logistics proved difficult. According to publicity, 50,000 feet of lumber was used to refit the 80 ships to 31 BCE authenticity. The battle took eight days to film, requiring meals to be trucked in. Extras were paid at a generous $5.00 per day in the form of silver dollars given to them as they boarded the train on the last day. Anywhere from 10 to 18 cameramen were used at a time; more than 100,000 feet of film was exposed.

During filming, measures were taken to cut down on the amount of sunlight falling onto the stages. Two glass roofs were installed at a price of $17,000. The film itself was publicized as having cost $500,000, with some 15,000 extras, 2,000 horses, and various wild animals. At the end of the shoot, four camels were donated to the Griffith Park Zoological Gardens in Los Angeles—now known as the Los Angeles Zoo

Noted dancer Ruth St. Denis and her company appeared in the banquet scene. Both of the picture's leading men were to have long careers on Broadway and as supporting players in the talkies. Thurston Hall ("Marc Antony") amassed more than 250 film and television credits, usually as a comical heavyset, overbearing boss, or other figure of authority.

Fritz Leiber ("Caesar"), the possessor of a true Roman nose, brought his distinguished theater-trained voice to more serious roles, including much Shakespeare. Art Acord, who played Kephren, was a popular cowboy star until his mysterious 1931 death in Mexico. All were still in harness at the time of their passing. This was the first film in which close Theda Bara friend George James Hopkins, known as Neje, assumed the multitasking of production, set, and costume design.

The film was a major feather in the cap of director J. Gordon Edwards, who had never before helmed a picture of this magnitude. In 1921 he directed the nine-reel *The Queen of Sheba* with Betty Blythe in the title role and Fritz Leiber as her co-star. Had

Cleopatra. Theda Bara is shown here in one of the 50 costumes worn—or barely worn—in Theda Bara's most famous role. The epoch ran for years after its debut and remains one of the most sought-after lost films. Only a few seconds out of its more than two hours running time are known to exist.

Theda Bara remained at Fox, she probably would have played this role too. Theda Bara was already one of the major silent stars; this film made her a superstar all over the world.

The Film

Directed by J. Gordon Edwards. Scenario by Adrian Johnson. Based on *Antony and Cleopatra* and *Julius Caesar* by William Shakespeare; *Lives* by Plutarch; *Cleopatra* by Victorien Sardou; *Cleopatra* by H. Rider Haggard; and *The Life and Times of Cleopatra* by Arthur Weigall. Cinematography by Rial Schellinger, John Boyle, and George Schneiderman. Edited by Edward McDermott. Production design, art direction, set decoration, and costume design by George James Hopkins ("Neje"). Released by the Fox Film Corporation on October 14, 1917. 11 reels.

Cast: Theda Bara (Cleopatra), Fritz Leiber (Julius Caesar), Thurston Hall (Marc Antony), Albert Roscoe (Pharon), Herschel Mayall (Ventidius), Dorothy Drake (Charmian), Delle Duncan (Iras), Henri De Vries (Octavius Caesar), Art Acord (Kephren), Hector Sarno (Messenger), Genevieve Blinn (Octavia).

Synopsis: While leading his forces in Egypt, Julius Caesar falls for the charms of the Egyptian queen Cleopatra. They plan to rule the world together, but he is assassinated. Because her subsequent rule is harsh, the priest Pharon plans to kill her; instead, he falls in love. He takes her to a tomb, where she violates a mummy and steals its treasures. Cleopatra travels to Rome to meet Antony, who also falls for her siren charms. They then go to Alexandria where they have a riotous celebration.

Antony is recalled to Rome and marries Octavia, but he is still besotted by Cleopatra. He tells her to arm her fleet of ships and sail them to Actium, where he hopes to defeat his enemies. Instead, they are vanquished, and they flee back to Alexandria. Captured by Octavius, who is Octavia's brother, Antony stabs himself and dies. Cleopatra is about to be executed by being dragged behind a chariot, but Pharon, who still loves her, brings her a venomous snake. She happily clasps it to her breast and receives its fatal kiss.

* * *

Not surprisingly, the Chicago censors led by the detested Funkhouser, had their knives out. So many cuts were demanded that in December 1917 the Fox studio's Chicago office withdrew the film and announced they would take the matter to court. The studio's $25,000 lawsuit and Theda Bara's $100,000 suit were both dropped when the office of the Chicago Corporation Counsel ordered the Major to issue a white permit that allowed the film to be shown in its entirety. When it was allowed to open there in May 1918, it was accompanied by a 25- to 30-piece orchestra.

Funkhouser had prevented the film from being screened because of the scantiness of the costumes and the sinuousness of Bara's movements. *Variety* joked: "By the time Funkhouser gets through with Cleopatra, she's going to look like Carrie Nation. In vain have the proponents of the picture pleaded with the obdurate Major that the dame Marc Antony went nuts about was not wont to attire in summer furs. Futile have been their references to accepted portraits wherein a southern exposure was invariably displayed." In December 1917 the Chicago City Council had asked to see the film both before and after the ordered excisions. At the time that body reserved judgment, but it provided the film with considerable publicity.

An Omaha women's club protested Bara's scant clothing. She replied that she had conducted considerable research and found that the actual queen sometimes wore no clothes at all. She also defended her portrayal. "Cleopatra was, according to history, a woman who used the prerogatives of her sex to gain political supremacy. In direct contrast did I show her with the same human feelings that dominate any other woman—her wonderful and true love for Antony. I progressed from low sensual love to spiritual love.... I have been faithful to myself as an artist, then to myself as a woman."

Fox publicity went all out. It touted Theda Bara as possibly being a reincarnation of the Egyptian queen. She went along with it, saying that she lived and breathed the role and that she believed that she could actually have been Cleopatra. "My portrayals of modern day vampires are but repetitions of the wiles practiced by Cleopatra." Bara wore a scarab ring, "which archaeologists declare to be an antique of extraordinary value."

The Company boasted to its exhibitors: "Witness the bombshells that will write new motion picture history, namely Theda Bara in *Cleopatra* and William Farnum in *Les Miserables*." Apparently, the studio was not far wrong. By August 1918 it was claimed that 5.2 million people had already seen *Cleopatra*. This was said to have exceeded the actual population of ancient Egypt by more than 200,000 people. Even if that claim should be taken with a grain of salt, the film was definitely a smash hit for Fox.

At the end of its 11-week New York run in December 1917, box office receipts were reported at $77,000, the equivalent of $1,677,000 in 2022 dollars. In its first two weeks in New York, 50,000 people were said to have seen it. Fox stated that many performances were standing room only. For all the people who got to see the film, half as many more were turned away—or so claimed Fox.

The film played on non-stop until at least 1919 and longer in some areas. Fox wanted 40 road companies to carry the film throughout the country. The National Board of Review gave it a commendation, and censorship demands were less onerous than might have been expected. It was officially reissued in 1921. Along with the preparations for the filming came a raise for Theda Bara. From a quite respectable $1,500 a week, she was jumped to $3,000. With the film's success, a further raise to $4,000 was granted. She received a two-year contract extension until mid–1919.

At one New York matinee screening it was reported that "vampires, real, amateur, professional, and imaginary" filled the Lyric Theatre. Theda Bara, seated in a stage box, was said to have favored them with a queenly bow.

Fox ads covered the ground from matter-of-fact to over-the-top. "The ancient critics agreed that Cleopatra was an interesting woman. See what the modern critics have said." To a more upscale audience: "You have read Plutarch and Shaw about Cleopatra, now see Theda Bara and know." On a lighter note: "Pharon, heir to Egypt's throne, gave up his father's jewels to see *Cleopatra*. You get off easier." A similar note read: "It cost Caesar an empire to see Cleopatra; it costs you twenty-five cents to a dollar."

A particularly perfervid ad that would have made Omar Khayyam blush: "Like a golden scarf heavy with the legends of antiquity, and rich with the luxuries and splendors of unbridled revelry woven of moonlight nights and pearl-studded days, of perfumed hours and lotus buds.... A wondrous picture of old Egypt that makes description beg words to portray, and [makes] an artist search his palette in vain for colors to picture its bewildering beauties." Taglines included: "Passions and pageants of Egypt's vampire queen."

Another ad compared the measurements of Theda Bara, the ancient Cleopatra, and Venus de Milo. Heights: Bara, five feet, six inches; Cleopatra, five feet, five inches; Venus de Milo, five feet, four inches. For Bara alone: Waist: 30 inches; Hips: 40.2 inches; Bust:

34.1 inches. The problem with these comparisons was that Venus de Milo is a statue of a mythological being, and the real Cleopatra's measurements were probably not accurately recorded. Chances are that Egyptian women of that era were probably somewhat diminutive.

In one theater a harpist furnished the music for emotional scenes. Publicity dubbed it an old Egyptian tune, but it was really "La Cinquantaine," composed by Jean Gabriel Marie in 1887 and often played at golden wedding celebrations.

In the main, reviews were positive, some glowing, some ecstatic. The often-critical New York newspapers (which were plentiful at that time) reviewed it positively. Some of them generally did not even review Bara films. Several New York papers chose to exercise self-censorship over some of the ads that Fox placed for its Big Apple run, including illustrations "by an artist of international fame." Of those that published the illustrations, two papers "removed certain marks on Cleo's bust."

The reviews that were less enthusiastic could be withering. Theda Bara's usual adversaries, such as *Photoplay*, were not assuaged. One of its reviews grudgingly granted her some credit, but another called her "a mangler of history" and averred that Cleopatra had always been wronged "but never more so than in the Fox picture." It seemingly invented a new adjective, "Sennett-izing," to describe what it considered the picture's distortion of history. *The Los Angeles Times* review credited Bara's eye-rolling as a sign of good acting, something that modern-day audiences would deem a sign of old-fashioned histrionics.

Variety compared Bara's *Cleopatra* with opera diva Geraldine Farrar's *The Woman God Forgot*, which opened a month later. The two had been rival *Carmens* back in 1915, Farrar having then been deemed the superior one. *Variety* commented: "Miss Farrar has lost considerable weight, looking all the better for it. The costuming is very much the same as worn in *Cleopatra*. Theda Bara would do well to watch Farrar. She could learn a lot. Miss Farrar was at all times bare of waist with the inevitable breast plates. The skirts were all transparent."

The best-known version of *Cleopatra* to have been produced earlier than 1917 was Helen Gardner's still extant 1912 film. About the time that Bara's film was released, it was announced that the Gardner film would have "a string of new scenes" added, would be revised to six reels, and would be distributed on a state's rights basis (where studios sold the films on a regional basis to so-called exchanges which then sold the film to individual theaters). Helen Gardner would personally appear in many cities where her film would be playing. The revised film was expected "to reap the benefits of the extensive advertising done for the Fox feature of that title."

An Italian-made film emerged in 1918. Other well-known Cleopatras were Claudette Colbert in 1934 and Elizabeth Taylor in the notorious 1963 version. Bara's film was also a target of parodies. Comic Larry Semon burlesqued it in his 1918 one-reel Vitagraph comedy *Romans and Rascals*, as did Toto (Armando Novello) in the 1918 two-reeler *Cleopatsy*. Comic vaudevillians Ray and Gordon Dooley announced their burlesque of the film to be called *Leo Patrick*.

Reviews

"If this movie version showed only one thing, it was that this photoplay, minus the beautiful lines of Shakespeare and the magnificent spectacular effects, is merely an expose of concentrated revolting sensuality and viciousness.... Miss Bara's portrayal savored strongly of Broadway, and what I imagine the notorious dancer known as Little Egypt might have been.... As far as acting is concerned, her death scene showed a pitiful lack of ability to express any strong dramatic feeling. A great deal of Miss Bara's work consisted of changing costumes." *Film Fun*, 1917?

In another review written in 1918, while *Cleopatra* was still playing in theaters, *Film Fun* was still grumbling: "Surely history lends itself, as few other subjects do, to screen portrayal. Then why must we all sit and suffer through such nonsense as Theda Bara pathetically attempting to interpret Cleopatra, and Geraldine Farrar in *The Woman God Forgot*?"

"The picture is so big that one is completely overwhelmed. One of the most sumptuous and sensational motion picture spectacles that has ever been produced. The spectacle simply beggars description, the greatest of all film spectacle plays.... It is Miss Bara's triumph too; her performance is at all times interesting. Never has she looked so regally beautiful. If the original Cleopatra was just half so lovely we do not blame Antony for renouncing Rome." *New York Herald*, 1917.

"An uncommonly fine picture. Miss Bara contributes a thoroughly successful portrayal. It is the finest sort of film fare and fans are certain to flock to it." *New York Times*, 1917?

"Historically correct in every detail." *Detroit Journal*, 1917?

"Miss Bara could not represent Cleopatra physically even if she should go into training, walk ten miles a day in a rubber sweater, and live on lemons and lettuce." *Boston Herald*, October 1917.

"Great white spaces of Theda Bara are alluringly exposed to the gaze of Antony, Caesar, and spectators.... Of her performance one might say without tempting contradiction that she has outstripped all other actresses who have played the part." *Detroit News*, 1917?

"Should have been a magnificent spectacle; the Fox picture is merely garish. Cleopatra herself was an irresistible little siren; Theda Bara is merely brazen in a ponderous way. The settings are bewildering heaps of fabrics. True magnificence is simple, dignified, not a clutter of expensive decorations. Historically the picture is incorrect without almost a single exception. Yet there is one inspired moment that redeems the entire production: Cleopatra returning from the defeat at Actium. Miss Bara rises to heights of tragic expression hitherto unsuspected, not by ravings and hysteria, but the sheer grace of despair. Had the entire picture been done in this spirit, it would be a thing of joy." *Photoplay*, 1917?

"An elaborate spectacle with gorgeous scenery.... It lacks the finish and dramatic force of *Birth of a Nation* and *Intolerance*.... Theda Bara is excellent and does some of her best work. She makes Cleopatra a sensual voluptuary of the most luring type. She plays the siren to perfection and yet she lacks the subtle charm which we are accustomed to attribute to the beautiful Egyptian queen. At no time did she impress me as being extremely beautiful, or charming, and her heavily painted black lips certainly did not add to her beauty. I got no glimpse of a great or powerful personality shining through. In spite of this, Theda Bara must be classed among the great players of the day for her creation." *Motion Picture Magazine*, 1917.

"Miss Theda Bara at her best; she is a real Cleopatra. As a picture the spectacle ranks second to none. The scenes were so gorgeous that they brought continuous applause. An enviable role for Miss Bara [who] gives a striking performance. The picture touches the top peak of films sirenic [sic]. Miss Bara is an immensely interesting Cleopatra, probably being the first actress to play the role whose eyes do the part. Surpasses even *Birth of a Nation*." *New York Telegraph*, 1917?

"This would be one of the great movies of the year if it were not for Theda Bara. She makes a burlesque of the Serpent of the Nile, and is never for one moment convincing. She could never tempt a man to be late for dinner, much less give up the throne of Rome. When she was not repulsive, she was funny." *Brooklyn Eagle*, 1917?

"Cleopatra lives again in the stunning characterization of Theda Bara in this production of overpowering import in the history of pictures.... Miss Bara achieves by the sheer force of her magnetic personality a brilliant star in the diadem of her many successes. Her work is daring in the extreme, human in understanding, and divine in beauty." *Exhibitors Herald*, 1917.

"An uncommonly fine picture. A distinct triumph for the production and the famous photoplay actress. Theda Bara has again scored one of the splendid triumphs of her conquering career. The star, by dint of much rolling of eyes and many other maneuvers, contributes a thoroughly successful portrait. Thus does the ill-starred Queen of Egypt become the well-starred queen of movies. A pageant-play of classic mold; the pages of history have been blazoned for us in gold and purple and red. Thus we shall never forget what we have seen. From a scenic standpoint it is quite a triumph. Miss Bara, to quote the program, wears fifty distinctly different costumes, many of which are so in attune [sic] with the period that they are likely to cause not a little comment." *Los Angeles Times*, October 15, 1917.

"There have been many mimic Cleopatras since the birth of the drama, but never before has a feigned Serpent of the Nile been given such a massive and artistic setting. A lucid and fairly authentic account.... Theda Bara is always satisfactory to the eye, save that a certain grade of spectators will criticize unfavorably the very frank display of her physical charms, and some of the seductive wiles she uses to ensnare her lovers. Technically, her acting demands respect without ever reaching any great tragic outburst, and she is best in the lighter scenes of the part." *Moving Picture World*, November 3, 1917.

"A stupendous offering with many magnificent scenes and gorgeous costumes. Theda Bara gives to her representation a [Broadway] touch which is not traditional. At no time does she appear queenly or dignified, but she makes a striking picture. The story is nearly historically correct. The production is not an artistic triumph due to overdressed interiors and shortcomings on the part of some of the cast. This is of little commercial importance as the picture is of the type to attract attention." *Motography*, November 3, 1917.

"Theda Bara in her most effective and impressive performance is creating little short of a sensation. Her seductive grace and her physical charms are revealed with frank yet artistic effectiveness. The production is parallel with the biggest things in the cinema art. For daring and luxurious splendor, Fox has accomplished nothing the equal. Her charm of manner, her beauty, and her splendid histrionic abilities are all revealed by Miss Bara.... A picture play of compelling fascination, but also a production worthy of closest study." *San Francisco Chronicle*, February 3, 1918.

"This played during the heaviest storm for three days, snow and rain. Still I had a fair house. All very well pleased; Theda Bara takes well here." Manager, Columbia Hall, Grace, Idaho. (This manager's comment was made two and a half years after the film's premiere. The picture was still drawing crowds, even though Theda Bara's career was fizzling out.)

"Played this as a special and got advanced admission. Good house and satisfied them all." Manager, Ryegate Theatre, Ryegate, Montana. (This was two years after its initial release.)

"This is an old one, but we put it over at fifty cent prices to three big houses." Manager, Chicago Theatre, Chicago, Illinois. (This was one-and-a half years after the film's initial release.)

"Cost a fortune to produce and is nicely done, but won't repeat. It's not raw enough for some and a little too rough for others, so the big business is the first day." Manager, Orpheum Theatre, Harrisburg, Pennsylvania.

"A real production. Theda not popular here, but this one got'em." Manager, Starland Theatre, Anderson, Indiana.

"Great picture; will get money anyplace. Broke record at Boston [Theatre]. Charged 25 instead of 15 cents. Good buy for a run." Manager, Boston and Rose Theatres, Chicago, Illinois.

"As a box office attraction it was great. Much time and money was expended.... You will find many of your patrons will not care for it; strictly a costume play. Admission 11 and 17 cents." Manager, Garfield Theatre, Chicago, Illinois.

"Drew a packed crowd at advanced prices. A beautiful and magnificent production, but I do not think Theda Bara is the right type for Cleopatra." Manager, Atherton Theatre, Kentwood, Louisiana.

"The picture of pictures. A picture that every exhibitor should run if possible. Theda Bara is by far the best emotional actress on the screen today in my opinion." Manager, White Way Theatre, Concordia, Kansas.

"Only drew fair. Pleased a certain element; others got tired of it." Manager, Empire Theatre, Winchester, Virginia.

"Fine business for two days. This is one of the pictures on which the argument for censorship is based. Nothing to it, go to it, it's a good one." Manager, Auditorium Theatre, Neligh, Nebraska.

The Rose of Blood (1917)

Background

It could not have been easy for Fox to decide on a Theda Bara film to follow the mega-success of *Cleopatra*. That film played for years after its initial release, and it is still being talked about more than 100 years later. The studio gambled that news of the turmoil in Russia would have sufficient audience appeal. The Russian Revolution had dethroned the Tsar earlier that year; and by the time this film was released in November 1917, the Bolsheviks had seized shaky power. Fox publicity could capitalize on the inherent drama of these momentous events.

The Rose of Blood would not be the first Theda Bara film in which Russia provided the setting. Earlier, *The Serpent* and *Her Greatest Love* also had their Russian settings. Also, *The Kreutzer Sonata* had been based on a Leo Tolstoy novella. Presumably to add to the authenticity of this picture, the story was devised by the flamboyant Ryzard Ordynski, known in America as Richard Ordynski (and born David Blumenthal?). He claimed that after seeing Bara in *Cleopatra*, he submitted his story "The Red Rose," and "it was immediately accepted by Fox and Miss Bara."

He was not Russian, but he had been born in the part of the Austro-Hungarian Empire which would become Poland. Therefore, he could be called at least a "Russian-adjacent." Fox claimed that "he has spent a great part of his life in parts of the Russian Empire." At least one review said Ordynski "was himself a Russian."

A multitalented actor, director, writer, and stage director at the Metropolitan Opera, Ordynski had been theater director Max Reinhardt's assistant in Berlin. A January 1915 article in the *New York Times* stated that Ordynski was coming to America for an indefinite period of time to introduce the methods of production which had made Reinhardt famous in Europe. He was quoted as saying: "My purpose for settling down in America for a while is to play a part in the development of the coming American drama. A young, fresh country like the United States ought to produce its own particular drama."

The Rose of Blood was the only Bara film to utilize Ordynski's talents, but that was enough for the Fox publicity flacks. In some of the publicity, he was given the honorarium of "Professor" Ordynski. The actual scenario was credited to Bernard McConville, who had been writing for films since 1915 and who would continue on with almost 100 credits into the mid–1940s. This was his only Bara film; most of his talkie credits were in "B" westerns.

Because Theda Bara had entrained to California to shoot *Cleopatra*, this film was also shot at the Fox studio in California. Yet again it was reported that she had averted a terrible accident. She narrowly escaped being trampled during a Cossack charge, and she was saved by an alert extra. She had been holding a little boy's hand at the time.

The Film

> Directed by J. Gordon Edwards. Scenario by Bernard McConville. Story [and art direction] by Richard Ordynski. Cinematography by Rial Schellinger and John Boyle. Released by the Fox Film Corporation on November 4, 1917. 7 reels, later edited to 5 reels.
> **Cast**: Theda Bara (Lisza Tapenko), Richard Ordynski (Vassya), Charles Clary (Prince Arbassoff), Herschel Mayall (Koliensky), Bert Turner (Princess Arbassoff), Joseph King (Prime Minister), Marie Keirnan (Koslya), Genevieve Blinn (Governess), Hector Sarno (Revolutionary).

Synopsis: Lisza Tapenko, though a commoner, has had a college education. She is in love with Prince Arbassoff, for whose child she is governess. When his wife dies, she takes the Princess's place in everything but name, but she is too lowborn to marry him. As a result of this rejection, she vows to become a revolutionary, as her former lover Vassya (known as The Firebrand) urges. She goes to Switzerland, the headquarters of the revolutionists, and takes an oath to save Russia from the aristocracy. Eventually, because of his son's pleadings, the Prince does marry Lisza.

The Prince's friend discovers Lisza's activities, but he agrees to keep silent providing that "she pays the price." She does not renounce her deadly activities, earning the sobriquet the Rose of Blood because she leaves a red rose on the bodies of her victims. When her husband is named prime minister, she is ordered to kill him too. Because of

The Rose of Blood. **A patriot has just killed the man she loves (Charles Clary) for the sake of Mother Russia. The actual revolution in Russia made this very timely.**

her love for him, she hesitates but finally decides to carry out her orders. She dynamites her own house, killing her husband and herself.

* * *

A Fox ad read: "A great 1918 vampire role with Theda Bara at the acme of her vamping…. Present crisis in Russia excitingly depicted." It was reported (accurately or not) that some exhibitors had paid as much as $1,000 to book the film, given the interest at that time in the Russian Revolution.

Fox publicity reported that a party of Russian scholars and members of a Russian commission that just happened to be passing through Los Angeles declared that it would be impossible to make a more accurately Russian picture.

The studio helpfully publicized the presumed fact that the red rose had always been the symbol for secrecy. When complete secrecy was ordered for any gathering of people, a red rose was suspended over their meeting place. It was considered a betrayal to disclose anything that had been discussed "sub rosa"—under the rose.

At about the same time that this film was released, Theda Bara sold more than $300,000 in Liberty Loan Bonds in front of the New York Public Library at 42nd Street and Fifth Avenue. The rally was organized under the auspices of the Stage Women's War Relief.

The Rose of Blood was the film which would eventually lead, indirectly, to the end of Major Funkhouser's reign (some would say reign of terror) as head of the Chicago Censorship Board. The 12 members of the Board had suggested only three or four minor cuts to the film, but the Major overruled them and ordered it banned completely.

One reason he gave was the number of bomb explosions in the film, saying that it might encourage bomb outrages in America. (The film had passed muster with every censorship board until it got to Chicago.) He further said: "It displays the revolutions which have occurred and are occurring in Russia, depicting the effects of bombs, firearms, and poison. It consists primarily of a series of unlawful actions of one mob after another."

The Federal Government intervened in the powerful person of George Creel, head of the United States Committee on Public Information. This committee had been set up as a propaganda arm of the government to monitor the content of American films during the war. Fox had cannily sent a print of the film to the Committee and the War Department to dispute Funkhouser's decision. Creel then sent a deposition urging that the film be released in its entirety.

Creel stated: "It violates none of the requests [i.e., commands] of the Government and seems to us to convey a patriotic message. There is the same right to a free film that there is to a free speech and a free press." The film was thereupon released with no cuts. Creel was being very disingenuous. During the war, films were routinely censored by the Committee; some film industry people were even prosecuted and jailed.

Fox once again sued Funkhouser, this time for slander. They asked $25,000 for his statement that the film was unpatriotic. Theda Bara filed her own lawsuit for $100,000, claiming Funkhouser had slandered her for *Cleopatra*. Although the court had usually sided with Fox's requests for injunctions against Funkhouser, this time it did not. The judge ruled that the film "tended to arouse the spirit of rebellion against organized government."

The Rose of Blood suit was still in court when on July 15, 1918, the Major and several aides were removed from office. He was no longer the Second Deputy Superintendent of Police and head of the Chicago Board of Censors. He in turn had sued the *Exhibitors Trade Review* for $100,000 for impugning his reputation.

Reviews

"It is a splendid role for Theda Bara. She is so much more convincing than her Cleopatra; you hardly knew her for the same actress. The story sweeps to a terrific tragedy." *Photoplay*, late 1917.

"We are firmly convinced there is only one way out of this Russian enigma, and that's to turn the job over to Theda Bara. We arrived at this conclusion after seeing the sinuous star vamp and bomb her way through [the film]. The star is, as ever, pleasing to the eye. There are moments, too, when her acting soars to artistic heights. We are frank to admit her skill surprised us." *Cleveland Leader*, late 1917.

"Ordynski has provided Miss Bara with a role rich in opportunities for her to display her special talents, and has built about it an action-full piece of fiction that has a wealth of popular appeal. A large audience, the majority of which probably know Russia better than the alphabet, was moved to applause several times when the story struck a popular note. Seems certain of finding favor." *Motion Picture News*, November 24, 1917.

"It has a good plot and holds interest without accomplishing any deeply convincing flight of the imagination that would set it above any other pictures.... The parts are well acted and the tale is made to run smoothly. It's a good picture." *Moving Picture World*, November 24, 1917.

Among the exhibitor comments were "Very good, but too much blood and thunder for these times" and "Bara good, but the picture did not please."

"Theda Bara doesn't take very well; picture only fair." Manager, Sherman Theatre, Sullivan, North Dakota.

"The picture is fair, but does not justify advance prices and did not draw here." Manager, Star Theatre, Talladega, Alabama.

"A good picture, but Theda Bara does not draw for me." Manager, Jewel Theatre, Red Lake Falls, Minnesota.

"As good as any, none better. Plenty of thrills; good business." Manager, Princess Theatre, Winnsboro, Louisiana.

"A very strong dramatic picture; business excellent." Manager, Columbia Theatre, Provo, Utah.

Du Barry/Madame Du Barry (1917)

Background

For Theda Bara's eighth and final film of 1917, Fox chose another historical character for her. The studio had managed to get that many Bara films out in 1917, even with the lengthy production of *Cleopatra*. As had happened with previous Bara films, another version of the story had been done within two years of this film. Theater diva Mrs. Leslie Carter had made, as her first picture, a six-reel version called *Du Barry* in 1915 for the Kleine studio.

That film was based on the 1901 David Belasco drama *Du Barry*, in which Mrs. Carter had starred on Broadway. The Bara film, which would alternately be known as *Du Barry* and *Madame Du Barry*, was supposedly based on the late 1840s Alexandre Dumas père novel *Memoires d'un Medecin*.

A Fox announcement breathlessly reported: "For the first time in her screen career, Theda Bara will become a blonde. In *Du Barry* the star wears an auriferous aura about her face. Searching through the memoirs of the French favorite character Miss Bara discovered that she was historically of blonde persuasion. In her search for accuracy and realism, she decided to follow in the footsteps of the woman she was portraying." As some reviews indicate, the film's level of accuracy was sometimes in dispute.

In the publicity that accompanied Theda Bara's rise to stardom, it was sometimes said that she was actually a natural blonde who was dyeing her hair black for the sake of her career. Although conceivably true, this is not borne out by any known photographs of Bara, beyond childhood, that show her with natural blonde hair. It was her younger sister Esther (Lori) who was seen as a blonde in photographs.

Bara claimed that her onscreen tears during the King's death scene were induced by the on-set musicians playing of Massenet's *Elegy*.

The Film

Directed by J. Gordon Edwards. Scenario by Adrian Johnson. Based on the novel *Memoires d'un Medecin* by Alexandre Dumas père. Cinematography by Rial Schellinger and John Boyle. Costumes by George "Neje" Hopkins. Released by the Fox Film Corporation on December 30, 1917. 7 reels.

Cast: Theda Bara (Jeanne Vaubenier, later Madame Du Barry), Charles Clary (King Louis XV), Fred Church (Casse-Brissac), Herschel Mayall (Jean Du Barry), Genevieve Blinn (Duchesse de Gaumont), Willard Louis (Guillaume Du Barry), Hector Sarno (Lebel), Dorothy Drake (Henriette), Rosita Marstini (Mother Savard).

Synopsis: Jeanne Vaubenier, an unknown young woman in Paris, attracts the eye of King Louis XV as he is riding through the streets. He arranges a meeting with her, at which she loses her garter and the King, his heart. He tells Jean Du Barry that he wants Jeanne near him, but that she lacks sufficient status to appear at court. Thereupon, Du Barry marries her off to his unappealing cousin Guillaume, who gives her the necessary status. The King showers her with riches and she becomes his favorite.

Du Barry/Madame DuBarry. Fox publicity raved about Theda Bara turning blonde for the very first time, and it also made much of the fact that she winked at the audience during the film. Shown with Charles Clary, she was just another doomed heroine.

Jeanne, however, has fallen in love with the dashing soldier Casse-Brissac, one of the King's guards. Du Barry tries to tell the King of the love affair, but instead he is banished from the court. The lovers narrowly avoid being caught by the King, and they carry on their affair until the French Revolution breaks out. After Louis dies, the couple hope to wed, but the vengeful Jean Du Barry incites the mob against her. She is convicted, along with other favorites of Louis. An unsuccessful attempt to escape leads to her lover's death. Although Madame Du Barry is not guilty of anything but vanity and avarice, she is sent to the guillotine.

* * *

The usually hostile Chicago Board of Censors only demanded two cuts, both in the very final part of the film: Elimination of Mme. Du Barry lying on the guillotine, and a close-up of its deadly blade.

Other actresses depicted Madame Du Barry. One who portrayed her successfully was Pola Negri. In May 1921 *Motion Picture Magazine* jokingly predicted that the German production of *Passion* with Negri was so successful that Fox would re-release the Bara version as *DuBarry's Passion*. *Du Barry, Woman of Passion* marked the end of Norma Talmadge's film career in 1930. In 1934 Dolores Del Rio made an uninspired *Madame Du Barry*. The most successful incarnation of that notorious lady was a comic one in the Broadway musical comedy and subsequent film *Du Barry Was a Lady*.

Reviews

"It is Theda Bara's own Du Barry, just as it was her own Cleopatra, just as anything she essays is her own.... A creation of decided originality.... Displays a remarkable degree of versatility.... Vastly entertaining as set down in this adaptation.... It has many, if not all, of these [qualities] which go to make the Theda Bara picture laid in the present time the popular thing that it is. This fact, together with the magnificent production, should establish the picture's success beyond the shadow of a doubt." *Motion Picture News*, January 19, 1918.

"Theda Bara has some very attractive moments in the part. She doesn't fill it, she often poses as herself rather than the character, but now and then she is most effective. It is a picture for Theda Bara followers, rather than for a college class or a literary club." *Moving Picture World*, January 1918.

"I have seen very few of the Theda Bara pictures and that few had left me comparatively chilly.... Without beating about the bush, I may as well remark at once that [the film] has converted me from a cynic to a Theda Bara admirer, and that I was splendidly enthusiastic about this picture.... It is not conceivable that a finer performance could have been given.... She was the siren that fascinated: light, vivacious, provocative, tense, and dramatic.... Throughout it was an impersonation of which any emotional actress might legitimately be proud. I doff my hat to this star whose art I have never appreciated before this. [She] proved to be an artist of the finest ray, and at last I can understand her amazing popularity." *Picture-Play,* early 1918.

"Without having been imbued with any great amount of enthusiasm with Miss Bara's impersonation of Madame Du Barry (maybe that's where she gets her name), I still maintain it is the best thing she's ever done." *Chicago Tribune* ("Mae Tinee"), early 1918.

"A splendid production, and should prove a good box office attraction.... Lavishly produced, well acted, has an entertaining story, and Theda Bara is cast in a very fitting role which she handles to excellent advantage." *Exhibitors Herald*, early 1918.

"The producers took liberties with the familiar story. It's a frivolous version of a big historical fact. Theda Bara makes Du Barry a kittenish, artful hussy instead of a clever, witty, intriguing woman. She is gorgeously overdressed. An attempt to make the costumes more than elaborate ended in making them junky.... Anyone who aims to improve a [David] Belasco production is aiming high. And so is Miss Bara when believing she can portray famous women of history with a 19th century wiggle." *Variety*, March 1918.

"Not up to Miss Bara's standards; we were disappointed in it. The audience was well pleased." Manager, Acme Theatre, Chicago, Illinois.

"Not for us. Theda will lose her prestige with many more of this kind." Manager, Olympic and Majestic Theatres, Bellaire, Ohio.

"This picture fell flat for us, but it's a fair picture and will please if they like costume stuff. My patrons don't." Manager, Orpheum Theatre, Harrisburg, Illinois.

"A good picture of its kind, but my people don't like costume plays." Manager, Dreamland Theatre, Chester, South Carolina.

The Forbidden Path (1918)

Background

Once again, Theda Bara plays an artist's model. The film would seem to be another of her standard melodramas, but the generally positive reviews indicate something more worthwhile. A reviewer opined: "One of the best pieces of work Miss Bara has ever done. Those who think she cannot really act will have to revise their opinions. Miss Bara has never risen to greater heights."

Based on the plot synopsis and reviews, scenarist Adrian Johnson presented a more modern woman. Bara had been quoted as saying, "I have the face of a vampire, but "the "heart of a feministe [sic]." This is probably the film that came closest to demonstrating that. The film produced two of her iconic stills: Theda Bara as Mary Lynde posing as a Madonna figure, halo above her head, and tenderly holding a baby, and the opposite, a dissolute Mary Lynde in a low dive with a bottle of cheap booze, wearing a man's battered hat and torn clothing.

Mary Lynde does not revenge herself on the man who has wronged her by vamping him, nor does she die for him. She outsmarts him. The denunciation scene that ends the film, the "J'accuse" moment ("She made him pay!"), must have been a satisfying culmination for many women in the 1918 audience.

The film was based on the E. Lloyd Sheldon story "From the Depths," which was the working title of this film. Sheldon wrote stories and scenarios for motion pictures from the mid-1910s to the end of the silent era. In the sound era he served mainly as a producer until the end of the 1930s.

A 1917 Paramount-Lasky film starring Sessue Hayakawa had the title *Forbidden Paths*. A 1913 one-reeler was called *On Forbidden Paths*.

The Forbidden Path. Theda Bara, again playing an artist's model, poses as the Virgin Mary. Bara claimed to have the "heart of a feministe." This is the film that came closest to showing it.

The Film

Directed by J. Gordon Edwards. Scenario by Adrian Johnson. Based on the story "From the Depths" by E. Lloyd Sheldon. Cinematography by John Boyle. Released by the Fox Film Corporation on February 3, 1918. 6 reels.
Cast: Theda Bara (Mary Lynde), Hugh Thompson (Robert Sinclair), Sidney Mason (Felix Benavente), Walter Law (Mr. Lynde), Florence Martin (Barbara Reynolds), Wynne Hope

Allen (Mrs. Lynde), Alphonse Ethier (William Sinclair), Reba Porter (Tessie Byrne), Lisle Leigh (Mrs. Byrne).

Synopsis: Although Mary Lynde lives in Greenwich Village, her parents have sheltered her from the art colony there. But when she is asked to pose for a portrait of the Madonna and Child, she happily accepts. While posing, she meets Robert Sinclair, the son of the man who has commissioned the painting. He seduces her, and her father throws her out. Sinclair falsely tells Mary that he will marry her and sets her up in his mountain lodge.

A child is born to Mary out of wedlock, and she is cast out by Sinclair. When she follows him to the city, she is sheltered by a poor family. Mary sinks into depravity. Several years later she is spotted living in a disreputable tenement by Felix Benavente, another painter. He asks her to pose for a painting of sin, to be called "The End of the Forbidden Path." Sinclair meets Mary again by accident. Fearful that she will expose him, he sets her up in luxury.

Sinclair is forced to steal in order to meet Mary's demands for money. He even tries to kill her, but Mary now insists that Sinclair marry her. He is engaged to a society girl; but fearing exposure, he breaks off his engagement and promises to marry Mary. At the altar she turns to the wedding guests and denounces Sinclair as a scoundrel unfit to marry any woman, even the disreputable one she has become. She throws the money he has given her in his face. She will now find happiness with Felix, whom she asks for forgiveness.

* * *

A Fox advertisement promised: "Dramatic masterpiece of passion and thrills. The greatest woman's picture ever filmed." Another posed the questions: "Suppose the Devil was at the end of the forbidden path. Would you follow him?" and "Suppose your betrayer drove you to the depths. Would you make him pay?" Another ad starkly answered that question: "She made him pay." Yet another promised: "One moral standard for men and women."

The opening of the film was delayed because of "Laboratory congestion due to the coal saving order by the Fuel Administration," a reminder that the Great War was affecting the home front.

The Chicago censors, led (or bullied) by the overbearing Major Funkhouser, asked for several cuts: All views of the interior of a house of ill-fame; all views of the statuary in the background (presumably due to nudity); the scene of a girl soliciting a male; close-up of an alleged "pervert" knitting; all views of other men "of the same character"; and a scene of a shooting. Apparently effeminate (i.e., gay?) men were pictured; being seen knitting was a signification of that.

Reviews

"A very trashy story. However, Miss Bara is doing better work in it than we have seen for some time. She understands this modern sort of heroine and she portrays her with great vividness in all her stages." *Columbus Journal*, early 1918.

"Theda Bara is used to 'point a moral and adorn a tale.' (This was one of the Fox taglines for the film.) She does both. The moral is the same moral found in all photodramas with a mission: Forbidden paths, like the paths of glory, lead but to the grave." *Photoplay*, February 1918.

"Miss Bara plays her part with feeling in all its many phases.... Always sincere and expressing her various emotions clearly, Miss Bara contributes yet another role of understanding force to the long list held in awe by her numerous admirers." *Motion Picture News*, February 16, 1918.

"A very melodramatic story. Should make good entertainment for the majority. There is an unexpected and more than usually vigorous twist for a melodrama.... It is beautifully staged and photographed. This kind of story gives Theda Bara a fine chance, and she appears to good advantage. Will almost certainly be a most popular release. Her large following will take especial pleasure in it." *Moving Picture World*, February 16, 1918.

"This latest vehicle for the queen of film vampires is not an altogether improbable phase of the depths of human degradation. The character around whom the story is woven is one that gives Miss Bara an opportunity to exhibit her unlimited capability. Somewhat different from her recent portrayals, yet equally as effective, the character is one of the best interpretations the star has done. She is seen in all the vividness and power that has made her such a universal favorite." *Motography*, February 23, 1918.

"Theda Bara has a role more human and understandable than she has played for some time. She gives a well-defined picture of a woman with ideals, and again with those ideals shattered.... The story enthralls you.... Miss Bara does not shine in modern dress at anytime, and this production is no exception." *Variety*, April 1918.

"Better than average Bara; star does fine work." Manager, Regent Theatre, Cleveland, Mississippi.

"Star is played out in this house; poor business." Manager, Rae Theatre, Ann Arbor, Michigan.

"A typical Theda Bara play, and as her followers like her best in pictures of this kind, did good business." Manager, Princess Theatre, Dubuque, Iowa.

"Drew better than usual on Bara subjects. Fine picture and pleased all." Manager, Empire Theatre, Winchester, Virginia.

"Pleased more on account of Miss Bara than the story. She never did better work. We ran this two weeks." Manager, Central Theatre, St. Louis, Missouri.

"Some picture and we did an excellent business. I think this is Miss Bara's best." Manager, Columbia Theatre, Provo, Utah.

Exhibitors' comments included: "A repeat picture, did big business."; "Extra good"; "One of the biggest moneymakers made by Fox; just the kind that this star shines in. We will repeat this, extra big business"; "Extra big and good show."

The Soul of Buddha (1918)

Background

Theda Bara followed the relative successes of *Madame Du Barry* and *The Forbidden Path* with yet another vampire film. Not only were such films losing their appeal in the midst of a war, where real horrors occurred daily, but also this was not a particularly good vampire film. And she proudly claimed the credit for the story.

Bara had been quoted as saying: "During the rest of my screen career, I am going to continue doing vampires as long as people sin. I believe that humanity needs the moral lesson and it needs it in repeatedly larger doses." This sounded pretentious—even sanctimonious—as she increasingly tended to sound in public pronouncements.

Whether or not Bara actually devised the story for this film as she claimed, or someone else like Adrian Johnson did (he is credited with writing the scenario), the results were disappointing. Reviews were split, but warning signs were evident. Former friends such as Louella Parsons were turning on her.

Theda Bara claimed to have written the story on the train from California to New York, and she was sometimes mistakenly credited with the scenario as well. She said she had appropriated some of the paste jewels from the production of *Cleopatra*, and this was her way of recompensing the studio. She presented the story to William Fox and confessed her "attack of conscience." "This is splendid!" Mr. Fox was said to have exclaimed, and the rest is vampiric history.

Her character Bava Mari was based on the recently executed Dutch spy Mata Hari. In an account not lacking in self-praise, Bara claims to have hired an authority on Eastern dances to teach her "Javanese forms." She supposedly was told she had the native instinct for the peculiar walk of Javanese woman, and she mastered the "wiggle" that allowed her to glide along without losing her batik slippers. She was not happy when a reviewer called it a "Broadway wiggle." Learning a new dance in such a short time left her with "muscles so stiff and sore that I had to be carried to my automobile." She claimed to have mastered in six lessons what the great ballerina Anna Pavlova had taken six years to master.

The Film

Directed by J. Gordon Edwards. Scenario by Adrian Johnson. Based on a story by Theda Bara. Cinematography by John Boyle. Costumes by George James Hopkins ("Neje"). Released by the Fox Film Corporation on April 21, 1918. 5 reels.
Cast: Theda Bara (Bava), Hugh Thompson (Sir John Dare), Victor Kennard (Ysora), Tony Merlo (Count Romaine), Florence Martin (Countess), Jack Ridgeway (Her father), Henry Warwick (Stage manager).

Synopsis: Fearing for Bava's morals, her widowed Buddhist mother gives her to the high priest Ysora as a sacred temple dancer. Bava is attracted to him and readily takes a vow to renounce the world, consecrating herself to the temple. During a religious festival she meets Sir John Dare, a major in the British army, who courteously helps her after she falls. Ysora and the temple priests want to kill Dare for defiling her, but Bava saves him. When she is ordered to pray to Buddha for the entire night, she leaves the temple at midnight to rendezvous with Dare. Ysora follows them to the barracks, but they escape on horseback. Bava and Dare are married by the army chaplain, and they move to Scotland.

The couple lives in Scotland for a while, but the climate makes Bava unhappy and they return to Java. There she gives birth to a son whom Ysora kills, leaving a Buddhist death sign on his forehead. Grief stricken, Bava and her husband go to Paris where she carries on a dissolute lifestyle. She tells her maid to take her "where life and death are the same." Two Apache dancers want to dance with her; she tells them to fight for the privilege with knives. When her husband is recalled to Scotland, she has an affair with

The Soul of Buddha. The story idea for this film was said to be Theda Bara's own, written on a train. The exotic heroine resembled spy Mata Hara. The perfervid melodrama featured the last full-on vampire role for Bara.

a French count, Count Romaine. Bava tells her husband she no longer loves him. The count's wife begs Bava to give him up; she refuses.

A theatrical agent, impressed by Bava's dancing, offers her a contract. The night she is to make her stage debut Dare shoots himself in her dressing room. She hides his body in a trunk, even sitting on it, and undaunted goes on with her dancing. It is a great success. While she is dancing one night, a background figure dressed like Buddha leaps on her and stabs her to death in front of the nightclub crowd. As her body falls to the stage, the audience, thinking it is part of the act, applauds wildly. Ysora has exacted his revenge.

* * *

Fox taglines included: "Strange, mystic, and grippingly intense tale of the Orient"; "From the temples of the most high comes death"; "The mysterious East and gay life in Paris. Breaking her oath meant death. A tense, mysterious, eerie, palpitating photodrama"; "Screen vampire turns to Buddha and is scornfully rebuffed."

One ad really seemed to be a reach: "Miss Bara's own original screen story has a tremendous home appeal to all who understand the Buddhistic culture of the East, and with her latest picture she will stretch hands across the sea into the homes of millions of new friends."

The film ran into censor problems in Canada. It was accepted in the province of Ontario, but it was banned in Manitoba and Quebec. In usually hostile Chicago, the censors ordered the following cuts: An attack on a female servant; all scenes of a woman's leg being shown above the knee; the framing of a woman's head with hands during the Apache dance and wiggling with her in a close embrace; a man kissing a woman's arm; and the love scene following the woman's stabbing.

Reviews

In its 20-year retrospective in 1938, *The Film Daily* summarized its 1918 review of *The Soul of Buddha*: "Nightmare meller with ever-present vamp who is funny at times. If your gang likes Theda, kid 'em along with this."

"Funny little Theda's back again with her bag of tricks in a funny picture built around a scenario she wrote herself. And she's a vamp proper this time. A look from her bedaubed eyes, a grimace from her be-jammed lips, one wiggle, and all men but Major Funkhouser are hers'n. As in all Bara pictures, the picture is all Bara—Bara making faces, Bara ogling, Bara wiggling, Bara shoulders, and everything." *Chicago Tribune* ("Mae Tinee"), May 1918.

"Theda Bara at her best according to her own light, and Theda Bara at her worst according to the public consensus of opinion, may be seen in [this film]. Now we know how Miss Bara likes herself: As a young woman whose life is one conquest after another. It is difficult to take either Miss Bara or the play seriously. To see it is to laugh." *Chicago Daily News* (Louella Parsons), May 1918.

"A pretentious (i.e., elaborate) feature.... It is a weird and quite fascinating tale.... Very artistically produced and perfectly clean. As a piece of pictorial handiwork it ranks high, judging it by the other Bara films. [Her] fans will not be disappointed in this picture." *Motion Picture News*, May 1918.

"Put on with all the lavishness, splendid sets, and impressive cast which have characterized her previous pictures, but does not come up to the standard." *Exhibitors Herald*, May 1918.

"It is about as mongrel a piece of film writing as has ever been known. A survey of the principal scenes will give a faint conception of this awful concoction.... Did you ever notice Theda's left eyebrow is higher than the right?" *Variety*, May 1918.

"Theda Bara has felt the itch for authorship in scenarios, yielded to the gentle tickling of the ego, and has written a photoplay.... It is herself. That it is not a very big photoplay is not her fault. She did her best. It has the touch of the amateur, and it is attractive in the way common to amateur performances. Their very weakness endears them even when they bore us. However this does not bore us; it really interests us. We enjoy seeing

Theda Bara sashay through the lightsome role. We like to watch her dancing on the stage in Paris, and we are not sorry when she is stabbed by the young priest of Buddha." *Los Angeles Times*, May 13, 1918. (As a "hometown" paper, *The Times* had up to now lavishly praised every Theda Bara film.)

"The same note of passion and physical desire as in *A Fool There Was* runs through the star's first attempt at scenario writing, and she is able to portray the same type of erotic womanhood.... The extent to which the spectator will be impressed by this grade of melodrama depends on his artistic instinct and his interest in seeing the unlovely passion of humanity." *Moving Picture World*, May 18, 1918.

"A wicked, wicked wamp [sic] concoction that will pull a lot of laughs." *Wid's Daily*, May 19, 1918.

"A typical Bara picture, a trifle lacking in spice. It was well received and drew extra good business. The audience was well pleased." Manager, Acme Theatre, Chicago, Illinois.

"Bara always draws and never disappoints. Give her more vampire stuff." Manager, South Side Theatre, Greensburg, Indiana.

"Theda Bara no longer draws here like she formerly did. Time was when the theater that had the vampire had the crowds, but the rule seems to be working the other way now." Manager, Lyric Theatre, Springfield, Illinois.

"Showed it to a big house. Some liked it, while several thought it not fit to be shown. The dances overdrawn." Manager, Central Theatre, Oberlin, Kansas.

"Program picture, drew fair. Bara never draws big here." Manager, Empire Theatre, Winchester, Virginia.

"Touch this one light; there's nothing to make a fuss about. Theda was loaded down with an uninteresting theme." Manager, Auditorium Theatre, Neligh, Nebraska.

"Good, but entirely too strong. Business good." Manager, Columbia Theatre, Provo, Utah.

"Pleased but a small percentage of patrons." Manager, Princess Theatre, Clare, Michigan.

"A high class production, but a bit slow for the average crowd." Manager, Atherton Theatre, Kentwood, Louisiana.

Under the Yoke (1918)

Background

Theda Bara now returned to the adventure-melodrama of such films as *Under Two Flags* and *Heart and Soul*. She was reunited with her *Cleopatra* and *Camille* co-star Albert Roscoe. Fox claimed that there had been innovations in how the film was photographed. Several reviews did note the excellent cinematography, then still widely called photography. Part of the picture was filmed in the San Jacinto Mountains of California. It was noted that the studio had problems finding enough bolo knives for use of the extras.

George Scarborough, who is credited with the story, was a Broadway playwright. Among his successes was *The Son-Daughter*, later made into a film. The working title of this film was *Spanish Love*.

The Film

Directed and produced by J. Gordon Edwards. Scenario by Adrian Johnson. Based on the unpublished, un-copyrighted story "Maria of the Roses" by George Scarborough. Cinematography by John Boyle and Harry Gerstad. Costumes by George James Hopkins ("Neje"). Released by the Fox Film Corporation on June 9, 1918. 5 reels.

Cast: Theda Bara (Maria Valverde), Albert Roscoe (Captain Paul Winter), G. Raymond Nye (Diablo Ramirez), Edward Booth Tilton (Don Ramon Valverde, Maria's father), Carrie Clark Ward (Duenna).

Synopsis: Maria Valverde, a *mestiza* (i.e., of mixed Filipino and non–Filipino heritage), comes home from a convent to live on her father's *rancho* in the Philippines. When Diablo Ramirez, the overseer, comes to court her, she rejects him, and Maria's father throws him out. Diablo comes to hate the family and stirs up rebellion among the natives. At a ball in Manila, Maria sees Captain Winter, with whom she had flirted while still at the convent. Her father takes her home and shortly afterward leaves for Manila on business.

En route he is stopped by Diablo's men and is murdered. The rebels invade the *rancho*, but Maria has time to telegraph Manila. When Winter's men arrive, they are taken prisoner. Maria and Winter try to escape but they are recaptured. The troops manage to wire for help, and fresh troops attack the fort in which the rebels are hiding. A battle ensues. Winter opens the gate for the troops and saves Maria from Diablo. Maria and Winter are then betrothed.

* * *

This film premiered a few weeks before Major Funkhouser, the Chicago censorship czar, was finally relieved of his responsibilities once and for all. Chicago censors asked for the elimination of the scene showing the execution of Don Ramon and the scene of Diablo kissing Maria's shoulder as well as the shortening of scenes showing torture of an American soldier.

The oddest thing about this production was not the movie itself, but one of the more dramatic movie posters. It pictures Theda Bara, who is in every way unlike the character she is playing. Draped in blood-red material that seems to leave her bosom bare, bedecked with Cleopatra-like adornments, and staring almost malignly at the onlooker, she looks much more the evil vampire than the heroic heroine. The shadowy gray-black background is not at all redolent of the sunny Philippines. It seems to come from an entirely different movie.

The film's often-used tagline "The battle for love of a woman with no regrets" could also be interpreted as a vamp allusion. It would not be cynical to think that Fox was trying to sell this as another Bara vampire production. An ad referred to the Bara character as "a little Spanish flirt." Fox tried to hedge its bets by trying to sell it in several different ways. Had Americans not been fighting overseas in 1918, the amorphous title of this film and its subject matter probably would not have generated much audience interest.

Some ads compared the picture to other notable Bara successes: "Combines all the good qualities of *Carmen* and *Under Two Flags*, two of her most popular dramas." Taglines emphasized that the heroine was fighting for the Stars and Stripes, so it was also sold as a patriotic film and as a romance: "Dark-eyed charmer dares American to plunge into conflict for love and treasure" and "Cupid's triumph when the Philippines were ablaze with revolt."

Another ad read: "America's greatest emotional actress in her most appealing role, a daughter of Old Glory.... Sweetheart of the man who fought for the flag.... A pulsing drama of the Philippines in the days of Aguinaldo.... Vibrant with the turmoil of insurrection." Although the film was set around 1902, American troops were fighting in Europe in 1918. A connection could be made about America's fighting spirit, wherever and whenever it was found.

One Fox ad read: "Depicts a situation utterly new to the screen." This was not the case. At the time of the Aguinaldo rebellion in the Philippines, several actualities (as newsreels were then called) were screened. The Edison Company and perhaps other studios also produced re-creations of the battles.

A supposed news account (or possibly the Fox publicity machine) reported that during a July 1918 Allied counteroffensive in the Marne Salient, American troops discovered that German troops had been watching three Theda Bara movies: *A Fool There Was*, *Cleopatra*, and *Under the Yoke*. An American YMCA in France had been showing the films. Captured "Huns" said they had enjoyed the films, which the Americans now proceeded to enjoy. The sight of an American actress, even on film, caused the soldiers to cheer.

In an effort to re-burnish Theda Bara's career, articles were planted by Fox in various movie magazines. One read: "In focusing the demand for an American film star who can fill the public eye in South America, the Antipodes, and Asia, foreign exhibitors have concentrated on Theda Bara as the one best qualified to fill the international bill. To meet these Asiatic audiences Miss Bara is reaching out across the Pacific in *Under the Yoke*."

By this time "The Queen of the Screen" seems to have replaced "The Bernhardt of the Screen" as Fox's encomium for "Theda Bara." Its publicity machine trumpeted: "With the 'Queen of the Screen' there is little doubt that [the film] will be another Theda Bara super-production worthy to be added to the list of wonder-pictures she has filmed in California."

A similar article in *Motography* read: "The worldwide and unceasing demand for Theda Bara pictures has stimulated Fox's 'Queen of the Screen' to almost superhuman efforts to meet the extraordinary situation, especially in foreign countries.... Foreign exhibitors seem to have concentrated on Theda Bara as the one best qualified by name, fame, and previous achievements."

Reviews

"A remarkable lack of plot is forgotten for the moment by the excellent photography, the unusually good lighting, and the general beauty of the production. The Spanish atmosphere is admirable. Miss Bara looks the part and acts with more naturalness and simplicity than she sometimes does." *Variety*, June 1918.

"A very pleasing picture. It has a good and plausible story, a lot of good acting and several scenes with the required punch to make it a thriller." *Los Angeles Tribune*, June 1918.

"Your enjoyment of the play depends largely on your attitude toward the star. If you are one of her admirers you will see here a picture which gives her an opportunity for depicting varied emotions. If you do not like Theda you will not find much to entertain you in the picture." *Chicago Post*, June 1918.

"Some exceptional bits of photography; some very well handled mob scenes; a story that has been handled with a great deal of intelligence, and a star whose mannerisms are entirely original and who is well-fitted to her part. Fast moving, logical, and interesting. Altogether a good offering." *Exhibitors Herald*, June 9, 1918.

"Excellent picture, but the star not suited to this play." Tokio Theatre, Morehouse, Missouri.

"A very good picture; plenty of action." Manager, American Theatre, New Ulm, Minnesota.

"About the best Bara picture yet; some wonderful battle scenes." Manager, Dreamland Theatre, Winchester, Virginia.

"An ordinary picture; business fair." Manager, Michigan Theatre, Chicago, Illinois.

"Pleased. Bad weather, business fair." Manager, Kozy Theatre, Villisca, Iowa.

"The poorest picture Bara ever appeared in. Audience walked out." Small-town theater manager.

Salome (1918)

Background

The year 2021 brought exciting news. About two minutes of scenes from the lost Theda Bara film *Salome* had been discovered by an intern at the Filmoteca Espanola, a Spanish film archive. From a viewing it seems clear that Bara, in the fourth year of her movie stardom, has not developed much subtlety as a screen actress. She is still using the exaggerated facial expressions and body movements of the early silent film days. This Delsarte acting method was satirized by Marion Davies in the 1928 film *Show People*. The more extreme the emotion, the more exaggerated, to modern eyes, the grand gestures.

The Bara figure is lithe, apparently having shed some of her Cleopatra plumpness. She could pass as the 28-year-old she claimed to be, rather than the 33 she actually was. It has been speculated that the clips are from a 1919 print, and they were to be used in a documentary or retrospective. The subtitles have been translated into English; among them "You must suppress Prince David" and "The arrogant figure of the prophet did not leave the lascivious mind of Salome for a moment."

With *Salome*—or *Cleopatra Part Two,* as Fox may have thought of it—Theda Bara's decline in popularity was temporarily slowed. Fox was still willing to lavish money on the production values and advertising of her films. In June 1918, a month before the premiere of this film, Fox had proudly announced that Theda Bara had completed 32 films since her debut three and a half years earlier: "A record which is looked on with pride by both Miss Bara and Fox Film Corporation." Touted as having "set a standard of film art which will take a long, long time to surpass" were the Bara films *Cleopatra, Salome, A Fool There Was,* and *The Two Orphans.* Considering that Theda Bara often complained about overwork and not being able to take vacations because of the frenetic pace of filming, this Fox statement may have been issued to mollify her.

In a February 17, 1918, interview with the *Los Angeles Times* Bara discussed her vision of *Salome.* She said the original scenario depicted her as a vampire "of the worst sort, the quintessence of vampirism" with no redeeming qualities. Bara on the other hand did not see *Salome* as a vampire at all, but as a "baleful pale-green flower," sort of a flower that the French call a *demi-vierge* (i.e., a half-virgin who behaves provocatively but doesn't actually surrender her purity). She also said it would be difficult for audiences to separate Salome from Cleopatra, but that she would be playing them completely differently.

Production began six months after *Cleopatra* concluded filming. Ancient Jerusalem was revived, supposedly with the help of 800 artisans. Publicity claimed that many of the 2,000 extras, a dozen camels, 12 burros, and 100 horses were used for scenes shot in Palm Canyon in Palm Springs, California. It was also claimed that the machines used for simulating a huge storm caused the camels to stampede, endangering the extras and Theda Bara, who avoided yet another accident. A special train was required to transport all the extras.

The film opened in August 1918 in a 2,000-seat theater in Seattle because of a labor dispute in New York. Under the headline "*Salome*, Countrywide Fox Success, Finally Comes to New York," a newspaper touted the New York engagement beginning that October. The New York premiere boasted a 24-piece orchestra with a score arranged by George Rubenstein.

Theda Bara claimed that when she had to film the scene of *Salome* kissing the dead lips of John the Baptist, she could not bring herself to do it. One night she had a dream vision of the sacred head with a divine sort of light upon it. After that she felt she could do the scene.

The crediting of first century CE Roman-Jewish historian Flavius Josephus with the story of this film is disingenuous. A much more contemporary figure, namely Oscar Wilde, is almost certain to have been the inspiration for the film. His scandalous 1891 play *Salome* was originally written in French and translated a few years later.

Perhaps Fox was afraid of adding to the censorship problems it must have known were coming. Nevertheless, reviewers all assumed it was based on the Wilde play. The libretto of the 1905 opera by Richard Strauss is also credited to Wilde. In 1877 novelist Gustave Flaubert had published a tale called *Herodias*, dealing with the execution of John the Baptist.

Vitagraph produced a four-reel version of *Salome* in 1908 with then major stars Florence Lawrence and Maurice Costello. Many other versions of the story have been made since then, including the 1923 Alla Nazimova film.

The Film

Directed by J. Gordon Edwards. Produced by William Fox. Scenario by Adrian Johnson. Based on an account by Flavius Josephus [and the play *Salome* by Oscar Wilde?]. Cinematography by John Boyle, Harry Gerstad, and George Schneiderman. Art direction, set decoration, and costumes by George James Hopkins ("Neje"). Released by the Fox Film Corporation on August 10, 1918. 8 reels.

Cast: Theda Bara (Salome), G. Raymond Nye (King Herod), Albert Roscoe (John the Baptist), Herbert Heyes (Sejanus), Bertram Grassby (Prince David), Genevieve Blinn (Queen Marian), Vera Doria (Naomi), Alfred Fremont (Galla).

Synopsis: King Herod, ruler of Judea, is hated because he gained his throne when Caesar displaced the former king. In an effort to solidify his hold, Herod married

Salome. Some critics dubbed this *Cleopatra*, Part Two, and Fox surely hoped it would be. It was Theda Bara's final big hit. Newly discovered scenes from the film show that Bara still relied on the "big" emotions favored in the Victorian era. She is shown here with an unidentified actor, possibly Herbert Heyes.

Marian, the heir's sister. Herod is petitioned to install Prince David, the rightful heir, as the high priest, but Herod is reluctant until his cousin Salome urges him to do it. She really does not want the heir to have so much power, but she sees the refusal as a political problem.

Salome solves the problem by seducing Sejanus, the captain of the guard, into drowning Prince David as he bathes. Now she sets her eyes on John the Baptist, who has condemned Herod's rule and has been imprisoned for sedition. She desires him but he rejects her. Next Salome plots to destroy Queen Marian by implicating her in false plots to poison and stab Herod. Marian is beheaded for treason. Still yearning for John, Salome offers to perform the Dance of the Seven Veils if Herod will grant whatever she desires.

It is still John whom she desires; but when he continues to reject her, she schemes to have him killed. Herod reluctantly grants her wish, and a triumphant Salome kisses John's dead lips. When a terrible storm arises, Herod sees it as an omen of God's wrath. He now orders Salome to be put to death under the shields of his guards.

* * *

In spite of Bara's interpretation of Salome as being no vampire but a baleful green flower, the film was publicized as an all-out vampire film. It would be the final picture in which she played the persona that had brought her fame, and her last really successful film.

A Fox ad read: "Sinuous, seductive Theda Bara in her greatest triumph: Salome, the Princess of Passion." Another ad reads: "Pagan Salome sees only the beauty and strength of John's body—In her hungry eyes he is sent but for caresses and love."

As usual, Fox ads poured on the super-superlatives: "*Cleopatra* outdone in dramatic power and drawing power, and the greatest spectacular drama that William Fox has produced. A tremendous, historically accurate story of the world's greatest vampire—The wickedest woman of all times." Another boasted: "Theda Bara, siren supreme of the screen, portraying the tremendous role of the wickedest woman of all times. The biggest box office triumph in the history of motion pictures." Yet another: "Outdrawing *Cleopatra* and equaling it in tremendous spectacular effects. Surpassing it in dramatic power and appeal." Another ad called Salome the "Female Nero, the wickedest woman of all history" who lived in "a setting of regal magnificence."

While Theda Bara was in Florida shooting scenes for *A Woman There Was*, the owner of three Miami theaters rebooked *Salome*. He papered the town with posters and built a special box for Bara to make a personal appearance. He did record business, estimating that 30 percent of Miamians had seen *Salome*.

The Chicago Board of Censors asked for cuts in scenes showing Salome's breasts; a scene of an executioner's sword descending, and two scenes of Salome bending over the dungeon where John is imprisoned. The St. Louis censors called Bara's performance "overbold and under-clad." As she often did, she responded about her films actually being lessons in morality. "*Salome* was a deterrent, not an inspiration to wickedness." She accused the censors of hypocrisy because her costuming was no worse than what was seen at the beach.

Director J. Gordon Edwards also asserted that the film carried "a big moral lesson." He addressed the criticism of John the Baptist being portrayed as clean-shaven, claiming to have old prints that showed a clean-shaven John. Edwards also admitted to some poetic license: "It would be impossible to expect an audience to be sympathetic toward a hero who wanders through eight reels pushing before him a clump of mattress material. We stand by the boyish John. There is no romance in whiskers."

In Boston a 30-foot-high painting representing a scene in ancient Judea advertised the film; above it was a cutout of Bara looking over the city. In Syracuse, New York, huge ads were carried on the front and rear of streetcars. A Harrisburg, Pennsylvania, theater manager printed facsimiles of the $5,000 check he paid for booking *Salome*, and distributed thousands of them. The gimmick resulted in long lines at his theater. Another theater manager got a story in the papers that said every "old bachelor and gay old dog in town" was crowding in to see the film. Many townspeople went to the theater to see that sight, resulting in packed houses.

The usually fervently pro–Bara California newspapers were split on this one. *The Los Angeles Times* was back with its accustomed fulsome praise; the *San Francisco Chronicle* was off the reservation. *Photoplay* was figuratively frothing at the mouth.

In two different interviews, Theda Bara argued on both sides of her interpretation of Salome's intellect. In a September 1918 interview with the *Los Angeles Times*, she gave one interpretation. "I arrived at the idea that the dominating note of her character was love of power.... While doubtless my conception has taken many liberties with the idea of Salome, I believe my characterization is logical. I'm sure I've made her more intellectual than the common ideal of her character. While vanity swayed her and love of conquest was ever present, yet there was a certain element of sincerity, the tiniest flame of real love."

In another interview she responded to a negative review. "Criticism hurts Miss Bara very much." Some critic had just intimated that her Salome was a fleshly conception and not the mental lady who would have upset the Roman court. "I ask you," demanded Miss Bara plaintively, "How can I portray a mental Salome? Can I show my mind working for the camera? Will I have subtitles tell my brainy sayings? Or will [I] get through the Dance of the Seven Veils (actually four in the film) with a finger thoughtfully pressed to my forehead?"

When the film was shown at Fox's Liberty Theatre in St. Louis, it was accompanied by a special presentation. On a throne of gold and white, a young dancer dressed as Salome half-reclined with two "Nubian" slaves in attendance. A soloist played Puccini's "My Bedouin Girl" and the dancer gave her interpretation of the Dance of the Seven Veils. The overture and other pieces from Strauss's opera *Salome* were played by 25 musicians.

The very amusing two-reel comedy *The Cook*, released a month after *Salome* in September 1918, featured a clever extended parody of Salome's dance by Roscoe "Fatty" Arbuckle and Buster Keaton. The head of John the Baptist was represented by a head of cabbage. A reviewer said it would "make any grouch laugh." *Salome* also lent itself to other forms of humor. One jingle read: "The Salome costumes Miss Theda Bara wore/ Would suffice to plug up tight the keyhole in the door."

A wag said: "William Fox says Theda Bara's costumes in *Salome* are worth a king's ransom. So, after all, a king's ransom amounts to but a few nickels." In a common trope on Theda Bara's surname, a jingle ran: "When you see *Cleopatra* and *Salome*, you'll say/ She's becoming Bara and Bara every day." Along the same lines: "During the premiere in Los Angeles the costumes worn by Miss Bara were placed on exhibition in a local department store. A careless clerk spoiled it all by dropping a handkerchief over them."

In 1923 Fox re-released the film in an edited-down "revised" version of five reels. On its circuit it was accompanied by a dancer, and it was being publicized as a Bible story even though much of the mayhem remained.

Prior to *Salome*'s New York opening, the National Board of Review of Motion Pictures gave its report. "Entertainment value: Excellent; Educational value: Good; Dramatic interest of story: Powerful; Coherence of narrative: Strong; Historical value: Considerable; Moral effect: Good. In the opinion of those present, this production was a serious and dignified portrayal: Imaginative, dramatic, and presented in a way that should rank with the best screen productions."

Reviews

"This is not a sin against morals, only a colossal assault on common sense. It means nothing.... As Salome Miss Bara does not resemble the tigerish Princess of Judea as much as a neurasthenic taking sunbaths. No wonder Herod killed Salome after her dance.... A story unworthy of even a nursery fable, a drama without a whit of dramatic interest, characters which are characterless. Miss Bara was not content merely to vamp the Prophet, she revamped him." *Photoplay*, 1918.

"Yet another of history's wicked women has been presented on the screen by Theda Bara, that arch wearer of chiffon veils and beads. [The film] is utterly uninspired, mainly a series of poses, some effective, some otherwise, combined with a change of beaded costumes every minute. Salome, one conceives, as a creature of flame, fire and imagination. Miss Bara depicts her as beautiful but cold, and utterly lacking imagination." *Motion Picture Magazine*, 1918.

"The story of the famous Biblical wanton should have provided a vivid screen panorama, but Theda Bara's *Salome* is uninterestingly inadequate. [It is] stupid. [It] moves turgidly and tediously. The Bara characterization is a below-stairs conception." *Motion Picture Classic*, 1918.

"*Salome* has been playing to packed houses; one of the great triumphs of the picture world. The very best work she has ever done. Doubtless, scores have marveled at the clearness of her conception that has succeeded in producing a marvelously fascinating and inexhaustibly interesting impersonation. There has never been a picture that has created the good impression that has been left by it, in spite of the fact that it is not a war picture and different from most of the releases shown today. The grandeur that was Jerusalem and the glory that was Rome are blended in the majestic scenes." *Los Angeles Times*, September 24, 1918.

"A photoplay for which richness and extent of pageantry, sumptuousness of setting, and color of details has few equals. Theda Bara in the title role was all that those who have seen her in other films might expect—every minute the vampire in manner, movement and expression. Her impersonation has no significance of good or evil, or strength or weakness. Miss Bara seems to have conceived of Salome as simply offering her an opportunity to register her well known, and not very varied, sets of expressions and to expose discreetly parts and lines of her body. While there is much on the screen that could not be included from either the opera or the play, it must be admitted that the story itself loses in dramatic power when limited to pictures." *New York Times*, October 7, 1918.

"William Fox's scrambled and completely disinfected film version of *Salome* was disclosed.... The fact that she is Herod's daughter was apparently deemed too strong a moral for the sensitive patrons of the movies, so she is called his cousin instead. Most of the other wicked features of the Wilde version are considerably played down. The famous dance of the seven veils is shown only for a moment, and even at the end she has at least three more veils to shed.... The star's *Salome* is far less fleshly than in *Cleopatra*. With all the wiles she exercises on John the Baptist she remains so unattractive that the prophet's invulnerability is not wholly to be wondered at." *San Francisco Chronicle*, October 7, 1918.

"*Salome* is a better production than *Cleopatra*. Its story is more compact. Mere bigness of space and numbers is not allowed to obtrude itself on the human interest of the theme. A more unlovely character than Salome never lived. She is drawn in all her hideous imperfection of heart and brain. It is this adherence to the psychological truth of Salome's nature that is the chief merit on its ethical side.... Theda Bara presents a figure that is without glamour of any kind. She seems a creature of evil from her birth. The actress reflected this conception of the character with varying degrees of success. Great tragic power is not yet hers, but her work is always interesting and her tricks of mannerism help to give the character the stamp of her time and environment." *Moving Picture World*, October 19, 1918.

"Told in the simplest, most direct language the screen knows. Because of this it is dramatic. This is *the* picture of all of Miss Bara's ... sufficiently sensuous and sufficiently real to play it above everything else she has done during her career." *Picture-Play Magazine*, November 1918.

"Great. Played to the largest Sunday crowd in the history of the house. Capacity business all week." Manager, Rialto Theatre, Des Moines, Iowa.

"Fine picture, and good run on two days. This sure is a money-getter; book it!" Manager, Wilson's Theatre, Astoria, Illinois.

"Not as good as *Cleopatra*; business did not hold up." Manager, Orpheum Theatre, Seattle, Washington.

"Did not go at all; people are protesting about vampire pictures." Manager, Ozone Theatre, Des Moines, Iowa.

"Wonderful spectacular picture, but our patrons like her best in the later pictures where there is less vamping." Manager, Dixie Theatre, Athens, Louisiana.

"Not a picture for a small town; too gruesome." Manager, Forest Theatre, Forest City, Iowa.

"A cleanup from every angle; capacity houses on both days which is unusual here. Satisfied patrons who came to me unsolicited and told me how much they enjoyed this attraction. So many are clamoring for a repeat booking. Two-day pictures in our town are usually losing propositions but *Salome* was different. Our brother exhibitors who do not book this beautiful feature are doing themselves and their patrons an injustice." Manager, Empire Theatre, Staten Island, New York.

"I have seen all the big picture spectacles and think few equal this. None surpass it. Theda Bara does the best acting of her career." Manager, Atherton Theatre, Kentwood, Louisiana.

"A 100 percent picture with a 30 percent draft. Biblical subjects won't draw in an age of flying machines, Fords, and hobble skirts. Its ability to pull is largely overestimated." Manager, Auditorium Theatre, Neligh, Nebraska.

"Fine picture, but did not draw as well as expected." Manager, Empire Theatre, Winchester, Virginia.

"Drawing fair, not as good as *Cleopatra*." Manager, Princess Theatre, Eastland, Texas.

"Full house at advanced prices. Elaborate production well put together." Manager, Oasis Theatre, Ajo, Arizona.

"Did not come near the box office receipts of *Mickey* and *Hearts of Humanity*. Picture will not please the masses. Lavishly staged with rich settings, but this type of picture does not appeal to our audience." Manager, Garfield Theatre, Chicago, Illinois.

"A stupendous and gorgeous production. Not liked by all." Manager, Pastime Theatre, Greenville, Ohio.

"A big, gripping drama of the Bible story. Theda Bara at her best. It will make you money if you have not run it." Manager, Wigwam Theatre, Oberlin, Kansas.

1923 Re-Release

"This old Fox special has been whittled down to five reels and I got a new print. May be all right for those who like this sort of entertainment. As it stands now there is a murder, drowning, decapitation, or a little hari-kari in every reel. A great number of patrons told me that too much of this stuff in one sitting is more than enough." Manager, Trag's Theatre, Neillsville, Wisconsin.

"This was a good picture and pleased, especially the churchgoers on account of its being a Bible story. Morals are good and it's suitable for Sunday. Attendance [was] 125 in a town of 700." Manager, Star Theater, Eglin, Iowa.

When a Woman Sins (1918)

Background

Following the success of the lavishly produced *Salome*, which did give her career a needed boost, Theda Bara was back to more standard melodrama again a little more than a month later. The film was kind of a hybrid. Its vampire aspect and the story of redemption were melded together well enough to draw some favorable reviews. This was the last known story credit for Betta Breuil, who had been contributing stories to the cinema for about five years.

Fox tried to finesse the difference between those who still wanted the evil Bara and those who had grown tired of it. This is reflected in the film's tagline: "The regeneration of a modern vampire," and also in some of the reviews. The working title of this film was *The Message of the Lilies*. A 16-page press book was issued to publicize the movie.

The Film

Directed by J. Gordon Edwards. Produced by William Fox. Scenario by E. Lloyd Sheldon. Based on the story "The Message of the Lilies" by Betta Breuil. Cinematography by John

Boyle. Costume design by George James Hopkins ("Neje"). Released by the Fox Film Corporation on September 29, 1918. 7 reels.
Cast: Theda Bara (Lillian Marchand, later called Poppea), Josef Swickard (Mortimer West). Albert Roscoe (Michael West), Ogden Crane (Dr. Stone), Alfred Fremont (Augustus Van Brooks), Jack Rollens (Reggie West), Genevieve Blinn (Mrs. West).

Synopsis: Lillian Marchand is nursing at a hospital when she gets a call to take care of the old, seriously ill Mortimer West. It turns out that he is less feeble than she supposed. She allows him to take some liberties because she has been told any shock would kill him. His son Michael, a divinity student, rescues her from his father's advances. He and Lillian fall in love, but a misunderstanding leads him to think that Lillian has caused his father's death. She is ordered from the house and eventually becomes the dissolute and notorious dancer calling herself Poppea.

Among her admirers is Michael's cousin Reggie, with whom Poppea amuses herself to hurt Michael. When Michael begs her to give Reggie up for his mother's sake, Reggie sees them embrace and kills himself. Michael again rejects Poppea. She hosts a party of wealthy men and offers herself at auction to the highest bidder. Just as that is about to happen, she receives a Bible and a lily from Michael. His love and faith redeem her; she goes to work in the slums among the sick. She and Michael are happily reunited.

* * *

The Chicago Board of Censors, no longer under the strictures of Major Funkhouser but still of a puritanical bent, ordered cuts of a girl wearing pajamas; an old man kissing his nurse's shoulder; and a subtitle that reads: "I am for sale to the highest bidder." The censors suggested that it be replaced by "I will marry the highest bidder."

Reviews

"Theda Bara at her best. An unusually strong story.... If Miss Bara would not persist in using so much black paint under and around her eyes, and did not make her lips to appear black as ink she would look more like a real character. She is always best in serious parts. When she tries to dance and coquette with flowers, and when she assumes a laughing rollicking girl she is not herself. Her gaiety appears assumed, her joy is not sincere. But otherwise she is a great artist, and her work in this drama is a triumph in spite of these shortcomings." *Motion Picture Magazine*, 1918.

"Theda Bara's latest offers her unusual opportunities for emotional acting and she takes full advantage of them.... Her popularity, more than the strength of the story, will draw patrons." *Exhibitors Herald and Motography*, 1918.

"There is nothing distinctive about this offering, being a routine vamp meller. It seems a pity that Theda Bara should come back to doing ordinary vamps, after having managed to get away with such hellcats as Cleo and Salome. It certainly seems like some comedown. Possibly your fans are still willing to come in and observe the large-eyed lady inveigle weak men a la movie vamp style. It sort of seems to me that this will register as a relapse after your fans have seen her in her undressed spectacles.... Theda's been getting away with it for a long time, but by cricky it seems to me that the gang is going to sour on this sort of thing before too long. The lowbrows have been fed up on Theda and her vamping to such an extent that it has become an old story. There ain't no way to tell just what some folks will like, and it's quite possible that there still remains a sufficient percentage willing to watch a vamp at work, to justify putting this over." *Wid's Daily*, September 15, 1918.

"Miss Bara has one of the most varied roles of her career. She carries her character from good to bad and back again. She is cynical, impulsive, calculating, lovable and repentant, all in one sensational drama. She acts the parts forcefully, yet with a delicate, touching appeal." *San Francisco Chronicle*, September 16, 1918.

"If you happen to be located in a wicked city inhabited by very, very bad people, this picture will make them see the light. It is a combination of a vampire play and a sermon.... The star is handicapped by a bad story." *Motion Picture News*, September 28, 1918.

"An expurgated version of a Theda Bara vamp story. It fairly oozes morality. The old time vamp, it would appear, has had her day: the sinuous lady without a soul or conscience, but with a long and lurid past. A surfeited public emphatically says that it has had quite enough of her. Mr. Fox has immediately proceeded to reform her. We can't quite believe in her, but we find her vastly interesting—in a photoplay." *Los Angeles Times*, December 4, 1918.

"Considering the way I'm landed on by ardent Bara fans, I think I'm a brave woman to venture criticism on a Bara picture. Being a brave woman, I've been to see [this film] and I think it's just as punk as most of the photoplays in which I have been so unfortunate as to witness Miss Bara.... P.S. She never did anything to me, and I'm not jealous of her shape!" *Chicago Tribune* ("Mae Tinee"), 1918.

"Drew the crowds. Satisfied, and drew favorable comment." Manager, Newberry Theatre, Chicago, Illinois.

"Fine, a remarkable production." Manager, Majestic Theater, Missouri Valley, Iowa.

"Great. Splendid picture for this star, and all her followers pronounced it her best to date." Small town theater manager.

"This is the best picture Theda Bara ever produced. A good sermon, big business." Manager, Grand Theatre, Lebanon, Ohio.

"Fair. Got good business on account of not having Theda for some time." Manager, Lorin Theatre, Oakland, California.

"Star is at her best in this one; audience well pleased." Manager, Gem Theatre, Higbee, Missouri.

"Usual vamp stuff with a sugarcoated finish. However, Theda is surefire at the B.O. [box office.]" Manager, Bijou Theatre, Carrollton, Illinois.

The She-Devil (1918)

Background

For her sixth and final film of 1918, Theda Bara and Fox were once again experimenting with a change in image. Instead of the serious vampire-redemption theme of her last film, this was a sort of a vampire film, but with a (hoped for) leavening of humor. Bara would not really be evil, but more playful—kind of a vampire/coquette. It appears that Fox could not quite let go of the vampire persona that had made Bara a star.

Yet again in this film she plays an artist's model whose beauty sets society on fire.

Theda Bara was enthused that there were some light moments in the film, and she told a reporter that she was actually making a Spanish comedy. A June 1918 article reported: "Theda Bara is to essay comedy in her next picture. This change of vehicle is due entirely to Miss Bara's own desire. Not only does she wish to appear in comedy because she believes cheerful entertainment is most needed in the world today, but as a result of the unenviable success achieved by her in the comedy touches in *Du Barry*."

Another article announced: "Theda Bara, forsaking villainy for the time being, has plunged into comedy and is assisted by her sister who is golden-haired and Theda-eyed, and by her namesake, a pet bear." Fox had its own ideas; the film was advertised and reviewed as strictly another straight vampire film. It was something which Theda Bara could well have considered a betrayal.

A Spanish town was constructed on Brown's Ranch in California with a large assemblage of farm animals and the contrary bear dubbed "Theda Beara." Scenes featuring more than 1,000 extras were expected to be filmed there. The nature of any participation of her sister Esther, later Lori, is not known.

This film is one of only four in which George James Hopkins ("Neje") gets credit for writing the scenario and/or story. He was far more renowned for being a set decorator, and during his long movie and television career he won four Oscars and was nominated for several others. He had previously worked with close friend Theda Bara on *Cleopatra* and *Salome*.

The adverse reception of Hopkins' scenario for this film, and later his story idea for *A Woman There Was*, possibly Bara's worst film, must have convinced him to quickly return to what he did best. That the Fox studio allowed a journeyman to write a Theda Bara film when her popularity was clearly waning, seems a clear indication of their decreasing interest.

The working titles of the film were *Spanish Love* and *The Little She-Devil*. The former title would have made the film seem like a romance; the latter, more like a comedy. Neither fit Fox's intention to market the film as another standard vampire melodrama.

The Film

Directed by J. Gordon Edwards. Story, scenario, and costume design by George James Hopkins ("Neje"). Cinematography by John Boyle and Harry Gerstad. Released by the Fox Film Corporation on November 10, 1918. 6 reels.
Cast: Theda Bara (Lolette), Albert Roscoe (Maurice), George McDaniel (Tiger), Frederick Bond (Apollo).

Synopsis: Peasant Spanish dancer Lolette lives in a small Spanish village. She entrances all the men, including the bandit Tiger, but not the Parisian artist Maurice, who has come there to paint. He seems immune to her charms, and she sets out to vamp him. He paints her picture but refuses to take her to Paris with him. Tiger proposes marriage; Lolette persuades him to steal some money for the wedding. Instead, she steals his stolen swag and pursues Maurice to Paris. She models for him and becomes the toast of the town. One evening she jumps on stage and interrupts another dancer to show how much better she is.

Tiger is in the audience. He has followed Lolette to Paris and forces her to return what she stole from him. Through a ruse she gets it back and Tiger escapes. As a result of her impromptu performance, she is offered many contracts to perform. She accepts all of them, taking advance payments from everybody. Maurice fears that Lolette will face arrest for breach of contract. He persuades her to return with him to her village. On the way, Tiger attacks their coach and takes them prisoner. Still besotted by Lolette, Tiger holds a feast in her honor. She feigns interest in him, then gets him drunk, ties him up, and she and Maurice escape.

* * *

The Chicago Board of Censors ordered deletion of two holdup scenes.

Any chance for the success of this film was dimmed by the announcement that an armistice had been signed ending the Great War. It went into effect just one day after the release of the film, and the news overwhelmed the publicity for the film. The rather feeble publicity suggested for theater managers included sending a man wearing a skirt and dressed as the Devil into the streets; i.e., as a she-devil. Another suggestion was finding images of the Devil, adding a red skirt, and using them in window displays. A third was to print and distribute cards reading "The Devil will get you if you don't watch out."

Suggested taglines read: "The story of a woman who raised havoc with a dozen lovers"; "Sensational story of a super-woman whose thrilling romance ruled an empire—Far sharper than a serpent's sting—This vampire's ingratitude to men from Paris to Spain"; "A woman without a conscience, without a heart, with sympathy toward none and malice toward all—With Theda Bara playing the role with splendid abandon."

A wag asked: "We are informed that Theda Bara portrays an improper lady with no visible means of support—meaning that, for now, Theda's costumes are opaque?"

A supposed "secret" was revealed that Fox cowboy star Tom Mix had driven a stagecoach in the film. According to the publicity it was not previously known because Bara's contract specified that no other performer's name could be included with hers in a story. To repay Mix's favor, Bara had agreed to accept a supporting role in his film *Fighting for Gold*. To no-one's surprise, when that film was released in March 1919, there was no Theda Bara.

A review in *Motion Picture Magazine* called into question the similarities between this film and *Revelation*, a Metro release of February 1918 starring Alla Nazimova. It not so subtly suggests that Theda Bara is imitating that Russian diva, who was beginning to be regarded as one of the great screen actresses.

Reviews

"Either there is a scarcity of stories or someone has blundered in selecting this for Theda Bara. Not only is it illogical, but unfitting of her particular talents as well. It belongs to the fiction class in which absurdity, inconsistency, and exaggeration are the fundamental features. No attempt is made to present it as a serious thing, resulting in a product that will hardly satisfy critical audiences.... The unconvincing construction of the story destroys all good effect. The heroine's Parisian activities are the most unconvincing of all, sometimes they border on burlesque." *Motion Picture News*, November 9, 1918.

"Theda Bara's loyal following will undoubtedly enjoy seeing their favorite. To discriminating audiences, it will not measure up to the standards of a first-class feature. A character based on most unattractive lines, coarse instead of frank, repulsive instead of convincing." *Exhibitors Herald and Motography*, November 24, 1918.

"Particularly suitable to the ability of Theda Bara, and this is what the photoplay amounts to. There is not much to the story aside from furnishing a vehicle which Miss Bara handles notably as a vampire.... There is much of sensation in the story." *Photo-Play World*, December 1918.

"If one had not previously seen Nazimova in *Revelation*, one would undoubtedly admire this more. The story and general environment constantly remind one of [that film], and Theda Bara looks and acts so much like Nazimova that we can almost imagine that one is the other.... Miss Bara's conception of the film is unlike any character ever done before by her or anybody else—except Nazimova. If [Fox] had kept just a little farther away from the general scope and scheme of the Metro masterpiece it would have been wiser and better all around.... Bara depicts every emotion with fidelity and skill. Her makeup too was a decided improvement. The film starts out like a racehorse, but it ends up like a horse car. It begins to look like merely a series of adventures or episodes." *Motion Picture Magazine*, 1919?

"This film is Theda Bara's own, and pray, what picture of hers isn't? Here she is a wild mountain maid of Spain.... Rather neat." *Picture-Play Magazine*, 1918?

"Star's work was poor; overacted. Theda Bara's popularity is fast waning." Manager, National Theatre, Cleveland, Ohio.

"Drew well, but not the kind of thing we like to see Theda in." Manager, Lyda Theatre, Grand Island, Nebraska.

"Played to a fair house. Picture not very well liked, too much vampire. Not good for my house." Manager, Opera House, Gardner, Illinois.

"If your patrons like Theda Bara, this should get the money. It is well produced and it pleased the majority." Manager, Regent Theatre, Cleveland, Mississippi.

"Another like this and I won't be able to get people in to see Bara on passes." Manager, Princess Theatre, Clare, Michigan.

"Regulation Bara production of a somewhat different type. Pleased better than usual. Theda Bara losing drawing power with me." Manager, Bijou Theatre, Carrollton, Illinois.

"Poorest Theda Bara picture yet. Rotten direction made Theda silly. More like this and Theda will be dead." Small town theater manager.

The Light (1919)

Background

The first Theda Bara film of 1919 follows the basic theme of *When a Woman Sins*, in that it features a wicked woman—this time the wickedest woman in Paris, no less—and her ultimate redemption. For the final time, she plays a woman so irresistible that an artist, in this case a young sculptor, must have her for a model. Following the poor reception of *The She-Devil*, Theda Bara needed a success. This lightly reviewed film (no pun intended) may be considered a slight improvement, but no more than that.

These trite melodramas, yet again with her as a vampire, would not be the solution to Bara's fading popularity. It seemed the public could accept her as a historical vampire like Salome, but not a modern one. It may be that Fox did not care any longer. Bara was making a good deal of money at $4,000 a week (more than $64,000 in 2022 terms) when the average *annual* salary was about $1,200. The Fox studio apparently felt she was no longer worth it.

Her triumph as *Cleopatra*, though little more than a year prior, now seemed an eon in Hollywood terms. (That epic was still playing in theaters and would be for some time to come.) It was a case of "What have you done for me lately?" However, the studio did film some exteriors in New Orleans, which, according to Fox publicity, was the place "where the proper French atmosphere could be properly duplicated."

The Light was also the title of a five-reel 1916 film produced by the American Film Production Company.

The Film

Directed by J. Gordon Edwards. Scenario by Adrian Johnson and Charles Kenyon. Based on a story by Luther Reed and Brett Page. Costume design by George James Hopkins ("Neje"). Released by the Fox Film Corporation on January 12, 1919. 5 reels.
Cast: Theda Bara (Blanchette Dumonde aka Mme. Lefresne), Eugene Ormonde (Chabin), Robert Walker (Etienne Desechette), George Renevant (Auchat), Florence Martin (Jeanette).

Synopsis: Blanchette, the mistress of the wealthy Chabin, is known as the wickedest woman in Paris. She selfishly pursues her riotous lifestyle while other Parisians dedicate themselves to the Great War. Etienne, a young sculptor, sees a real soul in her face and asks her to pose for his Madonna-like figure to be called "A Soul's Awakening." Chabin refuses to allow it and has Etienne thrown out, but Blanchette experiences an unexpected awakening of virtue. She has seen "the light" and volunteers to work with wounded soldiers. When the hospital realizes who she is, they refuse her services; the nurses shrink from her.

She returns to her wanton ways, throwing Chabin over and taking up with Auchat, a rough Apache dancer. They flee to a remote cottage to escape Chabin's jealousy. At a railway station, Blanchette sees Etienne among the returning soldiers; he has been blinded. Something good once again stirs in her; she deserts Auchat to take care of Etienne. He sculpts her again, this time just by touch. Auchat finds them and tries to kill Etienne; Blanchette kills him instead just as Chabin arrives. When Chabin sees the reformation that Blanchette has undergone, he takes responsibility for Auchat's death, claiming that he was shot trying to rob the house. The lovers are free to pursue their happiness.

* * *

A Fox publicity tagline: "A tale of the wickedest Madonna ever to wear a halo." Another: "A production of illimitable candlepower. To see it is to see one of the season's brilliant offerings. And Theda Bara is the brightest ray in the entire production."

In February 1919, between the release of this film and that of her next, *When Men Desire*, it was reported that "Theda Bara may leave the management of William Fox when her contract expires. The general belief is that the star is unwilling to remain with the company that first exploited [i.e., publicized] her."

Although it was damning Theda Bara with extremely faint praise, the ever-censorious *Chicago Tribune* critic "Mae Tinee" finally had positive word to say about a Bara film.

Reviews

"Miss Bara is really rather nice in this picture. I'm honestly glad to make that announcement. To me Miss Bara's besetting screen sins have been too much makeup, too much grimace, too much pose, too much claptrap of all kinds. In [this film] she deals sparingly with the jam-pot and the blacking [i.e., her makeup]." *Chicago Tribune* ("Mae Tinee"), 1919.

"Theda Bara is up to her old tricks again ... and Theda can be some wicked on the screen. She is just as gosh-darned wicked, that's all. This is one of the feverish vamp stories that she can do so well, and Theda certainly walks away with the honors.... A fairly good type of a Bara vamp production." *Variety*, January 1919.

"From nearly every photoplay standard, this is a cheap production catering to the least worthy element among picture fans. They can't even boast of first-class settings and a well-photographed film. This will seem pretty poor entertainment.... The entire story is so removed from life that it would be a waste of time to point out minor inconsistencies." *Wid's Daily*, January 12, 1919. (This review was published under the headline: "The Same Old Theda in a Picture True to Type; Poorly Produced.")

"The story of this picture is much better than any furnished the star for some time. It is interesting, and though of the vampire sort, is clean. Although some parts of it are improbable, and some of the situations awkward, it appeals to the emotions. Theda Bara fans should be pleased with it." *Motion Picture News*, January 25, 1919.

"Feverish is the word to apply to [this film] ... Theda Bara is its shining star; passion unashamed is the dominant note of the story.... Theda Bara makes [her character] the accepted type of French kept woman as she is drawn in popular melodrama and wears many changes in unconventional gowns." *Moving Picture World*, January 25, 1919.

"Star was wonderful drawing power here. I did well on the picture considering the hot weather. This is a very poor story and the whole audience was dissatisfied." Manager, Newark Opera House, Newark, Delaware.

"Keep her away from these vampire parts and she will build a reputation that will eclipse them all. Good picture, good business." Manager, Dixie Theatre, Athens, Alabama.

When Men Desire (1919)

Background

Years had passed after the end of Great War before classic films about the conflict began to be produced. Many pictures made during the course of the war were crude propaganda about the horrible Hun. By the time Theda Bara made this film, other top Hollywood names had already come out with their own war movies: Mary Pickford in 1917's *The Little American*; in 1918, Charlie Chaplin in *Shoulder Arms* and D.W. Griffith's *Hearts of the World*. This film from Fox and Theda Bara fell into the crude propaganda class, as the taglines and reviews indicate.

So soon after the war's end, it is likely that much of the movie-going public wanted lighter entertainment. Plenty of jingoistic anti–German sentiment still remained though. Playing into this, a Fox tagline read: "Singing the American anthem is what Theda Bara does in Germany during her portrayal." A reviewer stated that the film's plot was almost exactly the same as that of 1918's *For Liberty*, directed by Bertram Bracken. It also re-uses the plot point of Theda Bara impersonating another woman from *Her Double Life*.

Stills from the film show her with less black eye makeup and more natural lip color. This may have been an effort to make her look younger for the role, and therefore more vulnerable. Reviewers had been increasingly commenting on the unchanging nature of Bara's heavy black makeup despite the role she was playing.

Once again, she suffered for her art. It was reported that "wounds and more wounds were Theda Bara's rewards for playing in *When Men Desire*. [In a fight scene] an Iron Cross scratched her arms which were bare. She counted nine long scratches which the Iron Cross had inflicted upon her. [She said,] 'I hate to be scratched, but of all things, I hate to be scratched by an Iron Cross, even if it is only a fake one.'"

When Men Desire. Much more sinned against than sinning, American girl Marie Lohr, is menaced by the Hun in this World War I melodrama. The troops had already come home, and audiences were getting tired of crudely done war films.

The Film

Directed by J. Gordon Edwards. Produced by William Fox. Scenario by Adrian Johnson. Based on the unpublished, uncopyrighted story "Scarlet Altars" by E. Lloyd Sheldon and J. Searle Dawley. Cinematography by John Boyle. Costume design by George James Hopkins ("Neje"). Released by the Fox Film Corporation on March 9, 1919. 5 reels.

Cast: Theda Bara (Marie Lohr), Fleming Ward (Robert Stedman), G. Raymond Nye (Major von Rohn), Florence Martin (Elsie Henner), Maude Hill (Lola Santez), Edward Elkas (Professor Lohr).

Synopsis: Marie Lohr is staying with her uncle in Strasbourg and is about to finish her musical studies. She is set to return to America but is prevented by her would-be suitor, Major von Rohn, head of the German Secret Service. She is in love with American pilot Robert Stedman, who is escorting other Americans out of Germany. Marie learns that her passport has been given to a German spy, who is headed to France to stir up pro–German propaganda.

For a while, Marie manages to stave off the Major's advances; finally, he locks her in his office. While she is there, a bomb wounds him, and the woman who has her passport is killed at a railway station. Marie assumes the identity of the dead woman and flees. She is stopped at the Swiss border, but not before she gets word to the Americans. Stedman returns and is hidden by Marie in a closet in von Rohn's office.

The the Major tells Marie that if she marries him, he will not denounce her as a spy. Stedman overhears him, but he is also heard by von Rohn, who heads to the closet with a drawn gun. Marie stabs him in the back, and Stedman dons his uniform. The Americans flee by car to get to Stedman's plane. Chased by the Germans, they manage to reach the plane and fly over the Swiss border.

* * *

The suggested Fox taglines resonate with the kind of crude poster propaganda familiar during the war. "Hun duplicity and brutality frustrated by Yankee genius"; "American girl in power of Hun beast rescued by fearless Yankee"; and "Womanhood outraged. The thrilling adventures of a woman who tried to be true." Some of the taglines tried an erotic appeal: "Rich men and poor men of noble birth fight like tigers to win one kiss from her lips." The most feverishly overheated one read: "They coaxed her; they tainted her; they tortured her; they threatened her; they kissed her."

A Fox publicity release for theater managers boasted: "Here is the most sensational Bara picture since *Salome*. A picture with a big human appeal. A picture packed with gasps and surprises. A moneymaker that will surpass your rosiest dreams of a big box office cleanup."

The Chicago Board of Censors forbade a Chicago theater from displaying the name of the film. (After all, who knew *what* things men might desire.) The manager put a sign in front of the theater displaying the order, and curious patrons packed the theater. Kansas censors ordered cuts in some intertitles.

Reviews

"One of the poorest of this star's long series." *Picture-Play Magazine*, March 1919.

"To be of interest at this time, the film that revolves around the recent war, German cruelty, and their famous spy system, must have the very best of preparation and a story of great strength to its credit. [This film] can hardly be said to possess these qualities in a measure sufficient to overcome the popular aversion.... Theda Bara is neither better nor worse than usual in the leading role." *Exhibitors Herald and Motography*, March 1919.

"A crude and improbable melodrama. There is plenty of excitement of an entirely obvious sort, but Bara fans will like the picture, for she is given plenty of opportunity to indulge in those characteristic bits for which she is famous." *Philadelphia Public Ledger*, March 1919.

"An inconsistent story of a female spy in Germany.... Brought laughs for its ridiculousness as a climax to a slow moving feature." *Variety*, March 1919.

"No-one is apt to consider this story seriously. It is melodramatic and decidedly unreal, but possesses elements that continue to make Theda Bara's photoplays popular with many fans.... It may be questionable to show the stars and stripes on the screen for so cheap a melodramatic purpose, but this did not bother the Fox producers.... There is plenty of action, bringing thrills of the obvious sort. The production is about on a par with a story that never advances beyond melodramatic crudeness." *Wid's Daily*, March 9, 1919.

"There is a striking climax.... The plot is clear and entertaining. Theda Bara has a role that fits her perfectly and wears many striking costumes." *Moving Picture World*, March 22, 1919.

"Doesn't contain as much substance as the usual Bara picture, and its inconsistencies are rather numerous.... The escape in the airplane is more or less a flight of wild imagination. The star's performance is up to the standards she always maintains." *Motion Picture News*, March 22, 1919.

"A fair picture, drew a small crowd. Star's popularity on the wane with us." Manager, Princess Theatre, Henderson, Kentucky.

"A good picture; better than Theda used to make. Not quite so strong." Manager, Lyric Theatre, Crete, Nebraska.

"Good picture; drew well." Manager, Grand Theatre, Lebanon, Ohio.

"An exceptional picture. Bara is a real actress." Manager, Newberry Theatre, Chicago, Illinois.

"This picture has done more toward putting Miss Bara right with my patrons than anything she has ever made." Manager, Dixie Theatre, Athens, Alabama.

"Drew fair, but did not think much of the picture." Manager, Tenth Street Theatre, Kansas City, Kansas.

The Siren's Song (1919)

Background

One reviewer called this film's story "moss covered." A still shows Theda Bara in what is supposed to be a French peasant dress, including a pointed cap, with thick black braids hanging halfway down to her knees. The costuming is a far cry from her slinky vampire gowns, and the role is even further from her most popular portrayals. In retrospect, it could be considered as a kind of rehearsal for her long-desired role as a simple peasant in *Kathleen Mavourneen*. Or, more realistically, assignments like this may well have led to her announcement in February 1919 that she would be leaving Fox.

Perhaps in reaction to that announcement, in March 1919 it was reported by the *New York Clipper* that "Theda Bara may shortly be furnished with an act tried out as a drawing card in vaudeville…. Fox had in mind the fact that such a venture would add materially to the prestige of their star." That, after four years as a major star, Bara needed a prestige boost reveals something about the studio's then-current attitude towards her. She did ultimately go briefly into vaudeville after her Fox career had ended.

This was publicized as her 30th film since she had become a star; in actuality it was her 33rd. Coincidentally, she was 33 years old, and still playing a naïve village girl dominated by her ignorant father. The role was more suited to a considerably younger and more ethereal actress along the lines of a young Lillian Gish. The film had apparently been scheduled for a January 1919 release, but it was held back until May. Instead, it was her film *The Light* that got a January release, perhaps because its plot touched on the just-concluded Great War. Despite its creaky premise, Bara's performance in *The Siren's Song* got some fairly positive reviews. It may be regarded as the final Theda Bara film to have earned such reviews. It was the final Bara film in which Albert Roscoe appeared.

A 1915 film with the same title was made by the short-lived Shubert Film Corporation.

The Film

Directed by J. Gordon Edwards. Scenario by Charles Kenyon. Cinematography by John Boyle. Costume design by George James Hopkins ("Neje"). Released by the Fox Film Corporation on May 4, 1919. 5 reels.
Cast: Theda Bara (Marie Bernais, later called Marinelli), Al Fremont (Jules Bernais), Ruth Handforth (Aunt Caroline), Lee Shumway (Raoul Nieppe), Albert Roscoe (Gaspard Prevost), Paul Weigel (Hector Remey), Carrie Clark Ward (Paulette Remey).

Synopsis: Marie Bernais, a peasant village singer, is in love with the clergyman Raoul Nieppe. His family disapproves of her because she is below his station; Marie then attempts suicide. Her father believes that her beautiful voice is a snare of the Devil. Hector Remey, once a well-known tenor in Paris, hears her sing and takes her away to be shaped into Marinelli, a famous singer. Her lessons have been paid for by Gaspard Prevost, who loves her but is already married.

Marie returns to her village to sing for the soldiers, although she is worried that it might ruin her voice. Her father and brother continue to scorn her until they both eventually die. Raoul re-enters her life and persuades her to give up hopes of Gaspard, saying he (Raoul) will now marry her. This time she spurns him. While singing for the troops, she does ruin her voice; she then returns to being a simple peasant girl again. Unexpected happiness comes when Gaspard returns to claim her. Gaspard's wife has died, and they can be together.

* * *

A song titled "The Siren's Song" was composed with words by Roy Turk and music by Ray Perkins, and it was dedicated to Theda Bara. The sheet music featured a half-figure photograph of a demure Bara.

Fox publicity suggested taglines such as "Story of a woman's soul redeemed by a woman's sacrifice."

Reviews

"A romantic tale flavored with considerable pathos, and interesting in plot and action. Miss Bara plays the heroine with considerable feeling that is marked by sincerity." *New York Review*, 1919.

"Here is another typical Theda Bara production.... Inconsistencies of the plot are counterbalanced by the elaborateness of the sets and intelligent direction. Few people are neutral as far as Miss Bara is concerned, she is either liked or disliked. If patrons like this kind of picture, advertising will bring them in." *Exhibitors Herald*, May 1919.

"Here is a film where Theda Bara does not roll her eyes and smoke a cigarette. And what is more, she isn't a sneering vampire and doesn't lure one man to his destruction." *New York Clipper*, May 7, 1919.

"It seems odd to see Theda Bara in one of these old-fashioned pictures of parental intolerance.... The star has usually had subjects that were based on unconventional plots and characterizations and, if they were far from being plausible, at least they were not conceived for this purpose. The film contains a moss-covered story that is far removed from truth.... Had the story and characterizations been treated more intelligently, the picture would have sounded a human note. The details are over-elaborated so that a semblance of life is not realized.... Miss Bara gives her usual good performance and makes the heroine quite sincere." *Motion Picture News*, May 17, 1919.

"Depends for its interest on one character, its heroine played by Theda Bara.... Her fates and the peculiar emotional tangles that bring them about are freshly imagined, and to some will be of gripping interest. How wide a circle of spectators will understand it is a question. She plays the singing girl with effectiveness. The average spectator will probably count it a good Theda Bara picture, but with a somewhat forced plot." *Moving Picture World*, May 17, 1919.

"A striking success is being achieved by Theda Bara in a soul-stirring play. Affords the star a wonderful opportunity to display the talents that have brought her fame." *San Francisco Chronicle*, May 22, 1919.

"No good from a box office standpoint." Manager, Lyric Theatre, Oxnard, California.

"Not Theda Bara's best by any means; ends abruptly. The star a favorite here; two days good business." Manager, Dream Theatre, Port Angeles, Washington.

A Woman There Was (1919)

Background

This is arguably one of Theda Bara's worst films and a throwaway for the Fox studio, which had already cut her loose. The title is deliberately reminiscent of Theda Bara's first success more than four years earlier. Its obvious purpose was to remind moviegoers of

A Fool There Was, still one of her most popular movies, and to hope that it would rekindle strong positive opinions of Theda Bara. Instead, it may have reminded many of how far she had fallen.

It also was the final Bara film to be directed by J. Gordon Edwards. They had been a team since mid–1916's *Under Two Flags*, one of her signal non-vampire successes. He went on to direct until ill health forced him to retire in 1924. He died the following year.

It marked the return of George James "Neje" Hopkins as the source of the story. He was supposedly a good Bara friend, but what she needed at this point was a good story. What she got was a melodrama that drew ridicule for her "shredded wheat" costume, curly black wig, and way of "speaking." To make matters worse, Hopkins flippantly claimed he had written the story in three nights, first as a comedy. By the third night he had decided to "kill everybody off" so he could get some sleep. Some of the fault also needs to be laid at the feet of scenarist Adrian Johnson.

Bara's leading man, William B. Davidson, worked in movies until his death in the late 1940s. In sound films he was often cast as figures of authority, such as prison wardens and irascible high-ranking police officers. He would have supporting or small roles in as many as 15 films a year, and he collected more than 300 movie credits during the course of his career.

The gimmick in the form of a rumor that Theda Bara supposedly wrote the Kipling-esque poem that opened the film might have stirred a bit of interest. The text of that poem would certainly be of great interest to modern-day film buffs. It is almost certain to have opened with the line "A woman there was." It was publicized as a woman's response to Rudyard Kipling's poem "The Vampire," one of the sources for *A Fool There Was*. Fox press agents suggested that her poem be distributed to the public on blotters and cards.

Three weeks were spent shooting scenes in Miami, Florida, and on William K. Vanderbilt's palatial yacht "The Water Witch." Fox publicity claimed that 40 planes had flown over the yacht and that the pilots had stood up and saluted Theda Bara.

A month before the release of this film, Theda Bara's contract with Fox expired. The studio refused her demand for a raise to $5,000 a week. *Variety* reported back in January 1919: "The Bara contract with Fox finishes in May, and the star has been flooded with offers through her attorney during the last fortnight. Just what Theda Bara is going to do in the future is not settled yet, but several managers have made offers for her services." This sounds less like independent reporting and more like a Bara publicity release.

The Film

Directed by J. Gordon Edwards. Scenario by Adrian Johnson. Based on the story "Creation's Tears" by George James Hopkins ("Neje"). Cinematography by John Boyle. Costume design by George James Hopkins. Released by the Fox Film Corporation on June 1, 1919. 5 reels. **Cast**: Theda Bara (Princess Zara), William B. Davidson (Rev. Winthrop Stark), Robert Elliott (Pulke), Charles Payton (High priest), John Ardizoni (Majah).

Synopsis: Zara is a half-savage princess on the South Sea Island of Kolpee. When the Reverend Stark comes as a missionary, they meet and she falls in love with him. Stark is already engaged and rejects Zara's ardency. During his sermon on brotherly love, Zara interrupts to tell him he does not know what love is. The chief pearl diver Pulke is in love with her. He tries to bribe the high priest to say that the gods have

A Woman There Was. In a black curly wig and "shredded wheat" skirt, Theda Bara hit bottom in this juvenile melodrama with William B. Davidson. Her attempt to portray a pagan South Seas princess was undercut by her "Fifth Avenue" lingerie and "Broadway jargon."

commanded Zara to marry him. When that fails, he jealously attempts to kill the missionary. Zara saves Stark from Pulke's spear.

When a typhoon hits the island, the chief orders Stark to be sacrificed. Zara offers herself instead as a way to appease the angry gods. She throws herself into the roiling waves but is saved by Stark. She nurses him back to health after his ordeal. Her father has died during the storm so she is now the reigning princess. Pulke still wants to kill

Stark, but Zara steals a rare black pearl from her father's tomb hoping to appease him. When the natives storm the hut to kill Stark, he escapes, but Zara is accidentally killed by Pulke.

* * *

Some reviews mentioned that Bara wore visible and modern, some called it Fifth Avenue, lingerie under her grass skirt, and this is clearly seen in some stills. That skirt was more than once unkindly compared to "shredded wheat." Some reviews also mentioned the anomaly that during the typhoon, the palm trees on the beach remained calm.

Reflecting the prejudices of that time, one suggested Fox tagline read: "How a woman of an alien race gave her life that a white man she loved might be saved." Another, with overweening optimism, read: "They will come miles to see her. The eternal question of the man and the woman." Other publicity played up the poem supposedly penned by Bara.

Reviews

"The role fits [Bara's] peculiar talents remarkably well…. The story does not differ materially from hundreds of triangle situations that have been enacted before the camera…. The picture has plenty of action; there is something doing every minute." *Exhibitors Herald and Motography*, June 1919.

"It is probable that the only feeling any audience that sees it will have is one of extreme happiness that the thing is over. The story and acting are as mediocre as possible. It was evidently made to be a tragic drama, but they have unconsciously succeeded in turning out a burlesque. Not content with torturing those who will see it, the death scene has been dragged out until the audience will pray for a bomb to blow up the whole bunch." *New York Clipper*, June 4, 1919.

"A more nonsensical concoction than this South Sea meller, containing a lot of bunk, could not be well devised. Allows the players to emote all over the place. Theda Bara is anything but attractive; some of her attempts at coyness are ludicrous. Almost all of it is old stuff, the kind of trash that fans were fed in the early days of photoplays. It can't be taken seriously at any time; introduces a lot of heathen hocus pocus…. Photography varies from fair to poor, a few scenes out of focus. Theda Bara appeals only to a certain definitely limited clientele. It would be unwise for an exhibitor aiming to build up a reputation for showing first-class productions, of a superior tone, to bother with her pictures except in rare instances. *A Woman There Was* is no exception." *Wid's Daily*, June 8, 1919.

"The film is one of a picturesque type, abounding in the special atmosphere of the South Sea Islands. The action is quite dramatic at times, and the incidents are typical of native island stories. Theda Bara fits very easily into the role…. As a whole, this lacks the intensity of some previous features, but with Theda Bara in the lead it carries good entertainment value." *Moving Picture World*, June 14, 1919.

"May strike a responsive chord in the hearts of impressionable juveniles, but to one out of swaddling clothes it is a pretty big pill to swallow. [Bara] has trespassed on juvenile domains with her present material since the subject matter resembles nothing so much as the goodnight story you tell your kiddies…. Garbed in a shredded wheat costume, the star plays a dusky princess of a South Sea island.... Before the climax there is a lot of comic opera business which is ridiculous to say the least.... The thing is so fantastic that one simply cannot take it seriously.... Theda Bara's language [i.e., in her character's intertitles] is the curbstone vernacular of Broadway. Could be vastly improved were it reedited; the only asset is the title." *Motion Picture News*, June 14, 1919.

A wag also commented on the way Zara spoke: "In her newest picture, Theda Bara takes the part of a wild woman who, strange to say, speaks a Broadway jargon. But it was the wild women of Broadway who started the jargon; perhaps all wild women speak a universal language."

"Now it's clad in shredded wheat and a curly black wig that Theda Bara vamps! It's a highly imaginative one in some respects, but fails in cumulative and, therefore, appealing human interest. A series of incidents loosely strung together, unconvincing and reminiscent, so that when Miss Bara dies, it's quite impossible to get excited about it. All of which is a pity because after all there is only one Theda Bara, only one such gorgeous, compelling, and imaginative personality." *Los Angeles Times*, June 17, 1919.

"So obviously and tiresomely a poor picture. It is so carelessly devised, so poorly directed, and so sloppily cut and strung together.... This is nothing less than remaking Theda Bara's reputation in picture circles. It will offend no-one, but it is so stupid and unattractive." *Variety*, June 19, 1919.

"Patrons disappointed. Not the right kind of play for Theda; she can do better. Too old for the part she took." Manager, Mystic Theatre, Marmarth, North Dakota.

"Poorest picture of the star we have ever run. People did not like it; business poor." Manager, Princess Theatre, Buchanan, Illinois.

"Short picture and not much to it. I have small houses on Theda." Manager, Lyric Theatre, Rugby, North Dakota.

"Theda Bara, once my best bet for a capacity house, is now the poorest. Will not use any more of her pictures. The last three have killed her." Manager, Queen Theatre, DeQueen, Arkansas.

"Comments very unfavorable; Bara has lost her following here." Manager, Rex Theatre, Bessemer. Michigan.

Kathleen Mavourneen (1919)

Background

This is the film that Theda Bara had long desired to make to finally separate herself from the vampire image. In an October 1919 interview with the *Los Angeles Times*, she had proclaimed that she went out on strike and "stayed struck" until given the chance to make this film. There was a new director in Englishman Charles Brabin, whom Bara would marry in 1921.

The story had been filmed before, and she had already played a "good girl" in films such as *The Two Orphans*, *Her Greatest Love*, *Under Two Flags*, and *Romeo and Juliet*. She was hardly the typical Irish lass in appearance, even with Mary Pickford curls, and was quite a bit beyond the young colleen stage at 34 years of age (officially 29 in movie star years).

In promoting the film, she was quoted as saying: "This is the best role I ever had. (She had also said that about *Cleopatra*.) There isn't the slightest trace of the vampire in Kathleen, so you see I have kept my promise about the type of heroine I'd portray when I was ready to forsake the ladies of highly emotional proclivities. How I did delight in that quaint little Irish girl. I adopted her heart and soul. She permitted me to take down my hair.... I no longer had to glide into a room and begin working the wiles of a trade as old as the call of sex. I could run and jump and skip and be happy."

It was probably about this film that in 1919, *Film Fun* wrote in its humor column: "Alice in Wonderland": "Alice knew she was in Wonderland because she saw Bill Hart [William S. Hart, actor and director] without a gun [and] Theda Bara acting like a human being."

Theda Bara said she loved playing "a simple mountain girl in short skirts." Five years of vampire roles had "drawn her nerves pretty taut and weighed her down." (All this talk about simplicity was quoted in the same interview in which she said her favorite reading was Sarah Bernhardt's memoirs in the original French.) To try to ensure authenticity, the Fox studio crammed the film full of farm animals, farm implements, and happy peasants. One review said the cast featured "a large number of correct types."

The previous incarnations of *Kathleen Mavourneen* included a one-reel version that had also been directed by Charles Brabin in 1913 starring Mary Fuller. That same year a three-reel version had appeared. Earlier one-reelers came out in 1906 and 1911. The former film was produced by the Edison Company and was directed by the pioneer Edwin S. Porter. It starred an actress calling herself the very Irish-sounding Kitty O'Neil.

Two sound versions, a "Poverty Row" modern-dress production in 1930 and a British production in 1937, both starred Sally O'Neil (no relation to Kitty). The UK production was O'Neil's final film; it was also known as *Kathleen*. "Mavourneen" is an endearment meaning "my darling" and is not meant to be Kathleen's surname, which differs depending on the film version.

The first stanza of the Julia Crawford song lyric, on which the story may be based, reads: "Kathleen Mavourneen! The gray dawn is breaking/The horn of the hunter is heard on the hill/The lark from her light wing bright dew is shaking/Kathleen Mavourneen! What slumbering still?" Unlike the Bara film, which ends in a pairing, the song ends in a parting: "Mavourneen, Mavourneen, my sad tears are falling/To think that from Erin and thee I must part/It may be for years and it may be forever...."

The Film

Direction and scenario by Charles Brabin. Based on song lyrics by Julia (Annie) Crawford and/or the play by Dion Boucicault and/or a poem by Thomas Moore. Cinematography by George Lane. Costume design by George James Hopkins ("Neje"). Released by the Fox Film Corporation on August 19, 1919. 6 reels, possibly edited to five reels.

Cast: Theda Bara (Kathleen Mavourneen), Edward O'Connor (Kathleen's father), Jennie Dickerson (Kathleen's mother), Raymond McKee (Terence O'Moore), Marc McDermott (Squire of Traise), Marcia Harris (Lady Clancarthy), Harry Gripp (Denis O'Rourke), Henry Hallam (Sir John Clancarthy), Morgan Thorpe (Father O'Flynn).

Synopsis: Irish peasant Kathleen and young blacksmith Terence plan their wedding. After seeing her dance a jig at the fair, the wealthy squire on whose land they work wants Kathleen to marry him. He threatens to evict her family if she refuses. She rebuffs

Kathleen Mavourneen. **Theda Bara finally got her way in playing a simple Irish peasant girl, even though she had played many a good girl previously. The Irish American community was up in arms, and Bara's starring career was just about at an end.**

him and falls asleep by the fire. When she awakens, she reluctantly agrees to marry the Squire. After some years he meets a noblewoman and, short of money, decides to rid himself of Kathleen.

She is lured into the forest, where she is set upon by hired ruffians. Having overheard the plot, Terence rescues her, but he kills one of the attackers and is tried for murder. False evidence has been planted that accuses him of being the one who lured Kathleen and that attests that the dead attacker was actually a rescuer. The Squire testifies against Terence, and he is sentenced to be hanged. Suddenly, Kathleen is awakened by Terence. It has all been a bad dream; they are free to marry after the Squire relents.

* * *

In Atlanta, a display to publicize the movie consisted of cut-outs of Bara and co-star Raymond McKee attached to gears that moved the figures into a kiss. In a Cincinnati movie theater, an Irish-American tenor sang old Irish ballads and folk songs.

Pro–Irish and anti–British feeling ran very high in 1919; Ireland had long been agitating for independence. Although Fox made much of the picture's historical correctness, it was innocently tangled up in the Irish politics of the time. It had been three years since the Easter Rising in Dublin, following which the UK executed the ringleaders. It would not be until three years after the film was released that Ireland (then known as the Irish Free State) came into being.

In what seems like a case of wishful thinking, an article in the *Motion Picture News* of September 20, 1919, read: "Publications devoted to Irish interests give the picture much praise.... Irish New York has supported the film with an enthusiasm that bespeaks its success in all cities of the United States. It is a true picture of an Ireland that is little known in the United States—the Ireland that every Irishman knows and loves and is ready to fight for."

The reality after the film's release was quite different. In December 1919, a letter written by the New York Local Council of the Friends of Irish Freedom was published in newspapers. Delegates from many Irish-American societies had passed a resolution to the managers of all movie theaters in the greater New York area. It called for them not to show *Kathleen Mavourneen*. The letter said the film was "a brutal caricature of Irish life, and not fit for exhibition in your theater. The request of this organization is reasonable *and will be complied with* [italics mine]. Irish and Irish Americans consider the picture an insult and strongly resent it being shown." One stated cause of resentment was the film's portrayal of Irish peasant life that showed farm animals living inside the house. Another source of discontent may have been Bara's Judaism.

In March 1920, the film was taken off the bill at a Newport, Rhode Island, theater because of protests from the state's branch of the Friends of Ireland and "other prominent Irish leaders." The worst reaction came in San Francisco where a mob, objecting to the scenes of Irish poverty, broke into the projection booth of the Sun Theatre. They beat the projectionist, smashed two new projectors, stole two reels of the film, and vandalized the balcony. They also pulled telephones from the wall, delaying the arrival of the police.

No arrests were made. During the riot, some women patrons grew hysterical and fainted. The American Committee for Irish Freedom had threatened trouble because they considered the film to be British propaganda. At a private showing, two priests had censured the film. Replacements for the missing two reels were flown up from Los Angeles. *Variety* called the rioters "pigs in a parlor" and claimed there had been $3,000 worth of damage—more than $48,000 in 2022 terms.

Although the theater manager said showings would continue with police protection, some scenes were cut. The manager ultimately decided not to continue the showings. Before all this happened, an ad for the San Francisco theater called the film "the sweetest Irish drama ever written—as sweet as the laughter of an Irish colleen."

On the lighter side, the "Fade-Outs" column of *Picture-Play Magazine* had some comical reactions to the film *(translations provided below)*. A quatrain was published under the heading "Wurra! Wurra!": "Lay off of Erin, oh Theda Mavourneen/Sure, is it someone you're tryin' to kid?/You vamps are the darlints—but you a colleen?/Arrah, acushla, it just can't be did!" The column went on with a supposed quote from William Fox: "Theda Bara will assume the part of a merry Irish colleen with flying pigtails, clumsy shoes, and roguish eyes."

It continued: "Well, anyhow we wouldn't miss this picture of Theda's for all the potheen in Ballyrag." The column went into another quatrain: "It may be for years, it may be forever/Before a colleen just like Theda we'll view/So by the same token we'll use all endeavor/To see her colleening, 'twill be something new."

Definitions: "Wurra": a word of lamentation, sometimes spelled wirra or whirra; "Potheen" (sometimes poteen): an alcoholic drink illegally made from potatoes; "Arrah": a word used to describe excitement or surprise; "Acushla": Darling, or other term of endearment; "Darlint": Irish dialect for darling.

Reviews

"Theda Bara is defying tradition and stepping out of her customary vamp roles. It must have taken a lot of courage on [her] part to throw off her usual mantle and appear as an Irish lassie, pure of heart and sentimental to a degree far removed from the soul-destroying roles which she usually assumes. If you can forget the Theda of the past, you will like her in this new atmosphere, though she does not suggest an Irish girl, even for a moment.... The picture itself abounds in Irish atmosphere and is entertaining quite apart from the star's part in it." *Picture-Play Magazine*, 1919.

"Wouldst see Theda Bara as an Irish colleen? Faith and it might amuse ye! Joking aside, however much Miss Bara may amuse you in the role, you cannot fail to realize how beautifully Fox has produced this picture.... Now Miss Bara has been funnier than she is in [this film]. So much for Miss Bara." *Chicago Tribune* ("Mae Tinee"), 1919.

"It contains Miss Bara acting tremendously in an endeavor to get a 'sweet girl' part across." *Photoplay*, 1919.

"Theda Bara, abandoning the characterization that has made her famous, surprises somewhat by her splendid portrayal of the title role. She delivers entertainment goods of high quality. The picture with the double attraction of quality and novelty; sure to satisfy is the result." *Exhibitors Herald and Motography*, 1919.

"Theda Bara scores a great triumph.... In this work, Miss Bara has a happy part and plays it with great feeling. Her role is a new one for her, but one which she invests with both beauty and charm." *Houston Chronicle*, 1919.

"Can you picture Theda Bara as an Irish colleen? No, neither could we." *New York Tribune*, August 21, 1919.

"A most excellently produced film. Here is a film classic that the self-appointed uplifters should welcome. The big exploitation angle for exhibitors [should be] through schools and literary circles, and of course through all Irish societies. The photoplay faithfully absorbs Irish atmosphere. Theda Bara made a captivating Kathleen Mavourneen. It is a light drama maintained to the finale in which a dream incident gives it the happy ending. The Irish folk dances, the happy and simple habits of the peasants, with many lovely sidelights, make an ideal entertainment." *Motion Picture News*, September 6, 1919.

"A beautiful touching story, well acted. House crowded and everyone satisfied. Just a little different than the usual Theda Bara pictures." Manager, Hudson Theatre, St. Louis, Missouri.

"Fell flat with our audiences; Bara no drawing card here. No story to put the picture over. If you play this, keep your foot on the soft pedal and do not promise much." Manager, Liberty Theatre, Washington, Indiana.

"Did good business; good Irish picture. Star draws very good." Manager, Marquette Theatre, St. Louis, Missouri.

"A very good Irish picture; unable to handle the crowd. Ran two days. A most pleasing and beautiful picture." Manager, Rialto Theatre, Vallejo, California.

La Belle Russe (1919)

Background

This film is based on the David Belasco play of the same name, and it is the last Bara film to be based on a story from another medium. It is considered Belasco's very first melodrama in what would be a long and storied career. Its premiere took place in his home town of San Francisco in May 1882, and it soon attracted the attention of stock companies around the United States. The Broadway run starred the famous theater actress Rose Coghlan.

By this time, cowboy actor Tom Mix had joined William Fox favorite William Farnum as one of his top male stars. As a marketing device, the studio now packaged their films and those of Theda Bara into so-called series. Within those series, films were either designated as "Standard" or "Special." Bara's "Specials" were her preceding film, *Kathleen Mavourneen*, this film, and *Lure of Ambition*, her final one for Fox. *La Belle Russe* was actually dubbed a "Super-Special" by the Fox studio, presumably to improve its chances at the box office. This was the second and last Bara film to be directed by her husband-to-be Charles Brabin.

Even though Bara was contractually finished at Fox, the studio still wanted to extract the last bit of positive publicity from its fading star. Stills showing her in a ballerina's tutu reveal somewhat more voluptuousness than she exhibits in the now-extant clips from the previous year's *Salome*. It is not known—but seems doubtful—that she is actually shown dancing in *La Belle Russe*. Once again, a Theda Bara character is called the most notorious woman in Paris.

Charles Brabin claimed that in order to get an authentic English look, he imported 35 pigeons "of a certain breed" and hired real "Picadillians" to play the British equivalent of stage door Johnnies. For the nobleman's palatial home, he photographed a "magnificent feudal-like manor on the Hudson River." The double exposure technique used to show both twin sisters simultaneously was, according to reviews, very effective.

The Metropolitan Opera Ballet Company is featured in the picture. The film's working title was *A Case of Identity*. The Belasco play also had been used as the basis of a 1914 five-reel version by the Regent Feature Film Company, with actress Evelyn Russell in a dual role.

La Belle Russe. Again resurrecting an old warhorse for Theda Bara (seen here with a minor player), Fox had obviously lost interest in its once great star. In hopes of spicing up the film, double exposure was used to portray Bara as twins. Her obvious miscasting as a lithe ballet dancer is apparent.

The Film

Direction and scenario by Charles Brabin. Based on the play *La Belle Russe* by David Belasco. Cinematography by George Lane. Costume design by George James Hopkins ("Neje"). Released by the Fox Film Corporation on September 21, 1919. 6 reels.
Cast: Theda Bara (La Belle Russe/Fleurette), Warburton Gamble (Lord Philip Sackton), Marian Stewart (Philip Sackton, Jr.), Robert Lee Keeling (Sir James Sackton), William B. Davidson (Brand), Alice Wilson (Lady Sackton), Robert Vivian (Butler).

Synopsis: Lord Philip Sackton, an English nobleman, marries Fleurette, a ballet dancer. She is sweet and innocent, although her twin sister, known as La Belle Russe, is called the most notorious woman in Paris. Sackton's family refuses to acknowledge Fleurette because he married beneath his station and because of her sister's reputation. He is disinherited, and the couple goes off on their own. Sackton becomes a painter, and

Fleurette teaches dancing to children. When she is expecting a baby, he leaves to fight in the war and is commissioned as an officer for his bravery. While in the trenches, he is told by his comrade Brand of an unfortunate love affair that he (Brand) has had. It appears that the faithless woman is none other than La Belle Russe.

Sackton goes into battle and is believed to have been killed. La Belle Russe shows up at the Sackton family home with Brand's child, impersonating Fleurette, who is too ill to travel. La Belle Russe is accepted by them because the family's other son, Sir James Sackton, has been killed and Lord Philip Sackton's son, Philip Sackton, Jr., is now the heir. Lord Sackton is actually alive, although he tried to commit suicide when he could not find Fleurette. He returns to the family home with his friend Brand. When Brand sees La Belle Russe, he insists that she is his faithless paramour; the family still believes she is actually Fleurette. Finally, both sisters appear together, and the misunderstanding is ended. All is happily concluded.

* * *

A wag joked: "In Theda Bara's *La Belle Russe*, her husband paints a picture to keep the wolf from the door. D'ja notice the painting? He should have set it out in the hallway where the wolf could see it."

Reviews

"The Fox press books will tell you that Belasco beat all records and wrote this play in six weeks. After seeing the picture, we are inclined to suggest that if he had written the play in the days of typewriters he could have beaten his own record by about five weeks and six days." *Film Fun*, 1919.

"An outstanding feature is the wonderful work of Miss Bara in a dual role. It is a new departure in double exposures on the screen. In several scenes the star is seen in both characters simultaneously, the two figures being seen in such close proximity as to perplex even the spectator to whom double exposure is no longer a novelty." *Exhibitors Herald*, September 1919.

"Theda Bara's latest offering harks back to the old school of fiction and drama. The development of the ancient plots was invariably about heroes when they condescended to marry below their station. The [Fox] producers had the foresight to turn the ancient material to advantage by making it up-to-date…. Theda Bara's performance is the chief point of interest in a story not conspicuous for any dramatic highlights. The plot is so obvious that the suspensive [sic] value is lost sight of completely. Forget its ancient vintage and you will like it." *Motion Picture News*, September 20, 1919.

"Shorn of its artistic staging and other production values, this is not so much. Holds up dramatically for some of its length, weakens when it slips into straightaway narrative, then misses fire very badly. The crudeness of the denoument spoils to a considerable degree much of the better stuff that had registered before. When everyone had gotten into too deep a dramatic hole, they dragged from nowhere at all a twin sister to account for some things that needed explaining. Miss Bara's work is by no means wonderful. It never showed enough contrasting characteristics to make the dual role convincing. The story itself is old stuff with old situations." *Wid's Daily*, September 21, 1919.

"Belasco's old play is not improved in this optic version. The fault seems to be nowhere in particular except for the staleness of the play, and the lack of any original ideas in the adaptation." *Photoplay*, October 1919.

"The screenplay is full of interest and suspense. These are the two main ingredients for a good picture. Theda Bara has two parts: one, a loving wife; two, she has her cigarette, rolling eyes and vamp movements." *New York Clipper*, October 1, 1919.

"Good business and gave satisfaction." Manager, Denison Theatre, Denison, Iowa.

"This is some picture. Pleased all who saw it; [Theda Bara] sure is some star. Book it, can't go wrong." Manager, Fox Theatre, Allen, Nebraska.

"Star plays a double role with clever photography and acting. Good picture, good crowd." Manager, Hudson Theatre, St. Louis, Missouri.

"Good picture of its type. Star does not draw here; poor business." Manager, Jefferson Theatre, Goshen, Indiana.

"One of the star's best. Held the audience spellbound; all were pleased. Ran two days." Manager, Rialto Theatre, Vallejo, California.

"A splendid picture. Bara is fine." Manager, Opera House, Camp Point, Illinois.

Lure of Ambition (aka *The Lure of Ambition*) (1919)

Background

Almost five years after her meteoric rise from total unknown to stardom in *A Fool There Was*, Theda Bara's film career limped to its virtual end in this tepid melodrama. It had been more than a year and nine films ago since she had had her last bona fide hit with *Salome*. Plot-wise, she once again was irresistible onscreen to a man far above her station, landing yet another nobleman—this time a duke. The scenario would have been a familiar one for Charlotte Bronte; it is reminiscent of *Jane Eyre*.

Although the correct of title of this film is *Lure of Ambition*, the initial article "The" was often added in reviews and articles. Her male co-star Thurlow Bergen also had had a role in Bara's first known screen appearance in *The Stain* in 1914. He then had a leading role; she had been an extra. For this last film, Bara had a new director, San Franciscan Edmund Lawrence (1881–1944). Although he had amassed scores of credits by the time he helmed this film, his output had been relatively undistinguished. This remained true for the rest of his career, which did not outlast the silent film era.

The Film

Directed and scenario by Edmund Lawrence. Story by Julia Burnham based on her unpublished and uncopyrighted story. Cinematography by H. Alderson Leach. Costume design by George James Hopkins ("Neje"). Released by the Fox Film Corporation on November 16, 1919. 5 reels.

Cast: Theda Bara (Olga Dolan), Thurlow Bergen (Duke of Rutledge), William B. Davidson (Cyril Ralston), Dan Mason (Sylvester Dolan), Ida Waterman (Duchess of Rutledge), Amelia Gardner (Lady Constance Bromley), Robert Paton Gibbs (Miguel Lopez), Dorothy Drake (Muriel Ralston), Peggy Parr (Minnie Dolan), Tammany Young (Dan Hicks).

Synopsis: Olga Dolan works in a hotel as a public stenographer. She comes from a very poor home, supporting a drunken father and a spoiled sister. At work she meets wealthy Englishman Cyril Ralston, who sees her squalid living conditions. He offers to set her up in a hotel suite and promises to marry her, but not just yet. She resists his offer for a time, but she then gives in because she has fallen in love with him. Breaking his promise, he decamps to England. She vows revenge in the best vamp style.

Olga lands a job as secretary to the titled Lady Bromley and also sails for England. Once there, she discovers that Ralston, her former suitor, is her employer's son and has married someone else. She forces Ralston to introduce her to the Duke of Rutledge and has hopes of becoming his Duchess. After Ralston renews his advances to Olga, his mother dismisses her. Olga becomes the Duke's secretary after she performs an important service for him.

Olga discovers that the Duke is already married to a woman who has become insane and who still lives in the castle. The Duchess escapes from the room where she is held and attacks the Duke in his sleep. Olga saves him. Eventually the Duchess is so overwhelmed by jealousy that she has a fatal heart attack. Olga realizes her dream and becomes the Duchess.

* * *

A Fox publicity tagline read: "Yesterday a child of the slums—Today the Duchess of Rutledge. How did she do it?" An ad inquired: "What about your wife? Does she fret for diamonds, limousines, fine clothes, and a life above your means? Does she hate domestic duties and long to be a lawyer, a doctor, or an artist? If ambition is leading her on, where will it lead her? If you would know the answer, see Theda Bara in *Lure of Ambition*."

In January 1920, censorship of the film was debated by the Boston City Federation of Women's Clubs. One scene recommended for a cut was Theda Bara's flashing of what was described as one-half of one percent of her silk stockings. Elimination of a presumably too-steamy kiss was also urged.

Reviews

"They were hanging from the rafters at [the theater] in New Orleans on Sunday when the theater established a box office record. The vaudeville held little drawing power, but the Theda Bara [film] did." *Variety*, November 1919.

"If this is the Fox idea of ambition's lure, then better not be ambitious. Why pick on this particular word when it's just an excuse for Theda Bara to get in a little of her vamp stuff. Then they had to ring in the poor stenog [i.e., stenographer] story…. Guess Theda herself is getting tired of such stuff. Her facial contortions expressing hate and disgust, and her vamping sure did lack the pep of former days. If you are particular, don't bother with this…. The only chance this will have is in the downtown houses where this sort of hokum is a part of their very existence and it sinks in." *Wid's Daily*, November 16, 1919. (This review was published under the headline: "Typical Theda Bara Production, Ludicrous and Fails Generally.")

"Feeble entertainment from an old-fashioned theme. This story would be more fruitful had there been some authority and observation behind it. [It is] not faithful to English customs or traditions. It is a made-to-order picture with the star interpreting her vampish role after a fashion. You cannot call it an example of present-day picture standards. In its favor is a faint whiff of suspense, a bit of conflict, and commendable acting. The offering would hit a higher mark if the scissors were applied in certain details since they only succeed in emphasizing the crudities." *Motion Picture News*, November 22, 1919.

"Theda Bara for a change has found a story here that is intensely human, plausible, and interesting. [The situation] might have happened to anyone, indeed. You who are in the habit of following the cinema's flickers will welcome a rest, no matter how brief, from an overworked imagination.... One of the best pictures Miss Bara has appeared in for some time." *Los Angeles Times*, December 1, 1919.

"Picture is a good one. People don't like Theda anymore, but they sure come to see her." Manager, Sugg Theatre, Chickasha, Oklahoma.

"This is one of the pictures bought about a year ago, and we played it just to get it off our hands. Theda Bara was all right in her day, but her day has passed." Manager, Palace Theatre, Hamilton, Ohio.

"Good average picture. Theda Bara always pleases here; settings and scenery very good." Manager, Princess Theatre, Winnsboro, Louisiana.

"Excellent; audience well pleased." Manager, Lyric Theatre, Stuart, Florida.

"Well acted drama with a plot that holds attention to the end. Large attendance." Manager, Hudson Theatre, St. Louis, Missouri.

"Star does not draw for us. Good picture; a Sunshine Comedy helped to put this one over. Business fair." Manager, Opera House, Denison, Iowa.

"Bara has had her day. She is yet a clever actress before the camera, but she does not draw the people." Manager, Opera House, Kenton, Ohio.

The Unchastened Woman (1925)

Background

The Unchastened Woman, a play by Louis Anspacher, opened on Broadway in October 1915 and ran for 193 performances, closing in March 1916. It starred Emily Stevens, a well-known Broadway and silent film star. Coincidentally, she had been in the 1908 play *The Devil* when Theda Bara played a small role in the rival version. On the heels of this 1925 film, there was a Broadway revival.

The story was adapted for Theda Bara's return to the screen. Actor/director James Young (1872–1948) was the "Young" in the names of both silent film diva Clara Kimball Young and the multitalented playwright/lyricist/librettist Rida Johnson Young. He had almost 100 films to his directorial credit going back to about 1912. By the time of this film, he himself was no longer young, and he would only make a very few more films to the end of the silent era.

The Film Daily Yearbook for 1925 announced that Chadwick Pictures was planning a series of films for Theda Bara. In an interview that year with *Picture-Play Magazine*, she talked hopefully about her future in the cinema. She was apprehensive about her return (she did not talk in terms of a comeback), but she believed she still retained popular appeal. As the interviewer noted, there was still the memory of some bad pictures which she must live down. "My final pictures for Fox were frightful," she said, "Quality and quantity are seldom twins on the best of relations. I want to make but a few films each year, if I succeed in defining the modern woman."

Now there came a couple of unwelcome reminders of her invented past. *Photoplay*, in its column "Things they Want to Forget," came back to needle her. What Theda Bara wanted to forget, according to the column, was her "ill-judged claim of being a daughter of the Sahara." In its review of this film, it does offer her a bit of sympathy.

Picture-Play Magazine joined the chorus. In an article titled "The Press Agent and What He Does," it said: "Another form of press agentry that has fallen into disuse is the building up of a fictitious personality, like the one that was deliberately created for Theda Bara during the height of her career.... It has been almost entirely abandoned." The article also made this observation: "This seems to be the time a few old favorites have chosen for returning to the screen. Fortunately, William S. Hart [in his farewell film *Tumbleweeds*] has been more successful than Theda Bara."

The return of Theda Bara to the cinema after six years naturally generated interest. But it was a cinema which had moved rapidly into the Jazz Age with its coterie of new and much younger stars. She played a matron in this comeback film and was indeed matronly, even retaining the outmoded hairstyle of the previous decade. She said she wanted this film to be a bridge between the old Theda Bara and the new one—i.e., a modern woman. She herself had defined the modern woman as a combination of wife and vampire. In its 1923 review of Pola Negri's *Mad Love*, *Variety* sneered: "All she does is to reproduce the Theda Bara type that American grinned off the screen some years ago."

Chadwick Pictures, the Poverty Row outfit that finally employed Bara, was not likely to work any miracles. It had been founded in 1920 as a distributing company, and in 1924 began to produce films as well. When sound pictures came, its productions were distributed through Monogram, another Poverty Row studio, until it ceased production in 1933. Its hopeful motto was "Each production an achievement."

Chadwick had become known as the studio that showcased (presumably at a discount) former stars whose reputations had diminished. Among them were action hero George Walsh, comic Larry Semon, leading man Charles Ray, and surprisingly Lionel Barrymore. One of the problems with a studio such as Chadwick was that, unlike the majors, it had no chain of theaters. Its films had to be shopped around to find theaters willing to play them.

Theda Bara could still look movie star attractive in *The Unchastened Woman*, but the plotline of her being the toast of Venice, with all those sophisticated European men vying for her affections and following her back to America, seems absurd. Mae West pulled it off in the next decade, but hers was a far different tongue-in-cheek persona.

A seven-reel adaptation of *The Unchastened Woman* had previously been produced by Rialto De Luxe Productions in 1918, starring Grace Valentine.

The Film

Directed by James Young. Scenario by Douglas Doty. Adapted from the play *The Unchastened Woman* by Louis Anspacher. Cinematography by William O'Connell. Edited by Sam Zimbalist. Art direction by Clifford Saum and Earl Sibley. Released by the Chadwick Pictures Corporation on November 15, 1925. 7 reels.
Cast: Theda Bara (Caroline Knollys), Wyndham Standing (Hubert Knollys), Dale Fuller (Hildegarde Sanbury), John Miljan (Lawrence Sanbury), Harry Northrup (Michael Krellin), Eileen Percy (Emily Madden), Mayme Kelso (Susan Ambie).

Synopsis: Overjoyed that she is to become a mother, Caroline Knollys rushes to tell her husband Hubert. She is shocked to discover him in a passionate embrace with his young secretary. Plotting a campaign to win him back, she leaves on a long trip to Europe without telling him of the baby. Once she is settled in Venice, numerous wealthy men become enamored of her, particularly Lawrence Sanbury, a young American architect. As she desires, they remain only platonic friends.

In the meantime, her husband has become tired of the secretary and is jealous of Caroline's new reputation. When she returns to America, he tries to regain her affections, but she still has not completely forgiven him. Thinking she is hiding a man in her boudoir, Hubert and some detectives stage a raid, seeking evidence for a divorce. Instead, he finally learns that he has a baby son. Husband, wife, and child look forward to a happy future together.

* * *

On August 9, 1925, three months before the film's premiere, *Variety* announced: "Theda Bara has renounced her latest picture. Miss Bara did the repudiating act after witnessing a pre-preview.... She said the cutters and producers had reassembled the continuity, titles, and motive in such a manner as to reverse the picture from the way it was filmed. 'For once in my life I had a chance to do as I wished, play a role which women could understand.' Miss Bara stated that she quit the screen five years ago because she was disgusted with the manner in which her pictures were prepared. She was compelled to make forty pictures in four years which accounted for their crudeness in the past, and she will not again subject herself to any conditions which will interfere with her career."

Theda Bara did not blame director James Young. Despite her preemptive rejection, in September 1925 the studio announced that it had lined up 72 first-run houses to show the film. The film reportedly had its premiere in Fitchburg, Mississippi. Bara had also planned to release her frequently self-publicized memoir *What Women Never Tell* in conjunction with the film. More than 100 years later, it remains a fragile wordy manuscript.

Publicity ads read: "Must a wife be a vampire to win back an unfaithful husband? You will find the answer in that absorbing drama *The Unchastened Woman* in which Theda Bara makes a triumphant return to the screen" and "Millions have been waiting for the return of the Star of Stars." Whatever publicity the studio could afford did not always work. A theater in Chicago ran the film for a week and reported the worst business ever seen at that theater. Reviews were almost all negative.

The Los Angeles Times, Theda Bara's "hometown" newspaper and always one of her biggest boosters, noted that the West Coast premiere was at the same theater as *A Fool There Was*. It loyally, if dubiously, called Bara "a player whose vogue has never been equaled by any star of the film firmament. This vogue has suffered no impairment by the retirement of the actress." It claimed that *The Unchastened Woman* had broken records in every theater it played. Curiosity certainly lured audiences, but it could not sustain attendance once word about the film had spread.

Reviews

"[Theda Bara] does wonders with a role that forces her to repress her emotional fire under a mask of coldness. Absolutely miscast.... The entire cast seems to have realized the hopelessness of it all.... A colorless offering lacking human interest." *Film Daily*, December 27, 1925.

"An unsuitable comeback for Theda Bara. The famous queen of vamps is just as attractive as days gone by and her work is excellent. But she is burdened with an unsuitable story, poor direction and continuity. Nevertheless, it looks good to see Theda again." *Photoplay*, 1926.

"Badly directed and badly acted film in which Theda Bara makes an unworthy return to the screen. Bara, a victim of the wrong kind of showmanship, did not survive partly owing to conditions over which she herself had very little control. The organization with which she was associated had built up about her a veritable pyramid of exoticism and mystery. The public gradually rejected all this wild fantastic publicity. They found it a case of too much Barnum. Theda unfortunately did not have the resistance to withstand the change of public opinion, especially since her professional accomplishments were at that time at a low ebb." *Picture-Play Magazine*, 1926. (**Review number one**.)

"When I saw [the film] and realized that it was actually Theda Bara's return to the screen, and not just one of her old pictures, my amazement knew no bounds. I had to be told over and over again that I was actually seeing a picture made during the last year. I have heard that Miss Bara has signed up with Hal Roach comedies—this might be the first one. Miss Bara's vamping is so childish that it is almost wholesome. The picture is filled with such titles as 'Caroline, little mother, won't you let me tell you how much I need you?' The picture is vulgar, badly directed, badly acted, and in every way perfectly hopeless. I enjoyed it!" *Picture-Play Magazine*, 1926. (**Review number two**.)

"There is little to remind you of the exotic Theda Bara of former years.... She wasn't to play a vampire any more, not the kind that allure with sex appeal, and she doesn't. But how we wish she would, if this is an example of the intellectual vamp.... She doesn't gain our sympathy, and we doubt if she'll gain yours. After you have seen this picture, you will not wonder that Miss Bara herself requested vainly that it not be released." *Motion Picture Magazine*, 1926.

"Once a star, always a star; one may safely say that of Theda Bara at any rate. Her heavy vampish ways of yesterday have been forgotten.... Miss Bara has done some of her best work. For a woman to retire from the screen as Miss Bara did and then return as triumphantly, really, she should be very proud of herself." *Los Angeles Record*, 1926?

"Honest to goodness, folks, Theda Bara can't help herself, she's got to vamp. She's made that way, and when you're made that way, what are you going to do about it? She comes back to the screen lovelier than ever, but as far as her screen characterizations are concerned, she has not reformed." *Wheeling News*, 1926?

"Tough break for Theda. She has an unsympathetic part calling for repression. A repressed vamp is a new idea, but she is absolutely miscast. The picture is stilted, artificial, and unconvincing; leaves you absolutely cold throughout.... A colorless offering lacking human interest. The thin story could have been told in two reels.... Asking Theda to play a cold, disdainful part will get few cheers from her fans who glory in her vampish fire and high-tension emotionalism. The entire cast seems to have sensed the hopelessness of it all and acted accordingly." *Film Daily*, December 27, 1925.

"Theda Bara just can't learn new tricks. That's no reflection on her age, maybe the taste in feminine beauty has changed. Anyway, Theda in sensuous poses fails to arouse the old interest." *Cincinnati Post*, 1926?

"The much heralded return of Theda Bara should bring the shekels to the box office. Regardless of the quality of the production, her admirers will flock to see what Father Time has done. They will find that he has indeed treated her kindly. Fair entertainment.... The adaptation, while lacking in subtlety, is interesting.... The most logical exploitation angle is the return of Theda Bara to the silver screen." *Exhibitors Trade Review*, January 2, 1926.

"Theda Bara comes back to the screen with physical charm undiminished, and displaying much of the emotional power and dramatic ability that distinguished her in the past. It would be pleasing if I could truthfully brand [the film] as a notable production, but it is unworthy of the talents of the star.... It doesn't register audience appeal on the screen.... None of the characters either deserve or receive a shred of sympathy. Not even Miss Bara's splendid acting wins pity or approval for the deceived wife. The direction is poor and the continuity a shabby mess." *Motion Picture News*, January 2, 1926.

"The players are well-suited to their roles, but one cannot grow enthusiastic over their characterizations, not even Miss Bara's despite her fine acting." *Cleveland Plain Dealer*, March 24, 1926.

"It certainly will not help her to regain her former popularity.... It seems as though those responsible for the production were undecided whether to make a drama or a light comedy. If they had stuck to the light comedy, they might have had something of it, but when the thing becomes dramatic, they get a good laugh, but not when they expected it. The action is slow and poor editing is in a great way responsible. The titles are very poor and detract. Miss Bara seemed charming at times, but the bad lighting detracted much." *Film Mercury*, March 26, 1926.

"This will probably get over all right in the city, but out here in the sticks it flopped with a dull, sickening thud, as it sure left a bad taste in our mouth." Manager, Osage Theatre, Osage, Oklahoma.

"Very, very good picture, Theda as ever. These kind help." Manager, King Tut Theatre, Rising Star, Texas.

"It was a comedy but it didn't mean to be a comedy. It was as serious as Louis Anspacher is going to be when he sees what the movies have done to his play." Manager, Randolph Theatre, Chicago, Illinois.

"Poor. Star lacks color and box office attraction of former years. Should be played as double feature to best advantage. Sunday and special, no." Manager, Normandy Theatre, Brooklyn, New York.

"Theda Bara retired several years ago, and I am sorry she didn't stay so. Theda's facial expressions give one a good laugh. Nothing to it but a style show." Manager, Capitol Theatre, Delphos, Ohio.

"It has to be said that Theda Bara is arresting.... She plays with an easy grace and a surprising knack for light comedy. She is a most sympathetic actor." Modern day commentator.

"It was a disappointment. This dumpy, matronly figure with the vapid, expressionless face was certainly no Cleopatra. She radiated no charisma at all." Modern day commentator.

The Short Subjects

Screen Snapshots, Series 3, #19 (1923)

Background

The *Screen Snapshots* series was initiated by Columba Pictures and ran from about 1922 to 1958. They purported to show Hollywood celebrities relaxing at home or away from movie sets in informal or glamorous settings. Far from being candid, they were carefully regulated by the studios.

The Film

Produced by Jack Cohn and Louis Lewyn. Released by Pathe Pictures on February 11, 1923. 10 minutes.

Cast: Theda Bara, Madge Bellamy, Jackie Coogan, Cecil B. DeMille, Douglas Fairbanks, Mary Pickford, Thomas Ince, Marcus Loew, Rudolph Valentino, Theodore Roberts, Thomas Meighan, Lois Wilson, Leatrice Joy.

Synopsis: Theda Bara is seen golfing and playing Pung Chow; Pickford and Fairbanks return to Los Angeles and appear on the set of *Robin Hood*; DeMille stages a Roman orgy for one of his epics; Loew takes a group of actors to Philadelphia; Coogan is in a speed race; Valentino relaxes at home.

* * *

Pung Chow, the game Theda Bara is playing, is a form of mah-jongg known as the "game of 100 intelligences." She is the only person shown who was not then currently active in the film industry. The majority of reviews did not mention that she was in this film.

Reviews

"There are several sketches of real interest to photoplay goers, but also there are several of them which are hardly timely on the news side." *Exhibitors Trade Review*, February 10, 1923.

"Certainly an entertaining single reel. Have played several of these and never noticed anyone walking out while being shown." Manager, Orpheum Theatre, Quinton, Oklahoma.

"Very interesting and entertaining single reel; a good bet once or twice a month. These are just right; my patrons like them." Manager, Majestic Theatre, Eureka, Montana.

Madame Mystery (1926)

Background

Taking a page from Chadwick's playbook, a May 1926 ad read: "Hal Roach has taken the most daring step in the history of comedy production. He is signing up the biggest feature stars available to appear in two-reel comedies [i.e., those forced to find work wherever they can]. Lionel Barrymore, Theda Bara, Mildred Harris, Mabel Normand, and others of like reputation are appearing in Roach comedies of a kind that has never been made before. Feature stars, feature production, feature stories, feature directors."

This film is one of those comedies, made under the banner of Roach-Pathe. They played on the major Keith-Albee Vaudeville Circuit that was comprised of some 50 of the larger urban cities. Theda Bara has a couple of comic moments, but essentially she is the straight woman to several talented comic actors.

In November 1925, after being signed by Hal Roach, Theda Bara was quoted as saying: "I am glad to return to the screen before the class of audience which this contract offers. Any actress loves to reappear before the best possible audiences, the sort which a combination of the Keith Circuit and the country's key-city theaters offers. It is an opportunity highly satisfactory to any actress, providing the elements of production quality are assured, which in this case is settled." The following month, *Variety* reported that Hal Roach would pay Bara $15,000 to appear in a feature film under his direction.

This film was one of director Richard Wallace's earliest efforts. He spent only a brief time directing short subjects before being promoted to feature films in a career that ran to 1950. He was equally adept at drama and comedy. A couple of late Shirley Temple films were among his final productions. Wallace was one of the founding members of the Directors Guild of America.

The Film

Directed by Richard Wallace. Assistant director, Stan Laurel [and others]. Produced by Hal Roach. Written by Carl Harbaugh, Krag Johnson, Grover Jones, Stan Laurel, Hal Roach, and Hal Yates. Cinematography by Harry Gerstad, Floyd Jackman, and Len Powers. Edited by Richard Currier. Costume design by Will Lambert. Released by Hal Roach Studios on March 12, 1926. 2 reels. (A five-reel "feature" version was released in the UK by Ideal Films in 1927. This presumably was padded out with material from other films.)

Cast: Theda Bara (Madame Mysterieux), Tyler Brooke (Hungry artist), James Finlayson (Struggling author), Oliver Hardy (Captain Schmaltz), Fred Malatesta (Man of a Thousand Eyes), Sammy Brooks (Sam Brooks).

Synopsis: A struggling artist and his author friend look for a way to survive. The exotic Madame Mysterieux, an agent of the American government, is followed by a villain who wants what she is carrying. When he crashes his car, he is rescued by the two starving men, who pull him from the wreck. Noting his great height, one says, "I didn't know Longfellow was in town." They discover that he has a Secret Service badge, and he is so confused after the accident that he thinks one of the men is a beautiful woman.

When the two men learn that there is a large reward for the package that Madame Mysterieux is carrying, they decide to go for it. She discloses that it contains enough material to blow up the entire city, making everyone around her fearful. She boards a ship operated by Captain Schmaltz, who is immediately enamored of her. She is followed on board by foreign agents and the two men, all of them seeking the package. They put on various disguises to spy on her, including peeking through the porthole of her cabin.

Madame Mystery. Theda Bara's "comeback" in the mid–1920s culminated in this two-reel comedy from Hal Roach. Surrounded by talented comics like Oliver Hardy and Jimmy Finlayson, Bara was a competent enough straight woman, but it could not have been a happy ending to a once legendary career.

The artist and author succeed in stealing the package, only to be held at gunpoint by the foreign agents. Madame Mysterieux begs them not to make any sudden moves because the whole ship could blow up. The author is so nervous that he swallows the package, discovering that it contains gas—a helium-nitrate explosive. The unfortunate men bloat up and ascend into the sky, only to return when a passing stork punctures them. The gas is harmless after all.

* * *

In an example of damning with faint praise, an ad for Hal Roach comedies read: "Theda Bara—remember her?—Great actress, more capable than ever."

Oliver Hardy was in front of the camera; Stan Laurel worked on the film. According to a 1931 article, the duo first got the idea of teaming up together while working on this film. This may or may not be true.

In February 1926 at a preview of the film, then still called *High Explosives*, it was reported: "Miss Bara was the recipient of a thunderous round of applause from the audience. Several offers to continue her screen career are now being considered by the former vamp."

The film was headlined at Keith-Albee's New York Hippodrome, then the world's largest theater, and was given prominent billing in front of the theater. The comedy was billed as if it were one of the vaudeville acts currently playing there. Theda Bara came from California to appear in person. Other vaudeville houses followed suit without the personal appearance of the star. A Yonkers, New York, vaudeville house gave the film the best place on the bill, proclaiming that "Theda Bara in a comedy is something new and different."

Bara got some of the best reviews she had had since her role in *Salome*, even from bête-noire *Photoplay*. In the week of March 6, 1926, the National Board of Review selected a feature film and three short comedies for special mention. One of the comedies was *Madame Mystery*; the feature was *Ben-Hur*.

Reviews

"Theda Bara's first two-reel comedy is little short of a riot. It proves in a highly satisfactory manner that the jump from heavy vamp roles in even heavier drama to the lead in the short subject field can be successfully bridged.... Miss Bara plays a somewhat straight lead it is true, but it is quite apparent that her ability as a comedienne is but a latent quality. It is self-evident, too, that the former vamp has lost none of her charm and attractiveness. Never has she appeared more beautiful than in this comedy. Her understanding of every situation, her grasping of every detail is indicated." *Los Angeles Times*, February 7, 1926.

"It is a bit bizarre to see the voluptuous arrogance of Theda Bara set to the antic pace of hilarious comedy. One has the feeling of something painfully reluctant in her, and not yet relaxed to the demands of the new medium." *Nassau Daily Review*, March 7, 1926.

"Lots of exhibitors have been yelling for something different in comedy shorts. Hal Roach must have heard for he comes right back with a laugh lifesaver built from a new pattern. Can you picture Theda Bara, the vamp, in a two-barreled scream? She plays her role straight as a woman of mystery, and out of her perfectly serious and legitimate efforts the funny situations develop most naturally and screamingly funny. One of these you have to see to appreciate." *Film Daily*, April 17, 1926.

"Theda Bara's appearance in the comedy field has been extensively advertised, and exhibitors may rest assured that her first offering will live up to their expectations in every sense of the word. An all-star comedy cast in a screamingly funny yarn which is entirely free of slapstick." *Motion Picture News*, April 17, 1926.

"The directors, with the aid of these high-class artists, have made this one of the best comedies on the Pathe circuit. No audience will be able to resist it." *Moving Picture World*, April 24, 1926.

"See it and howl. It's Theda Bara's first comedy and not once is her face garnished with custard pie. One long scream from start to finish, with Theda furnishing the charm." *Photoplay*, May 1926.

"Not only is a feature star presented, but she plays a straight serious part all the way and gets roars of laughter from it. Here is the answer to those showmen who say there is nothing new in comedy." *Film Daily*, May 30, 1926.

"Very good comedy with same old Theda Bara of early days." Manager, Liggett Theatre, Madison, Kansas.

"Not so good; star had nothing to do." Manager, Community Theatre, Ridgeway, Iowa.

"A dandy comedy, different from anything lately. Pleased all adults as well as children." Manager, Manzanita Theatre, Carmel, California.

"Why was this ever released?" Manager, Illinois Theatre, Sullivan, Illinois.

"This comedy is classic; out of the ordinary." Manager, Silver Family Theatre, Greenville, Michigan.

"Something different in the comedy line, with Theda Bara taking the honors." Manager, Tivoli Theatre, Knoxville, Illinois.

"The old favorite back in a good comedy." Manager, Gem Theatre, Green River, Utah.

"Pretty good comedy, and it was interesting to see the old star back in a novel setting." Manager, Star Theatre, Menard, Texas.

"A moderately amusing short, entertaining for what it is but a tad disappointing considering all the talent involved. How rare it is to see Theda Bara in anything at all…. A pleasant bit of nonsense." Modern day commentator.

Archival Appearances: Film and Television

Forty-Five Minutes from Hollywood (1926)
[Motion picture short subject]

Directed by Fred Guiol. Produced by Hal Roach. Written by Walter Lantz and Hal Roach. Released by Hal Roach Studios on December 26, 1926. 21 minutes.
Cast: Live appearances include: Glenn Tryon, Charlotte Mineau, Sue O'Neil (aka Molly O'Day), Rube Clifford, Oliver Hardy, Edna Murphy, Jerry Mandy. **Archival appearances include**: Theda Bara, Joe Cobb, Mickey Daniels, Johnny Downs, The Hal Roach Bathing Beauties, Allen "Farina" Hoskins.

This is one of the Glenn Tryon comedy series. Among the uncredited players is the soon to be famous Janet Gaynor; Stan Laurel, who will team up with Oliver Hardy to become one of the greatest comedy teams; perennial comedy foil Tiny Sanford, and character actor Claude Gillingwater.

Synopsis: A rural California family lives only 45 minutes from Hollywood, but they are real country bumpkins. They owe a debt to a company's Hollywood office, so they all go in for the day. En route to the train, they are chased by horses and a cow. On a bus tour of Hollywood, they spot Theda Bara and the Our Gang kids, and they see a Hal Roach chase comedy being shot on the street. They also run into real-life bank robbers, one of whom is dressed in drag. The family thinks this is part of the movie until the robber changes places with the hero, putting him into the woman's clothing. Further complications ensue; they decide they have had their fill of moviemaking.

* * *

The few seconds-long clip of Theda Bara is an outtake from her previous Hal Roach comedy *Madame Mystery*. She had intended to appear live when she signed with Roach for two comedies. Her husband's objections to her continuing career, and probably her own misgivings, make this her first archival appearance instead.

This marks one of Stan Laurel and Oliver Hardy's very earliest appearances in the same film. Hardy was in one of his "thin" periods, and he is seen clad in a bath towel running through the hotel at which he is a guest. Laurel plays an occupant of another room who gets involved in a fight between the young hero and a bank robber. Laurel and Hardy did not share any scenes, and Laurel is uncredited.

Reviews

"There are touches here and there, which in the guise of showing the town to the passengers of a 'rubberneck wagon,' exploit some of the Roach personnel. This is all in the picture's favor. [It] makes the grade without particularly distinguishing itself." *Film Daily*, December 26, 1926.

"A movie with zero story, and is only filled with some slapstick and comical moments.... Also works pretty well as a satire on Hollywood.... Well constructed and good for some laughs." Modern-day commentator.

Stars of Yesterday (1931) [Motion Picture Short Subject]

Supervised [i.e., produced?] by Murray Roth. Master of Ceremonies: Walter O'Keefe. Vitaphone reel #178. Released by Warner Brothers/Vitaphone on February 28, 1931. 11 minutes.
Cast: Theda Bara, Broncho Billy Anderson, Roscoe "Fatty" Arbuckle, Sarah Bernhardt, Betty Blythe, Mary Fuller, Texas Guinan, Mildred Harris, William S. Hart, Helen Holmes, Mary Miles Minter, Mabel Normand, Charles Ray, Rudolph Valentino, Clara Kimball Young.
Synopsis: Scenes from silent films.

* * *

"Prepared at the Flatbush studio under the supervision of Murray Roth."

At the time of the film's release, a Warner Brothers announcement stated that this was to be the first of six one-reelers to be released under the same title, presumably with all different stars. No other Vitaphone films were to bear this title, perhaps due to lack of interest in silent films? Listings in contemporaneous periodicals for this film summarized its subject matter as "old film stars."

The clip from the Theda Bara film is taken from 1925's *The Unchastened Woman*. In 1931 most, if not all, of her now-lost Fox films were probably still in existence. Presumably they were not available for such uses.

Film Parade (U.S. Title: *March of the Movies*) (1933) [Documentary/Motion Picture Short Subject]

Directed by J. Stuart Blackton. Written and edited by Howard Gaye. Narrated by Kent Stevenson. Released by Alliance Films in the United Kingdom on December 21, 1933. 55 minutes; United States release. 25 minutes.
Cast: Live appearances: Marian Blackton, Violet Blackton, Marjorie Bonner, J. Stuart Blackton, Jr., Albert E. Smith. **Archival appearances**: Theda Bara, Charles Chaplin, Marlene Dietrich, Tom Mix, Broncho Billy Anderson, Clara Bow, John Bunny, Francis X. Bushman, Harry Carey, Marguerite Clayton, Mathilde Comont, Gary Cooper, Dolores Costello, Viola Dana, Bebe Daniels, Priscilla Dean, Billy Dooley, William Earle, Thomas Edison, Louise Fazenda, Flora Finch, Corinne Griffith, Alan Hale, Oliver Hardy, Tony (the horse), Phyllis Kennedy, Tom Kennedy, Barbara Lamarr, Harold Lloyd, Wallace MacDonald, Mae Marsh, Victor McLaglen, John Miltern, William Mong, Bull Montana, Harry Morey, Mae Murray, Mabel Normand, Ramon Novarro, Jean Paige, Mary Pickford, Marie Prevost, Esther Ralston, Charles Ray, Irene Rich, Larry Semon, Norma Shearer, Milton Sills, Anita Stewart, Edith Storey, Mack Swain, Gloria Swanson, Blanche Sweet, William Howard Taft, Mary Thurman, Ben Turpin, Rudolph Valentino, Bobby Vernon, Henry B. Walthall, Earle Williams, Woodrow Wilson.

Synopsis: J. Stuart Blackton harks back to the ancient Egyptians to talk about his theory of the genesis of movies, and he includes such eminent personages as Leonardo da Vinci. He credits Thomas Edison and George Eastman, but he ignores such early silent film pioneers as the Lumiere Brothers and George Melies. In general, he overlooks large segments of the silent cinema (but not his own contributions), while praising the early efforts in sound.

* * *

Blackton was a British-American director and producer during much of the American silent film era. He was considered a pioneer in film animation and was a founder of the Vitagraph Studio. His 1915 film *The Battle Cry of Peace*, despite its ironic title, urged America to join the Great War and caused much controversy among peace advocates.

Reviews

"An entertaining picture of its type, instructive and picturesque.... Scenes from old silent films are very entertaining." *Motion Picture Reviews*, 1933.

"Chiefly noteworthy for the fact that there are more shots of past and present film stars than has been offered before.... The result is very entertaining, is ideal for double bills, and should appeal anywhere." *Film Daily*, December 20, 1933.

"This is distinctly a novelty. It is interesting, educational, authoritative, and generally quite entertaining.... A splendid attraction for art houses." *Hollywood Reporter*, December 14, 1933.

Screen Snapshots, Series 16, #11 (1937) [Motion Picture Short Subject]

Directed, produced and written by Ralph Staub. Executive producer, Harriet Parsons. Released by Columbia Pictures on June 25, 1937. 10 minutes.
Cast: Theda Bara, Constance Bennett, Joan Bennett, Betty Bronson, Lew Cody, Gary Cooper, Jackie Cooper, Myrna Loy, Ben Lyon, Marx Brothers (Chico, Harpo, Groucho, Zeppo), Marie Prevost, George Raft, Wallace Reid, Charles "Buddy" Rogers, Gloria Swanson, Rudolph Valentino.

Synopsis: A number of people are at the home of series producer Harriet Parsons (daughter of Louella Parsons) to celebrate the series' 17th anniversary. A portion of the very first film is shown.

* * *

Hundreds of the short subjects in the *Screen Snapshots* series were produced between the early 1920s and 1958, often as many as 20 or 25 annually. For many years they were made under the personal supervision of Jacob "Jack" Cohn, younger brother of studio head Harry Cohn. Earlier ones were often narrated by Eddie Lambert.

Later ones were given titles along with the series numbers, and then the numbering was discontinued. They purport to show informal scenes of the stars at work and play, but in actuality they are carefully manufactured to safeguard the stars' images. They depicted stars from every studio, not just from Columbia. Art Baker often narrated the later ones in the series.

An early promotion to theater owners read: "Behind the Scenes with Stars of the Screen! There isn't a man, woman, or child in any of your audiences who wouldn't do a good deal to get behind the scenes of filmdom. *Screen Snapshots* does just that. It shows the stars as they are on the lot, off the lot, at work, at home, and at play."

A 1937 advertisement boasted: "Through kaleidoscopic changes, *Screen Snapshots* has devoted itself to the intimate doings of the stars in a brilliant, bright, and always entertaining manner." This issue of *Snapshots* was made to celebrate the series' 17th anniversary. *Film Daily* announced that it was booked in 6,000 theaters across the country and that it would play over the entire Fox West Coast Circuit.

Reviews

"Very good. [The series] is always enjoyed here." Manager, Plaza Theatre, Tilbury, Ontario.

"Very interesting. My attendance has improved since I started showing them." Manager, Grand Theatre, New Hamburg, Ontario.

Screen Snapshots, Series 17, #1 (1937) [Motion Picture Short Subject]

Directed and written by Ralph Staub. Produced by Harriet Parsons and Ralph Staub. Released by Columbia Pictures on September 17, 1937. 10 minutes.
Cast: Theda Bara, Agnes Ayres, Constance Bennett, Joan Bennett, Constance Binney, Clara Bow, Betty Bronson, Lew Cody, Gary Cooper, Jackie Cooper, Marion Davies, Janet Gaynor, Myrna Loy, Ben Lyon, Jeanette MacDonald, The Marx Brothers (Chico, Harpo, Groucho, Zeppo), Marie Prevost, George Raft, Charles Ray, Gene Raymond, Wallace Reid, Buddy Rogers, Ruth Roland, Anita Stewart, Gloria Swanson, Norma Talmadge, Ben Turpin, Rudolph Valentino.

Synopsis: A compilation of well-known stars at work and play from 1921 to 1937.

Reviews

"The highlights of a brand of film activity that will appeal to the general run of audience for the past 17 years is run off in this issue. The names, events, and what-have-you that made good publicity in years gone by is unreeled. Everything of importance from Rudolph Valentino to the Gene Raymond-Jeanette MacDonald wedding." *Motion Picture Daily*, September 24, 1937.

"Very good. This issue has dug deep into the recesses of the library for shots and scenes of the stars of yesteryear. [It] starts from Mack Sennett's bathing beauties, up to the 1930s." *Motion Picture Herald*, October 16, 1937.

"[My] audience hasn't gotten excited over this series yet. They can take it or leave it." Manager, Federal Theatre, Denver, Colorado.

The Movies March On (The March of Time, V. 5, #12) (aka 1938–1939 Season, #12) (1939) [Motion Picture Short Subject]

Produced [and directed] by Louis de Rochemont. Narrated by Jackson Beck. Released by RKO Pictures on July 7, 1939. 22 minutes.
Cast: Theda Bara, Renee Adoree, Broncho Billy Anderson, Joseph Breen, Charles Chaplin, Cecil B. DeMille, Walt Disney, Marie Dressler, Douglas Fairbanks, Greta Garbo, Mary Garden, John Gilbert, Lillian Gish, Hermann Goering, William S. Hart, Will Hayes, Adolf Hitler, Al Jolson, Buster Keaton, Keystone Kops, Raymond Massey, Paul Muni, Mabel Normand, Mary Pickford, Will Rogers, Rosalind Russell, George Schaefer, Mack Sennett, Rudolph Valentino, Walter Wanger, Harry Warner, Jack Warner, Darryl Zanuck.

Synopsis: The evolution of the movies as shown in film clips from the silent film era to 1939. The highlight is the opening of sections of the Museum of Modern Art (MOMA) in New York City. MOMA would become instrumental in the preservation and screening of rare films. The Theda Bara clip is taken from *A Fool There Was*. This is the first of two times that Theda Bara appears in the same film with Adolf Hitler.

The March of Time began as a radio series that ran from 1931 to 1946, and it was also a film series from 1935 to 1951. Almost all of these series were produced and/or directed by brothers Richard and Louis de Rochemont, and they were narrated by the authoritative baritone voice of Westbrook van Vorhees. The series were Oscar nominated several times. The rise of television news programs ultimately made them unprofitable.

In 1949 *The March of Time* produced another film of the same name. It consisted of much of the 1939 version, but it showed less of the MOMA segment and more of Hollywood's evolution.

Reviews

"A laudable piece for the industry as a whole. It should hold audience interest throughout.... This reel is worthwhile film fare for every age and type of patron." *Motion Picture Daily*, July 7, 1939

"An excellent subject from any and all angles. While it does an outstanding instructional job on behalf of motion pictures at large, it achieves this important objective without sacrifice of dramatic entertainment." *Boxoffice*, July 1939.

Flicker Flashbacks #2, Series 5 (1947) [Motion Picture Short Subject]

Directed, produced, and written by Richard Fleischer. Narrated by Knox Manning and Harry von Zell. Released by RKO Pictures on December 12, 1947. 9 minutes.
Cast: Theda Bara, Agnes Ayres, Lionel Barrymore, Francis X. Bushman, Christy Cabanne, Harry Carey, Lon Chaney, Charles Chaplin, Maurice Costello, Nigel de Brulier, Lillian Gish, Robert Harron, Helen Holmes, James Kirkwood, Marion Leonard, Harold Lockwood, Charles Hill Mailes, Mae Marsh, Claire McDowell, Walter Miller, Owen Moore, Mabel Normand, Mary Pickford, Wallace Reid, Blanche Sweet, Florence Turner, Rudolph Valentino, Henry B. Walthall.

Synopsis: Featured clips are from *Weighed in the Balance* (1913) and *Mile a Minute Kendall* (1918) and *Brave Girl Does Her Duty* (1915). The 1913 film was about a Northern female spy during the Civil War who learned about the South constructing an ironclad ship.

* * *

There is at least one source that states this short was made in March 1945. Like the later television series *Flicker Flashbacks*, this series consisted of edited and sped-up segments of obscure silent films accompanied by "hilarious" commentary, usually by Knox Manning. It served to relegate silent films to objects of ridicule. The shorts played in theaters from 1943 to 1948.

A mini-review in *Motion Picture Daily* said of another 1947 entry in the series: "The camera turns back to scenes of another day to get laughs out of what was taken seriously then."

Also in 1947, *Film Daily* said of another entry in the series: "Sequences are sure to give audiences a laugh, especially when the satirical narration of Knox Manning is added. With all the distorted 'drah-ma' of the silent screen, this should prove a boon on all bills."

Under the headline "Nostalgic Film Series Running Out of Oldies," *Variety* reported: "*Flicker Flashbacks* may soon have to [be] dropped because of the shortage of early day films.... When the series was first started, RKO found enough material in public domain to keep things perking. That has since been used up.... A bunch of early U.S. films were found in Buenos Aires, and some were uncovered at the Pathe-Cinema library in Paris." *Variety*, April 30, 1947.

Richard Fleischer (1916–2006) was the son of famous animation pioneer Max Fleischer. He wrote and produced the entire *Flicker Flashbacks* series, and he later became a respected cinema director, notably in the film noir genre.

Reviews

"Although we have played only two of this series they are becoming very popular. Knox Manning's narration is outstanding. These are good substitutes for cartoons." Manager, Ojai Theatre, Ojai, California.

"I play these only because I have to." Manager, State Theater, Rivesville, Wisconsin.

The Ford 50th Anniversary Show (1953) (CBS and NBC) [Television Program]

Directed by Clark Jones. Produced by Leland Hayward and Lawrence White. Written by Howard Teichmann. Hosted by Edward R. Murrow and Oscar Hammerstein II. Announcer, Don Pardo. Dances and musical sequences conceived and staged by Jerome Robbins. Costumes by Irene Sharaff. Broadcast live by the CBS and NBC networks on June 15, 1953. 120 minutes.

Cast (Live/Filmed appearances): Marian Anderson, Wally Cox, Bing Crosby, Eddie Fisher, Henry Ford II, Oscar Hammerstein II, Leland Hayward, Howard Lindsay, Mary Martin, Ethel Merman, Franz Rupp, Frank Sinatra, Dorothy Stickney, Lowell Thomas, Rudy Vallee.

Cast (Archival appearances): Theda Bara, Charles Chaplin, Winston Churchill, Marie Dressler, Greta Garbo, John Gilbert, Anna Held, Al Jolson, Vladimir Lenin, Charles Lindbergh, Franklin D. Roosevelt, Theodore Roosevelt, Joseph Stalin, Leon Trotsky, Rudolph Valentino, Orville Wright, Wilbur Wright.

Synopsis: A survey of the 50 years of the Ford Company from 1903 to 1953, as represented through the music of America. Puppets Kukla and Ollie, courtesy of puppeteer Burr Tillstrom, introduce some sequences. Lowell Thomas reminisces about old-time radio. A scene from the play *Our Town* is presented. Mary Martin and Ethel Merman present a medley of Americana in duet; other well-known singers contribute songs as well.

* * *

The show is said to have cost $500,000 to stage, and was reportedly viewed by 95 percent of all homes tuned in to television that night. The *Los Angeles Times* reported: "One of the more lavish presentations in the short life of television; programs on both networks were pre-empted. Broadway producer Leland Hayward was given practically a free hand in selecting talent."

Henry Ford II, President of the Ford Motor Company, whose anniversary was being celebrated, specified that there were to be no actual Ford commercials during the two-hour running time. Of course, the whole show is virtually an advertisement for the automobile company.

The enduring hit of the show was the dynamic duo of Broadway powerhouses Mary Martin and Ethel Merman. Decca Records released an album of their medleys, and the clip of their performances from the broadcast can still be viewed.

Review

"All things considered, some pretty wonderful things happened when the Ford Motor Company threw a lavish TV party as a climax to its 50th anniversary. It packed a terrific wallop in its re-creation of events, both large and small. There were inevitable shortcomings in a production of this size and scope. Timing was off [but] Ford's 50th birthday party turned out to be a very gala and enjoyable affair." *Broadcasting-Telecasting*, June 22, 1953.

Hollywood: The Golden Years (1961) (NBC) [Documentary]

Directed by David Wolper. Produced by David Wolper and Jack Haley, Jr. Story by Sidney Skolsky. Written by Malvin Wald. Narrated by Gene Kelly. Music by Elmer Bernstein. Edited by Philip Rosenberg. Released to NBC Television by Wolper-Sterling Productions on November 29, 1961. 52 minutes.

Cast: Theda Bara, Renee Adoree, Roscoe "Fatty" Arbuckle, Mary Astor, Albert Austin, Agnes Ayres, John Barrymore, Lionel Barrymore, Richard Barthelmess, Leon Bary, Wallace Beery, Henry Bergman, Billy Bevan, Clara Bow, John Bunny, Francis X. Bushman, Vilma Banky, Lon Chaney, Ronald Colman, Jackie Coogan, Gary Cooper, Dolores Costello, Maurice Costello, Marion Davies, Nigel De Brulier, Marguerite De la Motte, Dolores Del Rio, Marie Dressler, Thomas Edison, Douglas Fairbanks, Greta Garbo, John Gilbert, Lillian Gish, William S. Hart, Sessue Hayakawa, Tony (the horse), Al Jolson, Buster Keaton, Rod La Rocque, Florence Lawrence, Carole Lombard, Montague Love, Mae Marsh, Tom Mix, Antonio Moreno, Mae Murray, Marshall Neilan, Mabel Normand, Eugene Pallette, Mary Pickford, Edna Purviance, Wallace Reid, Rin Tin Tin, Will Rogers, Mack Sennett, Norma Shearer, George Siegmann, Gloria Swanson, Ben Turpin, Henry B. Walthall, H.B. Warner, Pearl White, Clara Kimball Young.

Synopsis: A history of silent films from their popularization by Thomas Edison to the creation of the star system, the growing artistry of the silents, and the early experiments with sound, which led to Vitaphone's *The Jazz Singer*.

* * *

This film preempted the popular series *Wagon Train* on the night it was aired. It spawned a sequel called *Hollywood: the Talkies*.

Review

"Industry-ites are agreed that it was one of the most effective plugs for motion pictures. A stirring documentary recounting of filmdom's history from its earliest days down to the first talkie. The wonders of motion picture entertainment were spread before the eyes of a vast TV audience." *Independent Exhibitors Film Bulletin*, December 11, 1961.

Hollywood and the Stars: Sirens, Symbols, and Glamour Girls, Part 1 [Television Program] (1963) (NBC)

Hollywood and the Stars was a weekly 30-minute show that ran for one season on NBC from September 30, 1963, to May 4, 1964. Each show highlighted a major star, a film genre, particular films, or even a significant time span. Jack Haley, Jr., produced and often wrote the shows, and the mellow voice of actor Joseph Cotten furnished the narration. This episode was the second show of the series, following its maiden episode on Humphrey Bogart.

> Directed and produced by Nicholas Noxon. Series producer, Jack Haley, Jr. Narrated by Joseph Cotten. Edited by John Soh. Music by Elmer Bernstein. Released to NBC Television by David Wolper Productions and United Artists Television on October 7, 1963. 30 minutes. **Cast**: Theda Bara, Joan Crawford, Linda Foster, Betty Grable, Rita Hayworth, Eileen O'Neill.

Synopsis: The changing image of women in the movies: the girl next door, the vamp, the blonde bombshell, and the sex kitten. What each generation of moviegoers thought of as the ideal woman.

* * *

The series was sponsored by Timex Watches and was sold to 30 countries and 65 markets in South America, Australia, Asia, and Europe. Some critics never liked David Wolper's method of putting together his frequent documentaries. One critic referred to them as "so-called entertainment documentaries" and to Wolper as a "snip and glue producer."

Reviews

"Ranks as one of the best of its kind behind-the-scenes look at classic Hollywood ever to be documented." *CB: Cinephilia and Beyond*.

"[The series] is the whole fabulous Hollywood story." *Broadcasting-Telecasting*, 1963.

"I remember this series as if I had seen it last night. Entertaining, informative, and breathtaking.... Equivalent to a course in film and Hollywood cinema." Modern-day commentator.

"Not a serious scholarly effort.... It would take much more sincere documentarians later to make something worthy of its subject." Modern-day commentator.

The Love Goddesses (1965) [Documentary]

Directed by Saul Turell. Produced by Graeme Ferguson and Saul Turell. Narrated by Carl King. Music by Percy Faith. Edited by Nat Greene. Distributed by Walter Reade-Sterling and Continental Distributing and released on March 3, 1965. 87 minutes.

Cast: Theda Bara, Agnes Ayres, Brigitte Bardot, Richard Barthelmess, Ingrid Bergman, Clara Bow, Clive Brook, Louise Brooks, Horst Buchholz, Maurice Chevalier, Montgomery Clift, Claudette Colbert, Gary Cooper, Joan Crawford, Marion Davies, Bette Davis, Lya de Putti, Marlene Dietrich, Anita Ekberg, Norman Foster, Clark Gable, Greta Garbo, Ava Gardner, John Gilbert, Lillian Gish, Louise Glaum, Betty Grable, Cary Grant, Jean Harlow, Laurence Harvey, Sessue Hayakawa, Rita Hayworth, Brigitte Helm, Audrey Hepburn, Emil Jannings, Ruby Keeler, Annette Kellerman, Deborah Kerr, Hedy Lamarr, Dorothy Lamour, Gina Lollobrigida, Carole Lombard, Sophia Loren, Myrna Loy, Jeanette MacDonald, Jayne Mansfield, Mae Marsh, Herbert Marshall, Adolphe Menjou, Ray Milland, Hayley Mills, Marilyn Monroe, Mae Murray, Nita Naldi, Pola Negri, Gregory Peck, Dick Powell, Esther Ralston, Ginger Rogers, Heather Sears, Simone Signoret, Barbara Stanwyck, Gloria Swanson, Sylvia Syms, Elizabeth Taylor, Shirley Temple, Gene Tierney, Lana Turner, Rudolph Valentino, Fannie Ward, Mae West, Henry Wilcoxon.

Synopsis: Features some of the so-called sex goddesses of their time, beginning with the silent movie era. The documentary shows the changes made in the depiction of sex in the cinema up to the 1960s.

Reviews

"There is much criticism to be leveled [at] another of those film clip compilations spanning the years. It suffers mainly from sins of omission, not inclusion. As a definitive full-blown work, the picture sags disjointedly.... Some of the prolonged vintage sequences are fascinating, yet historically the picture is wobbly." *New York Times*, March 3, 1965.

"A bit more interesting than anticipated, largely because of some interesting footage from the silents and early talkies. The trouble with pictures like this is that they tend to build their theories around the footage they have available." *Village Voice*, May 20, 1965.

Hollywood Babylon (1972) [Docudrama]

Directed by Van Guylder. Produced by Marvin Miller. Written for the screen by L.K. Farbella; Based on the book by Kenneth Anger. Music by Allan Alper. Cinematography by Henning Schellerup. Costumes by Kay Schellerup. Produced by I.A.E.; distributed by Aquarius Releasing and released to theaters on February 7, 1972. 87 minutes.

Cast: Live appearances include: Roger Gentry, Myron Griffith, Ashley Phillips, Uschi Digard, Marland Proctor aka Lloyd Allen, Maria Arnold, Dave Hagle, Matt Hewitt, Al Ward, Joe Stinson, Jane Allyson, Nora Wieternik, Suzanne Fields, Bunny Bronstein. **Archival appearances**: Theda Bara, Clara Bow, Al St. John, Roscoe "Fatty" Arbuckle, Buster Keaton, Wallace Beery, Raymond Hatton, Marie Dressler, John Bunny, Charles Chaplin, William S. Hart, Tom Mix, Tony (the horse), Buck Jones, Ava Gardner, Henry Ford, Audrey Hepburn, Brigitte Bardot, Sophia Loren, Marilyn Monroe, Mary Pickford, Elizabeth Taylor.

Synopsis: Using film clips, live re-creations (including some quasi-soft porn), and an uncredited narrator, it purports to tell the true story behind some of Hollywood's most salacious scandals. It is based on the book of the same name, first published in France in 1959 and in the United States in 1965. An updated and expanded version was published as *Hollywood Babylon II* in 1984.

* * *

Beginning in 1947 Kenneth Anger made a series of controversial short films, often with homoerotic themes. He also gained a solid reputation as a film historian, although some of his assertions over the decades have been called into question. That includes much of what is included in the book and this film.

Review

"Most sexploitation pictures are beneath criticism and [this] is no exception. But it cannot go without comment because it portrays the boudoir activities of actual people, some of whom are still very much alive.... It is a trashy pseudo-documentary interspersed with orgies and other starry peccadilloes.... Made on the cheap." *New York Times*, February 18, 1972.

Hollywood (U.S. Title: *Hollywood: A Celebration of the American Silent Film*) (1980) [Television Documentary Mini-Series]

Directed, produced, and written by Kevin Brownlow and David Gill. Narrated by James Mason. Music by Carl Davis. Edited by Trevor Waite. Initial episode released in the United Kingdom by Thames Television on January 8, 1980; released in the United States on February 9, 1980. 13 episodes in 676 minutes.
Cast: Live appearances include: Colleen Moore, Lillian Gish, Douglas Fairbanks, Jr., Leatrice Joy, King Vidor, Gloria Swanson, Blanche Sweet, Bessie Love, Hal Roach, Frank Capra, George Cukor, Janet Gaynor, Louise Brooks, Dolores Costello. **Archival appearances include**: Theda Bara, Renee Adoree, Bebe Daniels, Marie Dressler, Victor Fleming, John Ford, William Fox, Joseph Kennedy, Charles Lindbergh, Nita Naldi, Ramon Novarro, Alla Nazimova, Warner Oland, Will Rogers, Norma Talmadge, Raoul Walsh, William Wellman.

Synopsis: Kevin Brownlow and David Gill, considered among the world's greatest experts on silent film, survey its history from its beginnings in the crude nickelodeon days to the final sophisticated flowering of the silent film art form. What went on behind the camera, as well as in front of it, is presented through numerous interviews with silent stars, directors, writers, editors, cinematographers, and stunt performers.

* * *

The series, consisting of 13 episodes of 50 minutes each, ran in the United States until April 1980, garnering rapturous reviews for its comprehensiveness, erudition, and entertainment value. It won BAFTA awards in the UK, where it aired on the ITV channel.

Reviews

"Abounds in priceless interviews.... A fascinating, meticulously developed, and passionate look at the early stages of the Hollywood film industry. An investigative odyssey through the stepping stones on which film was transformed from a technological curiosity to a vibrant entertainment and business industry." *CB: Cinephilia and Beyond.*

"Here is the definitive video history of the art of the American silent film. This documentary was literally produced in the nick of time, as many of those interviewed would be deceased in a few short years, their wonderful memories lost forever." Modern-day commentator.

Hollywood Sex Symbols (aka *Hollywood's Sex Symbols*) (1988) [VHS Documentary]

No production data was available.
Released by Front Row Entertainment on August 5, 1988. 40 minutes.
Cast: Theda Bara, Brigitte Bardot, Richard Burton, Errol Flynn, Clark Gable, Cary Grant, Rita Hayworth, Sophia Loren, Jane Mansfield, Marilyn Monroe, Paul Newman, Tyrone Power, Elvis Presley, Robert Redford, Elizabeth Taylor, Rudolph Valentino, Mae West.

Synopsis: Using clips from interviews, publicity events, premieres, and photographs—but no film clips—so-called male and female sex symbols are shown. Most footage is given to Sophia Loren and Marilyn Monroe, but screen time for each performer is very brief.

* * *

The advertising tagline was "Meet the beautiful people of the Hollywood screen." Canada-based Front Row Entertainment was a distributor of VHS programming.

Review

"A thrown-together mess.... The footage is of poor quality and of little interest. The film quality is uniformly bad.... Very poor and easily skipped." Modern-day commentator.

The Casting Couch (1995) [VHS Documentary]

Directed by John Sealey. Produced by John Sealey and Alan Selwyn. Written by Selwyn Ford [i.e., Derek Ford and Alan Selwyn]. Based on the book *The Casting Couch: Making It in Hollywood* by Selwyn Ford. Presented by Susan George. Music by The Letherbridge and the

Parker Ellis Trio. Cinematography by Freddie Beach. Edited by Marc Corrance. Released in the United Kingdom by Lumiere Video on November 13, 1995. 57 minutes.
Cast: Theda Bara, Tallulah Bankhead, Elaine Barrie, John Barrymore, Clara Bow, Charles Boyer, Louise Brooks, Charles Chaplin, Joan Crawford, Marion Davies, Cecil B. DeMille, Marlene Dietrich, Greta Garbo, Paulette Goddard, Betty Grable, Jean Harlow, Will Hayes, William Randolph Hearst, Grace Kelly, Hedy Lamarr, Carole Landis, Florence Lawrence, Louis B. Mayer, Marilyn Monroe, Louella Parsons, Mary Pickford, Ginger Rogers, Jane Russell, Barbara Stanwyck, Gloria Swanson, Rudolph Valentino, Lupe Velez, Mae West, Darryl Zanuck.

Synopsis: Many women who became stars in the 1920s and 1930s had to endure the so-called casting couch, which meant being intimate (willingly or not) with influential movie men. Aspiring starlets were often exploited. The long-rumored and supposedly genuine Joan Crawford stag movies and a Marilyn Monroe striptease are featured.

Review

"Well-worn tales of a Hollywood for which the parade had long passed by.... If you're a nostalgia nut this is worth seeking out.... Covers much of the same ground as Kenneth Anger's *Hollywood Babylon* books." Modern-day commentator.

Empire of the Censors (1995) (BBC)
[Television Documentary]

Written and directed by Saskia Baron. Produced by Paul Kerr and Nigel Algar. Hosted by Richard E. Grant. Edited by Andy Taylor. Released by Barraclough Carey Productions to the BBC on May 27, 1995. 120 minutes.
Cast includes: Theda Bara, Marlon Brando, Louise Brooks, Ellen Burstyn, Leslie Caron, Kevin Costner, Joe Dallesandro, Mia Farrow, Bridget Fonda, Mel Gibson, Graham Greene, Adolf Hitler, Dustin Hoffman, Mick Jagger, Boris Karloff, Deborah Kerr, Stanley Kubrick, Bela Lugosi, Malcolm McDowell, Vanessa Redgrave, Ken Russell, Max Schreck, Quentin Tarantino, Dirk Bogarde, Roman Polanski, Margaret Thatcher, Oliver Stone.

Synopsis: Part One deals with British censorship leading up to the 1990s, and the frequent attempts to cut or ban films as diverse as *Battleship Potemkin, Last Tango in Paris,* and *A Clockwork Orange*. Part Two deals with the 1990s efforts to scissor what the censors called the "nasties" in current cinema and video releases. Interviews were held with filmmakers, censors, and journalists.

* * *

Presumably, Theda Bara's films were as much scrutinized by British censors as they were by American censors in the 1910s. This is the second film in which she inadvertently appears with Adolf Hitler.

The program was televised as a part of the BBC's "Forbidden" weekend.

Review

"The medium may have changed, but the hysteria of moral panic and censorship remains as present as ever.... Most interesting are the interviews with censors going over the editing and approvals process of various films, classic, tawdry or both." Modern-day commentator.

Woman with the Hungry Eyes (2006) [Documentary]

Directed and narrated by Hugh Munro Neely. Produced and edited by Andie Hicks and Hugh Munro Neely. Executive producer, Hugh Hefner. Cinematography by Hugh Munro Neely. Released by Timeline Films on May 2, 2006. 100 minutes.
Cast: Live appearances include: Robert Birchard, Edward Brabin, Dana Delany, Miles Kreuger, Phillip Dye, Eve Golden, Ronald Genini, Daniel Selznick. **Archival appearances include**: Theda Bara, Charles Chaplin, Alice Eis, Douglas Fairbanks, James Finlayson, Mabel Frenyear, D.W. Griffith, Runa Hodges, Stuart Holmes, Edward Jose, Fred Malatesta, Eileen Percy, Mary Pickford, Wyndham Standing, Norma Talmadge, Pearl White, Claire Whitney.

Synopsis: The well-detailed story of Theda Bara, told with extant film clips, and reenactments. A discussion of her films and highlights of her life story are provided by several experts.

Reviews

"Well made, supported by interviews with film historians, solid research, and creative use of stills and sound." *Kamera.co.uk*.

"Traces the mystique and magic of Theda Bara, and discovers a great deal of wonderful surprises along the way.... Offers a rich lineup of experts." *Filmthreat*.

Why Be Good: Sexuality and Censorship in Early Cinema (2007) [Documentary]

Directed and produced by Elaina Archer. Written by Elaina Archer and Scott Eyman. Narrated by Diane Lane. Music by Maria Newman. Cinematography by Todd Friedrichsen. Editing by Todd Friedrichsen and Elaina Archer. Produced by A & F Productions and Playboy Enterprises; distributed and released by Alta Loma Entertainment on May 23, 2007. 70 minutes.
Cast: **Live appearances**: Diane Lane, Chris Basinger, Jeanine Basinger, Carl Beauchamp, Richard de Mille, Leatrice Joy Fountain, A.C. Lyles, Bob Mitchell, Barry Paris, Maria Riva, Michael Schlesinger, Budd Schulberg, Kevin Thomas, Mark Viera, Marc Wanamaker, William Wellman, Jr., Michael Westmore, Holly Madison, Betsy Moore, Paul Tucci. **Archival appearances**: Theda Bara, Roscoe "Fatty" Arbuckle, Louise Brooks, Clara Bow, Charles Chaplin, Joan Crawford, Bebe Daniels, Bette Davis, Cecil B. DeMille, Marlene Dietrich, Douglas Fairbanks, Greta Garbo, John Gilbert, Cary Grant, D.W. Griffith, Texas Guinan, Ann Harding, Jean Harlow, Sessue Hayakawa, Will Hayes, William Randolph Hearst, Leslie Howard, Myrna Loy, Mary Miles Minter, Colleen Moore, Owen Moore, Pola Negri, Mabel Normand, Mary Pickford, Edna Purviance, Virginia Rappe, Theodore Roosevelt, Barbara Stanwyck, Gloria Swanson, Rudolph Valentino, Fannie Ward, Mae West, Woodrow Wilson.

Synopsis: In the days before the introduction of the restrictive Production Code in the 1930s and the current-day ratings system, there were some state and city censor boards. Frequently, there was nothing to prevent the movies from being as "wide open" as they chose to be. Interviews with former leading ladies and movie clips look at an era where often anything went.

Ultimately sex scandals, such as that which befell Roscoe Arbuckle, led to a closer scrutiny of Hollywood by church and community groups. In the 1910s the films of Theda Bara were often drastically cut or even banned outright in some localities by censors.

Review

"More a compilation of mini-biographical profiles than a scholarly history of the period.... Largely told piecemeal through the careers of a number of significant actresses, with Rudolph Valentino being the only male actor discussed in any depth. Nevertheless [the film] does feature some solid interviews." *Videolibrarian.com.*

Sex, Censorship and The Silver Screen. Disc One: *The Early Decades* (2007) [Documentary]

Released by Films for the Humanities and Sciences, 2007. 51 minutes.
No production data.
Cast: Theda Bara, Rudolph Valentino, Erich von Stroheim, Greta Garbo, Joan Crawford, Marlene Dietrich, Jean Harlow, Busby Berkeley, Mae West, Barbara Stanwyck.

Synopsis: The discovery of sex as a surefire way to attract audiences, and the reactions of censors, civil authorities, and religious institutions. Covers the rise of Will Hays and the reactions to such scandals as the Roscoe Arbuckle case. Includes footage from *A Fool There Was, Possessed,* and *Klondike Annie.* First part of a four-part series that examines censorship into the 1990s.

The Many Faces of Cleopatra (2009) [Documentary]

Directed and written by Phillip Dye. Produced by Phillip Dye and Dante Pugliese. Narrated by Brinke Stevens. Edited by Kent Hagen. Released by Passport International Entertainment on December 8, 2009. 90 minutes.
Cast: **Live appearances**: Robert Birchard, Rhonda Fleming, Anthony Slide, Leonor Varela.
Archival appearances: Theda Bara, Colette Colbert, Florence Lawrence, Virginia Mayo.

Synopsis: Cleopatra, fabled queen of Egypt, has been portrayed in the silent cinema by Theda Bara, Helen Gardner, and Florence Lawrence, and later by Claudette Colbert, Elizabeth Taylor, Sophia Loren, Rhonda Fleming, and Leonor Varela. This documentary focuses on both the actresses and those behind the scenes who brought the films to life, including Cecil B. DeMille, and the writers, cinematographers, producers, and directors.

Fragments: Surviving Pieces of Lost Films (2011) (TCM) [Documentary]

Written by Randy Haberkamp. Produced by Randy Haberkamp and Jeffrey Masino. Music and sound by Michael Mortilla. Released to television by Flicker Alley on April 3, 2011. 110 minutes.

Cast: Live appearances: Diana Serra Cary, Heather Linville, Mike Mashon, Michael Pogorzelski. **Archival appearances:** Theda Bara, King Baggot(t), Clara Bow, Louise Brooks, Lon Chaney, Betty Compson, Stan Laurel and Oliver Hardy, Emil Jannings, Harry Langdon, Winnie Lightner, Nick Lucas, Victor McLaglen, Colleen Moore, George Raft, Lawrence Tibbett.

Synopsis: Among the fragments featured are the final reels of John Ford's *The Village Blacksmith*, Victor Fleming's *The Way of All Flesh* (the only lost film containing an Oscar-winning performance), George Loane Tucker's *The Miracle Man*, and the only known remaining few seconds of Theda Bara's *Cleopatra*, directed by J. Gordon Edwards.

* * *

Diana Serra Cary (1918–2020), was the 1920s child star Baby Peggy. The film preservationists are Heather Linville, Mike Mashon, and Michael Pogorzelski. Cary discusses her mostly lost film *The Darling of New York*.

Reviews

"What we see here are priceless little bits of rare films now lost to time…. The facts that the clips are short makes us wish we could see more." Modern-day commentator.

"Fascinating documentary that was almost more frustrating to watch than enlightening. I want to see the full versions of some of these films! What we saw was tantalizing." Modern-day commentator.

Arena, Series 34: "Screen Goddesses" (2012) (BBC) [Television program]

Arena is a British television show, produced by the BBC, which has run since 1965 and has produced many hundreds of programs about the arts. It has collected numerous awards, including several British Emmys and a Grammy.
Directed and produced by David Thompson. Narrated by Elizabeth McGovern. Edited by Alex Jones. Released to television by Illumination Films on December 22, 2012. 60 minutes.
Cast: Theda Bara, Brigitte Bardot, Ingrid Bergman, Clara Bow, Louise Brooks, Julie Christie, Joan Crawford, George Cukor, Bette Davis, Dolores Del Rio, Catherine Deneuve, Marlene Dietrich, Anita Ekberg, Jane Fonda, Greta Garbo, Ava Gardner, Lillian Gish, Jean Harlow, Rita Hayworth, Audrey Hepburn, Grace Kelly, Hedy Lamarr, Florence Lawrence, Sophia Loren, Marilyn Monroe, Barbara Stanwyck, Gloria Swanson, Elizabeth Taylor, Joseph von Sternberg, Mae West, Billy Wilder, Anna May Wong.

Synopsis: "Documentary about the early female movie stars…. The star system was born with an archetypal bad girl, the vampish Theda Bara…. The era drew to a close with the supreme fame of Elizabeth Taylor and the tragic death of Marilyn Monroe." *Digiguide.tv*

* * *

Theda Bara is shown in a very brief clip from *A Fool There Was*.

Russia Not Today: October 1917 (2017) [Television program]

This was a satirical Russian program which ran for 111 episodes over 10 seasons from October 2013 to January 2020. Theda Bara is seen in stills taken from *Cleopatra*. Her inclusion comes because the release of *Cleopatra* in October 1917 occurred in the same month as the Bolsheviks' final seizure of power. Defeated Russian social democrat leader Alexander Kerensky is also featured.

> Directed by Irek Ibatulin and Vitaly Kosarev. Produced by Irek Ibatulin. Written by Vitaly Kosarev. Released to television on November 7, 2017. 25 minutes.
> **Cast**: Theda Bara, Alexander Kerensky, Vitaly Kosarev.

Lost Cleopatra (2017) [Documentary]

> Directed, produced, edited, and written by Phillip Dye. [Original film of *Cleopatra* written by Adrian Johnson, with assistance from William Shakespeare, H. Rider Haggard, Victorien Sardou, and Emile Moreau.] Narrated by Brinke Stevens. Released by Trench Art Productions on October 14, 2017. 87 minutes.
> **Cast**: Theda Bara, Art Acord, Genevieve Blinn, Henri De Vries, Dorothy Drake, Delle Duncan, Edith Emmons, Thurston Hall, Fritz Leiber, Virginia Leiber, Herschell Mayall, Albert Roscoe, Hector Sarno, Ruth St. Denis.

Synopsis: A reconstruction of the lost 1917 epic *Cleopatra*, starring Theda Bara as the Egyptian queen, with the last known surviving clip of the original film and more than 500 stills taken from the 1917 film.

* * *

This documentary was released on the 100th anniversary of the release of the original 1917 film. A companion book, also titled *Lost Cleopatra* by Phillip Dye, about the production of the 1917 film, was published in 2020. The original film is one of the most sought-after "lost" silent films. Any remaining prints are believed to have been lost in a 1937 fire at the Fox studio vaults in New Jersey.

Onstage

In 1908, 23-year-old Theodosia Goodman headed to New York with the ambition to become a theater actress. She was said to have been involved in amateur theatrics in Cincinnati. How she fared in the years between 1908 and 1915, when she suddenly morphed into the improbable Theda Bara, is still not known with complete certainty. Rumor had it that she might have worked in that era's rich Yiddish theater, based around Manhattan's Second Avenue. If she did know any Yiddish, it would have been through her Polish immigrant father. She did travel to England in 1910, where she sometimes claimed to have toured with a Shakespeare company.

In 1918 an interviewer told Bara that a friend had seen her playing minor roles in a New York City Yiddish theater years before. At first she replied with a non sequitur, then icily responded that she had never been on any stage except in Paris. At other times she also claimed that she had worked with stock companies for a season or two. She always remained vague about specifics. They might not have fit in with the star image she so carefully nurtured.

According to Hollywood gossipmonger Hedda Hopper, they were together in a 1911 touring company of a musical called *The Quaker Girl*. Hopper describes Miss Goodman, or De Cappet as she was calling herself, as trying to use a bad French accent. "Theodosia played a Frenchwoman with an accent that wouldn't fool a five year old …. She was then a believer in spiritualism and read about it constantly."

She did attain an appearance on Broadway in 1908's *The Devil*. Later, she would most often "forget" about this small role, claiming she had begun on Broadway already a star in *The Blue Flame*—just as she "forgot" being an extra before she became a star in *A Fool There Was*.

The Devil (1908)

The Devil was the first major success of Hungarian playwright Ferenc (later Franz) Molnar. Its subtitle was *A Tragedy of Heart and Conscience*. There were two versions of the play on Broadway at the same time in 1908. The more successful was the one with George Arliss in the title role. It opened on August 18, 1908, and ran for 175 performances. Appearing with Arliss was his wife Florence Arliss (sometimes billed as Mrs. George Arliss) and leading actress Emily Stevens.

The Edwin Stevens version opened on the same day, running for 87 performances. In her first known Broadway appearance, Theda Bara played a small role as Madame Schleswig, a party guest. In the cast list she appeared as Theodosia De Cappet. Since she had been spelling her stage name De Coppet, this was either a typographical error or she was trying out alternate spellings. She did not join the touring company of the play.

The Quaker Girl (1911)

The Quaker Girl was a musical which opened on Broadway in 1911 and ran for almost 250 performances. Theodosia De Cappet played French model Diane in the touring company. The actress playing the same role on Broadway was Olga Petrova, who would be a rival vampire in films.

Just Like John (1912)

Just Like John was a three-act comedy which opened and closed on Broadway in August of 1912, lasting a mere 16 performances. It was written by George Broadhurst and Mark Swan, and it was coproduced by the famous impresario William Brady. Broadhurst later built the famous New York theater which he named after himself. Theda Bara was part of the 1912 touring company, which essentially languished in the theatrical backwaters.

The Blue Flame (1920)

Background

Theda Bara was out of pictures for the time being, but her name still had cachet among certain audiences. Broadway producer Al H. Woods (born Aladore Herman in Hungary) had been a Broadway producer since the very early days of the 20th century. Judged only by the schlocky nature of *The Blue Flame*, he might have seemed little more than a hustler, but he had brought many respected plays to Broadway and would continue to do so until the early 1940s.

No doubt Theda Bara was anxious to establish herself as a "legitimate" actress after her less-than-stellar final year in the movies. Her early publicity, which claimed that she had had a distinguished Paris stage career, had long been debunked. During the Fox years, she had said she wanted to perform "heavy emotional roles" in the theater. In a January 14, 1920, interview with the *Los Angeles Times*, Bara said that the play, still called *Lost Souls*, would open its run in New York. That was the usual order of things; plays opened on Broadway and if successful went on tour.

That could have been her hope, but Al Woods surely knew better with a play of this low caliber. She also now claimed that she had never appeared in "the spoken drama" in all her life. Bara had already been contradicted by her own publicity. On January 7, 1920, the *New York Clipper* ran an advertisement for the play which referred to her as a "screen star and former stock actress."

The play was bought from its author, Leta Vance Nicholson, a scenario writer. Woods estimated that the play and a film version would bring in at least $250,000. When it opened, it was credited as being written by George V. Hobart and John Willard, based on a play of the same name by Leta Vance Nicholson. *The Blue Flame* was variously described as being in four acts and as being in three acts and seven scenes. Theda Bara had a half-interest in the play. Even though she had said many times that years of vampire roles had worn her down, Bara and Woods could hear the cha-ching of box office gold.

Synopsis: Scientist John Varnum has developed a device to resurrect the dead. His innocent fiancée Ruth Gordon loves him, but she is unhappy that he is an atheist. A stranger (perhaps a heavenly messenger?) reproaches him for his godlessness. At the height of a storm, his beloved Ruth is electrocuted by one his machines. Varnum uses his invention to resurrect her, but her soul has visibly left her body as a blue flame.

She is now changed from a pious girl to a wanton vampire. She and Varnum marry, but Ruth pursues young Larry Winston. She seduces him, gets him addicted to cocaine, and while in Chinatown steals a valuable emerald from an idol. Told it is sacred and that she will be killed for her sacrilege, Ruth manages to have another woman killed in her place.

Now she goes after another victim, Ned Maddox. She kills him for his insurance money and pins the murder on someone else. She is finally arrested. Just as it seems she could not become any more evil, the whole sordid business turns out to be a dream that John Varnum is having. Ruth has not been killed, nor has she lost her soul. It is now Varnum's turn to embrace the true faith; he destroys his machine.

* * *

This could have been the plot of any of the deep-dyed vamp movies in which Theda Bara had appeared. Ferdinande Martin of *Destruction*, Juliette De Cordova from *Gold and the Woman*, or the Princess Petrovich of *The Tiger Woman* would have welcomed Ruth Gordon as a sister in sin. John Varnum, the unwitting cause of Ruth Gordon's rampage, was played by Alan Dinehart, who had a worthy career on the stage and in films.

Broadway playwright Owen Davis claimed *The Blue Flame* was based on his 1910 novel *Lola*. He had written it as a play the following year, and staged it in a series of matinees with such stars as Laurette Taylor. It was then made into a film re-titled *Without a Soul*, starring Clara Kimball Young.

Beginning in February 1920, the play had some very remunerative runs in cities like Boston, Washington, Pittsburgh, and Philadelphia. Curious crowds lined up to see their former screen idol. In Boston, *Variety* reported, the show was "one of the theatrical events of the season.... It was necessary to call for extra police to hold the crowd in check. House is sold out for the entire two weeks, but it is believed that Theda can be prevailed on to play extra matinees." When an associate of Al Woods was asked what made Theda Bara such a draw he replied: "William Fox paid $2 million to make her the best-known picture actress in the world. The result of that is now being reaped by Theda Bara."

Indeed, she did reap. Her guarantee for *The Blue Flame* was a minimum of $1,500 per week plus 50 percent of the net profits. In the two weeks of the Boston run she earned $10,700. Bara was, so publicity said, to have been taken to and from the theater in a coach pulled by several pairs of milk-white horses. The idea of that queenly conveyance was dropped. Police had to be called to control the crowds at the stage door. If the weather had not been inclement it is estimated that several thousand people would have gathered. In Pittsburgh the play drew in $19,000 in one week, equivalent to almost $262,000 in 2022 terms.

Theda Bara insisted on bringing the play into New York where, according to Al Woods, she had been assured it would be a smash hit by a fortuneteller. One reason she may have wanted to open there (besides misplaced optimism) was this report: "Theda

Bara, it is said, is not finding trouping to her liking, even in a play which attracts such bad notices and good receipts, and is accordingly thinking of ending her tour. It is being extended week by week as Miss Bara's permission is obtained." In 1935 Al Woods was still claiming that he had advised against a New York run.

The play opened at the Schubert Theater on March 15, 1920, and closed a bit more than two weeks later after forty-eight performances. Little did she dream that she would virtually be laughed off the stage by the New York critics. Acerbic Alexander Woollcott said of Bara's performance: "She speaks her lines distinctly and rather like a young girl at a high school commencement. She displays a fine self-possession which enabled her to proceed with unflinching gravity even when the audience lost control of itself and shook with laughter."

He called her performance "punk." He also pointed out the Mid–Atlantic accent (he did not call it that) which she increasingly used. Some have attributed it to her English husband, but she was not then married to Charles Brabin. It can be heard in her radio interviews in which she pronounces words like "chance" as "chahnce."

Woollcott seemed personally offended by the play. In a review of John Barrymore's *Richard III* he said it was 962 times more worth seeing than *The Blue Flame*. He also compared it to Eugene O'Neill's *Beyond the Horizon* which had been a failure on the road, but a hit on Broadway. About *The Blue Flame* he went on to say: "No doubt sales on the road happened in advance of the play's arrival, before it dawned on each city what manner of actress in what manner of play has passed by."

Theda Bara reacted by placing the blame not on the play or on herself, but the audience. "The first night was a terrible ordeal. I had a cold and was so nervous that my voice went back on me. I thought I wouldn't live through some of the long speeches. My throat was tight and I felt I couldn't make a sound. Someone told me to go out and apologize for my voice, but I wouldn't. I suppose my fighting blood was up. Many of those in the audience were people who hated me. I don't know why they hate me but they do. They do not know me personally and I haven't done anything to them, but they hate me. And I wouldn't go out and apologize to them."

This sounds like a reworking of her claim, during her movie star days, about children and jealous wives avoiding her, or even hurling imprecations at her. It was a case of crying all the way to the bank because Bara still profited. After the first week of the run her profit-sharing agreement netted her $4,400. Among the reasons given by Bara for the play's sudden New York demise was that sudden illness caused her to end the run prematurely. It was falsely rumored that there was a bright side to all this: Theda Bara had married one Tom Bodkin in Pittsburgh in February 1920.

Variety reported that after the big New York opening attendance during the first week was 25 percent below what it had been on the road. The top price was $3.00 (equivalent to $42.00 in 2022), quite a bargain when Broadway prices can now be in the hundreds of dollars. A four-week ticket agency buy helped, but it was not going to be extended. Most of the money from the New York run came from agencies stuck with tickets and offering them at cut-rate prices.

The Woods office had wanted the play to open at the end of the New York season and then go back on the profitable road. If it had opened at the beginning of the season and flopped another road tour would be compromised. At the end of the run in April 1920, Theda Bara announced her return to the screen as head of her own company. It was reported that "she has been busy gathering a number of stories for her use. Her plan is to make at least two films during the summer and then return to go on tour with *The Blue Flame.*" The films and a further tour were never made. Before her New York fate was known it had been reported that she would appear in an unnamed historical play in the fall 1920 season.

* * *

Supposedly quoting a headline that read "1,200 Insane Saved at a Theater Fire," an April 1920 *Moving Picture World* quipped, "Maybe it was at *The Blue Flame.*"

The play's reputation continued to haunt it. More than two years after its New York fiasco, *Variety* referred to it again in their review of another poorly-received play. "The Cherry Sisters, *The Blue Flame*, and other inconsequential theatrical concoctions have no need to bear odious comparisons when bad plays are discussed." The five Cherry Sisters had been known for their deliberately bad vaudeville act, causing audiences to hurl vegetables and other nonlethal missiles at them.

In a 1920 article intriguingly titled "Confessions of Theda Bara," *Photoplay* writer Agnes Smith continued the magazine's attitude of antipathy toward the actress. Written at the time *The Blue Flame* was still running, Smith muses about Bara's film career and her present stage appearance. She claims to be "afraid" to meet Theda Bara for an interview. An excerpt from the article follows; other excerpts are quoted elsewhere.

"Only a few nights before I had heard her [Bara as Ruth Gordon] pronounce in a hideously strained voice these immortal—and immoral—lines: 'Let's get married. All I need is a legal pretext and then I will show you how cold I am. Kiss me, dearie.' ... Theda Bara's artistic sins have been many. In *The Blue Flame* she hasn't reformed artistically. She still blames it on the public. That is her greatest sin—this taking for granted that the public likes the cheap, the impossible, and the vulgar."

Besides the lines quoted above by Agnes Smith, another oft-quoted line from the play was: "I want to be so bad that I shall be remembered." (That sounds like a summation of Theda Bara's film persona.) Other favorites were: "Did you bring the cocaine?" and "I've got to have $85,000 in a hurry!" and "You make my heart laugh, and I feel like a woman of the streets."

If some of these quoted lines were not unintentionally comic enough, there were some more official gags going the rounds. All of them used her surname: "Could Theda Bara another set of criticisms?"; "Theda Bara's share of the gate will require a wheelbara to move"; "Despite the terrible reviews the pallbaras haven't been selected"; and "Seems the New York critics can't Bara a scream queen on the stage." This next one actually came from the review of the *New York Tribune*: "Perhaps *The Blue Flame* is not a perfect title for Miss Bara's play. Why not 'Tenting on the Old Vamp Ground'?"

Another aspect of the play that might draw laughs from a modern audience was the unimaginative names of the Chinese characters: Ah Foo, Quong Toy, Wung Ming, and Ling Foo. At least three of them were portrayed by white actors.

In 1914 a film with the same title was released by the Selig Studio. It was described as a detective drama.

Reviews

"A.H. Woods is one of the theatrical producers who is menacing motion pictures. He took Theda Bara and put her into a play which is probably the worst show ever produced.

He doesn't explain that Theda Bara as a motion picture star is no more. She wouldn't do any longer in motion pictures, so she went on the stage." *Picture-Play Magazine*, 1920.

"To see a crude actress, no matter how famous she is in the films, unfamiliar with the rudiments of dramatic art, strutting about in a series of maudlin episodes is not really worth fifteen minutes of time." *New York Dramatic Mirror*, 1920.

"The audience that had assembled to greet Theda Bara was divided into two factions: her friends and those who had come in the same spirit that sends people to bullfights. It was a terrible opening and a terrible play. It was considerably worse than anything Theda Bara attempted in pictures. It looked like a stage burlesque of one of her films." *Photoplay*, 1920.

"'Did you bring the cocaine?' demanded Miss Bara as the heroine. It was such a determined, boldfaced intention of being an immediate and unmistakable vampire that the audience fairly shouted in gleeful recognition. The vampire of vampires on the screen was going to be as devilish on the boards in spoken drama." *New York Evening Telegraph*, March 1920.

"The thing is not indecent, it is only offensive in its silliness. The most encouraging feature of the evening's exhibition is that it was received with derisive laughter by the curious audience which packed every corner of the large theater." *New York Evening Post*, March 1920.

"The first showing proved Miss Bara has some histrionic ability, but that is also true of the sixteen year old amateur who takes part in the school play.... The play surely does play on the credulity of the auditor, and then to top it off the incredulities are made a dream which converts the unbeliever to a believer. It surely does look as if the piece with its star will attract excellent business as a freak attraction." *Variety*, February 18, 1920. (Washington, D.C., review.)

"Miss Theda Bara played the role without violating any of the city ordinances, but she was not so very good either. At no time during the evening did the earth open up and swallow up the author, the star, and all the company, but Jonah was eaten by a whale for much less." *New York Tribune*, March 1920.

"Don't let any highbrow kid you into thinking Theda Bara isn't worth seeing. In it, around it, over it, on it, all of it; literally Miss Bara was the show.... [She] showed careful training. She has not quite learned how to get around the stage, but otherwise she was satisfactory enough. Her voice, while it was to an extent still self-conscious and a bit affected, had nevertheless pleasant even notes in it.... Miss Bara tried to sustain an emotional climax that was way beyond her." *Variety*, March 1920. (New York review.)

"Picture a soulless woman gallivanting around New York. Nothing is too bad for her to do. *The Blue Flame*, a crude, timeworn melodrama that it is, is entertaining when the lead role is played by Theda Bara. Her voice is pleasing and at times she is almost pretty. Miss Bara deserves a great deal of credit for her work in this, her first legitimate show of importance." *Camera!* April 1920.

In a retrospective review written six months after the play's opening, the *New York Times* recalled: "Last Spring there came to us from the road an unbelievably preposterous play, a melodramatic monstrosity concocted to exhibit on the stage one Theda Bara, a movie celebrity.... The piece was so wildly ludicrous that all through its most serious scenes the first New York audience fairly shook with laughter. Thereafter, the disposition of the New York public not to attend at all became so apparent that the play took the hint and, after a brief and defiant engagement, departed."

Serpent of the Neva (1929)

Theda Bara developed and began touring the RKO Circuit with a fifteen minute vaudeville sketch called *Serpent of the Neva*, in which she played a Russian spy out to decoy and capture a Bolshevik mastermind. It seems like a retread of her 1917 film *The Rose of Blood*. The sketch apparently debuted in Newark, New Jersey, on August 31, 1929, and in the RKO Jefferson Square Theater in New York City on October 15, 1929. It was mistakenly publicized as her first turn in two-a-day vaudeville. Given the very negative reaction to the sketch it was scrapped.

Review

"An inane, rambling and almost meaningless playlet.... It's utterly ridiculous. What a pity! If there were any reason to believe it, the thing might be accepted as deliberate satire. That Theda Bara should be detached from all the glamorous connotations of her name and seen in surroundings so devastatingly stupid. What transpires is so jumbled it is doubtful whether the average audience will make head or tail of it.... This turn is useless and for Miss Bara a disappointment.... Not that Theda Bara was a bore. On the contrary it was rather delightful as an example of how terrible pseudo-dramatics can be." *Variety*, October 20, 1929.

The Red Devil (1929)

On November 13, 1929, it was announced that a new sketch would replace *Serpent of the Neva*, called *The Red Devil* by playwright and screenwriter Edgar Allan Woolf. It was tried out on November 25, 1929, at RKO Proctor's 86th Street Theatre in New York. The sketch was also played in Yonkers and Buffalo, New York, in November 1929.

Fata Morgana (1931)

Theda Bara was the guest star in *Fata Morgana* with the Bainbridge Stock Company in Minneapolis. She was also reported to be playing it in one night stands on the West Coast. She cut her appearance short when a movie role was supposedly offered. The Ernest Vajda drama had run on Broadway for 120 performances in 1924 with such notables as Emily Stevens and Josephine Hull.

Bella Donna (1934)

Bella Donna was one of the final attempts of Theda Bara to be a presence in the theater, if only in a local Los Angeles-area production. Based on a 1909 novel of the same name by Robert Hichens, *Bella Donna* opened on Broadway in 1912, starring Alla Nazimova. It was made into a silent film three years later with Pauline Frederick; another movie version with Pola Negri came along in 1923.

The perfervid plot involves a London woman who loves luxury, but finds it harder to get men to provide it as she attains middle age. She manages to snare a decent man as her husband and goes with him to Egypt. There she takes up with a decadent potentate, and with the help of a servant plots to poison her husband. The plot is foiled by a surgeon.

In its announcement of the play, *Variety* reported that Theda Bara had last done a "bit" on a stage three years earlier (i.e., *Fata Morgana*). In May 1934 the paper revealed that the producer had had to replace four different casts because they had all been signed for pictures. The play ran for five nights at the Little Theatre in Beverly Hills.

Review

"Miss Bara, despite the melodramatic tone of the character, played with admirable restraint and poise. She was alluring throughout, and especially when highlighted by the golden light of a huge candle. At times her performance was marred slightly by lack of suavity, doubtless induced by first night nervousness, and there was a slight inclination toward older stage technique. Her voice was throatily pleasing." *Los Angeles Times*, May 24, 1934.

Miscellany

This section contains a sampling of Theda Bara-related miscellany: Theda Bar-iana to coin a phrase. These date from the period of her stardom, continuing well into the present day. Because her image from stills and photographs has remained so iconic, there have been many hundreds of items bearing Theda Bara likenesses.

FILMS

Meeting Theda Bara (1918)

Background

The popular newspaper cartoon *Mutt and Jeff* began about 1907 and had made it into the movies about 1916. By the time the movie cartoons ran their course in the 1920s almost 300 of them had been produced. The characters names came into popular usage as a slang term for a couple who are of mismatched height: Mutt being tall and skinny, Jeff diminutive and chubby.

The Film

Directed, written, and produced by Bud Fisher. Released by Bud Fisher Film Corporation; distributed by the Fox Film Corporation on June 23, 1918.

Synopsis: When Jeff inherits a fortune Mutt decides they will become movie producers. After seeing a Theda Bara movie, they want to sign her for a vampire role. Even though she is under contract to Fox, Jeff says he will meet her at the stage door of a movie theater. Mutt laughs at the idea that Bara will emerge in person from a movie theater. He waits for Jeff in a restaurant, not realizing that Theda Bara and Jeff are having dinner behind a screen at the next table.

* * *

American soldiers were still fighting in France when this cartoon screened. A publicity release aimed at the patriotism of exhibitors read: "Captain Bud Fisher's *Mutt and*

Jeff Animated Cartoons: Straight from the trenches to the American people. A weekly message of cheer that will make every soldier's family and friends interested in your theater. Start a good habit! Show them today!"

An attractive colored poster for this film shows Theda Bara in her Cleopatra garb looking demurely out of an apartment window. Jeff stands on a box and barrel waiting to serenade her with a ukulele. Mutt's hat flies off, presumably in excitement at the sight of her.

[Theda Bara: First of the Great Vamps Who Reigned from 1914 to 1919] [Title reconstructed] (1922?)

These clips are purportedly from some test shots made by the Selznick Studio about 1922. At the time Theda Bara was under consideration for a film role, but the studio went into bankruptcy in 1923. One clip shows her looking at some dress material; in the other she is getting ready to shoot a scene with an actor in a tuxedo, and is talking to the cameraman. They are not, as previously misidentified, from *Lure of Ambition*, from which no footage is known to exist. It is possible that these clips were originally shown in the *Pack o' Fun* newsreels produced by *Film Fun Magazine*.

Theda (2007)

This is a 40-minute, black-and-white, silent film/video. It is both an homage to, and a send-up of, the acting styles of Theda Bara and other stars of the silent era. It was originally conceived as a multimedia installation in which Theda Bara mourns for all her lost films, with performance artist Starr reconstructing a prototypical Bara film. This film consists of three parts, "Prelude," "Act" and "Epilog." "Prelude" features Starr using an array of exaggerated facial expressions used by Bara and contemporaries to express emotion. "Act" features Starr as an innocent model posing for a sculptor, a plotline often used in Theda Bara films. Starr plays all the characters, including a cat burglar modeled on French silent star Musidora.

An advertising poster pictures Starr holding a séance as a Theda Bara–type vampire with kohl-rimmed eyes. Her headdress is obviously modeled after the half-veiled hat worn by Theda Bara's vicious vampire Princess Petrovich in *The Tiger Woman*.

Radio

Lux Radio Theater (1936)

On June 8, 1936, during the broadcast of *The Thin Man*, starring William Powell and Myrna Loy, Theda Bara chats briefly with MGM director Woody Van Dyke. Reminiscing about silent picture-making, she claims she would soon be in pictures again and was sorting through many offers.

For Men Only (1939)

At least one source claims that Theda Bara appears on this half-hour radio show in March 1939. The date would fit; the show ran on New York's WEAF station and on the NBC Red Network from 1938 to 1940.

Texaco Star Theater (1939)

Theda Bara appears on the program of November 9, 1939. Also featured are Ken Murray, Irene Ryan, and Kenny Baker. Murray and Bara talk about her career. After she says that she has kept most of her money, Murray hints that he would like her to be co-signer on a bank loan. Kenny Baker (in his "dumb" character days) asks a "dumb" question, and Irene Ryan asks to play Cleopatra after Bara turns down the chance. Murray mistakenly claims this is the first time Theda Bara has been heard on radio.

Theda Bara possibly also appears again with Ken Murray in early 1940 in a sketch called "Seven Ways to Be a Vamp."

TELEVISION

Theda Bara and William Fox (2001)

Directed and written by Lucien Preyale. Produced by Antoine Disle and Hoang Le Van. Music by Maximilian Mathevon. Edited by Ghislain Vidal. Released to television by Europe Images International, 2001.
Cast: Paul Bandey (Voice of William Fox), Heather Wilcox (Voice of Theda Bara), Patrick Floersheim (Narrator).

A dubbed-into-English version of the original French documentary *Theda Bara et William Fox*; part of the documentary series *Couples and Duos*.

THE STAGE

The Vamp (1955)

A musical comedy in two acts and 10 scenes, the show opened on Broadway on November 10, 1955, and closed after 60 performances on December 31, 1955. It starred Carol Channing as farm girl Flora Weems turned Hollywood vamp. In the cast were veteran actor Will Geer and movie strongman Steve Reeves. It had originally been titled *Delilah*; the title was changed so it would not be thought of as a Biblical show. It received generally poor reviews.

While the musical was being written, silent screen actress Nita Naldi (born Donna Dooley) acted as an advisor. Often portraying vamps onscreen, she was quoted as saying that Theda Bara had been her idol. Bara had died earlier that year.

Review

"It surely needs a lot of glueing together.... Carol Channing is pretty wonderful as usual, but the show needs a lot of whittling, especially the dance sequences which never seem to know when to stop." *Los Angeles Times*, October 27, 1955.

Theda Bara and the Frontier Rabbi (1993)

New York critics called this "a lively little charmer of a musical comedy" and "a thoroughly delightful new musical." A Chicago critic said it was "brash, goofy, and sweetly comic." This off-Broadway show featured the character Theda Bara in 1917. She does not want to be a vamp any more. She just wants to be the nice Jewish girl Theodosia Goodman again and to meet a nice rabbi to marry.

PODCASTS

You Must Remember This (2014)

#17, October 7, 2014: Theda Bara: Hollywood's First Sex Symbol
The writer and narrator Karina Longworth discusses how Bara's "Goth" look influenced the styles of performers decades later.
June 2015: [Can We Please Talk About Theda Bara: The Hollywood Silent-Era Sex Symbol (and Off-Screen Bookworm) Who Allegedly Inspired the Idea of the Vamp?] [Title constructed by the author from podcast content.]
This podcast series described itself as "about the secret and/or forgotten history of Hollywood's first century. Two grad students chat about popular culture, fandoms [*sic*], and general oddities."

Horror Heroes (2018)

February 24, 2018: Women in Horror Month: Theda Bara.

The Dead Ladies Show (2018)

#8, April 25, 2018: Theda Bara.
Podcast produced and presented by Susan Stone and Alix Berber.

Internet

Walk of Fame Wednesdays with Todd Pickering (2017)

May 24, 2017: Theda Bara.

An 11-episode internet series in which Todd Pickering discusses the celebrity named on one of the stars of the Walk of Fame in Hollywood. It ran in 2017 and 2018.

Humor

During the time of Theda Bara's stardom, newspapers and magazines were sources of both news and entertainment. Many of them had humor columns that printed poems, puns, and limericks. Those about Bara could be a bit ribald, and there was not infrequent wordplay on her surname and the word "bare." Some had more literary pretensions and were composed out of admiration.

It was inevitable that something would be written about Theda Bara and two other actresses who also made their careers vamping on the screen, Olga Petrova and Valeska Surratt. In 1917 a *Film Fun* columnist composed "Theda, Valeska, and Olga." It read, in part:

> "Valeska and Theda and Olga one day/Met, and they smiled together/
> Left home their daggers and went out to play/Out in the sweet June weather/....
> There wasn't a trace of those murderous frowns we're accustomed to see on the screen/
> From Theda, Valeska or Olga....
> But now we must haste to our arduous labors/As fully attired in a comb/
> We've four men to kill before six with our sabers/Then sadly departing for home/
> Did Theda, Valeska and Olga."

* * *

In another of *Film Fun*'s humor columns "Whim-Whams and Wheezers," Theda Bara was quoted as saying that "one may shape one's ends." The columnist inquired: "Does this mean each of us should be our own manicurist and chiropodist?"

* * *

"Poem to Theda: In Tribute to Your Art—

To Err Is Human, To Act It, Theda Bara, Is Divine"

"Theda, you make sinning far too beautiful/I cannot seem to loathe it as I should/
The outraged wife, so virtuous and dutiful/Quite surfeits me with too much good/
But you, no feeling vastly melancholy/For your abandon grips the heart of me/
I cannot scorn your victim for his folly/I only sit and wish that I were he."

* * *

For this poem, Mr. Oscar Williams of Brooklyn, New York, won the fifth prize of $1.00 in the "Favorites of the Screen" contest. His favorite was Theda Bara, for whom this was written.

"The pen must stop, for when the soul is full/No earthly thing can show the gratitude/
I feel for you who animate the dull/Monotony of life's long interlude/
You show to me the sordidness of dust/And when I see Earth's purity I know/
And tho' you use the evil seed of lust/I reap the harvest of the good you sow."

* * *

This is the last part of a poem called "To Keep Warm":
"To a movie I'll be going/Where I sit with warmth a-glowing/
While Miss Theda Bara acts!/Hotter than the hottest crater/
She could warm up the Equator/With her incandescent glow/
For the sands of the Sahara/Are as ice compared to Bara/
When she starts to vamp."

* * *

"Theda Bara has such an appeal/Bowls you o'er like an automobile/
I heard of a cove/Who went dippy with love/After watching one-eighth of a reel."

* * *

"Old Mother Hubbard, she went to the cupboard/To get herself some clothes/
And when she got there, Theda was Bara/So she gave them to her, I suppose."

* * *

"Theda Bara is forced to wear smoked glasses while reading, in order to prevent her burning
   eyes from searing the paper."

* * *

"Beware of those alluring orbs/They may prove your undoing/
Don't pick out Theda Bara/When you'd start to go a-wooing."

* * *

"There was a young lady named Theda/She had all the men so they'd feed her/
She's a regular scamp, a naughty, bad vamp/The directors all seem to need her."

* * *

"He told of his loves of the stage/Why they got him 'twasn't beauty or age/
Theda Bara I love/All the others above/With Geraldine Farrar compare her/
Geraldine, I admit she is Farrar/But Theda, oh Theda is Bara."

* * *

This was written for Theda Bara's 1919 role as *Kathleen Mavourneen*.
"It may be for years, and it may be forever/Before a colleen just like Theda we'll view/
So, by the same token we'll endeavor/To see her 'colleening'—it will be something new."

* * *

"A youth with a weak heart said 'Great Scott'/When the screen showed a gown that did not/
Cover half the wearer/Then saw Theda Bara/And gave up the ghost on the spot."

* * *

"There was an old maid quite narrow/ Who never would look at a sparrow/
Unless fully dressed when he came from his nest/I wish she could see Theda Bara."

* * *

"Your honor, cried Michael O'Hara/I want to divorce my wife Clara/
But why a divorce?/Said Hara because/She can't imitate Theda Bara."

* * *

"What's the name of Theda Bara's brother?": "Paul Bara" [Pallbearer].

* * *

From the *Photoplay* column "Tabloid Scenarios" came:
"Wife invites young sister for a visit/Husband's glad/
Sis makes eyes at husband/Really, things look bad/

Sister makes an awful scene/Puts a bullet through his bean/
What a lovely part for Theda Bara."

Fiction

Altman, Diana. *In Theda Bara's Tent.* Tapley Cove, ME: Tapley Cove Press, 2010.

DiGrazia, Christopher. *The Director's Cut (The Theda Bara Mysteries, v. 1).* Haverhill, MA?: Theodosia Tramp Publishing, 2015.

DiGrazia, Christopher. "Thirteen Moons: a Supernatural Story, Starring Theda Bara."

In this 2017 short story, Theda Bara acts as a kind of detective to track down one of her lost films.

Songs

Theda Bara's photograph graced many a sheet music cover, as did those of many other celebrities of the day. This was common, whether or not the song had anything to do with them.

In January 1917 the comic song "Since Sarah Saw Theda Bara" was published, written by Alex Gerber and Harry Jentes. It was described as a "Yiddisher character song." It ran, in part:

> "Every night Sarah Cohen would go/To a moving picture show/
> And there she saw upon the screen/Miss Theda Bara, the Vampire Queen/....
> Then Sarah said 'It's an easy game'/I think I can do just the same....
>
> Since Sarah saw Theda Bara/She became a holy terror/....
> She's a wera, wera dangerous girl."

Later the same year, another comic song was composed in conjunction with Theda Bara's blockbuster *Cleopatra*. Called "Cleopatra," it was composed by Alfred Bryan and Harry Tierney. It ran, in part:

> "You've heard of Cleopatra who lived down beside the Nile/
> She made a mark of Anthony [sic] and won him with her smile/
> They say she was Egyptian, but I've reason to construe/
> She was Jewish and Hawaiian, with a dash of Irish too/....
> Her mother's name was Cleo and her father's name was Pat/
> So they called her Cleopatra, now what do you think of that?"

Merchandizing

Louis Vuitton, maker of luxury luggage, called its "Theda" bag the shining star of its 2004 collection. It came crafted with "an abundance of artistically mixed textures, skins, and fabrics. One of them was an ecru toile trianon with golden ostrich trim." It was named for Bara's performance in *Cleopatra* and was purportedly a steal at $6,000.

For the price of 200 pounds, Giulia Barela Jewelry featured a Theda Bara pendant, handmade in Italy. It was described as "a golden pendant with stones and a tiny hand engraving of an ouroboros, an ancient symbol of eternity and renewal." It was 24-carat, gold-plated bronze with semi-precious stones: nacre (for white), onyx (for black), malachite (for green), and lapis (for blue, with golden sprinkles).

Etsy, specializing in handmade craft items, sells a wide range of items picturing Theda Bara. Besides the usual mugs, posters, hats, and T-shirts, they include: Glicee art prints, earrings, cutting boards, key racks, pill boxes, silver pendants, pencil cases, pillows, Peroxide cream, compacts, zipper bags, and necklaces.

Postage Stamp

On April 27, 1994, in San Francisco, the United States Post Office unveiled a set of 10 stamps designed by cartoonist Al Hirschfeld and honoring silent film stars. Theda Bara was included, along with such other luminaries as Harold Lloyd, Rudolph Valentino, Charlie Chaplin, Buster Keaton, and the Keystone Kops.

Paper Dolls

"Theda Bara Paper Dolls: Vamp of the Silent Screen," designed by Brenda Sneathen Mattox with fashion commentary by Randy Bryan Bigham, was issued by Paper Studio Press in 2017. Featuring both a photograph and a drawing of Bara as Cleopatra on the cover, it contains two cutout paper dolls, one full face and one side view, with 15 outfits, including Cleopatra.

Culinary

It was commonplace at one time for restaurants and delicatessens to name sandwiches after celebrities. The Theda Bara sandwich is so named because it was supposedly her own recipe. It was included in a 1916 *Photoplay* article by Lillian Blackstone called "Sandwiches a la Movie." The recipes were reprinted in the 1929 book *Photoplay's Cook Book: 150 Favorite Recipes of the Stars*. The ingredients of this spicy sandwich (fit for a vampire!) were minced ham, mayonnaise, sliced pimento, and sliced sweet pickles. These ingredients were layered on toasted bread and served warm.

Appendix: Film Censorship in the Mid-1910s

In 1915, the year Theda Bara became an instant star, the question of film censorship was still being actively, and often hotly, debated. Nearly every issue of industry-related magazines such as *Motography, Motion Picture News*, and *Moving Picture World* had articles reporting the establishment or the rejection of censorship boards in many U.S. cities and states from Maine to California.

The "tut-tutting" about immorality in films had begun back in the 1890s over the often racy (by Victorian standards) little film clips of this emerging form of popular entertainment. As the film industry began to be taken more seriously as a potent communication medium to the masses, possible standards for censorship also began to be taken more seriously.

The *American Motion Picture Directory* for 1914/1915 wrote: "The most perplexing question in connection with the motion picture industry is that relating to the censorship of films. The legal and ethical questions involved are many and complicated. All reputable film manufacturers recognize the necessity for some form of voluntary control or legal censorship, [but] who shall have jurisdiction covering censorship of films?"

In February 1915, debate began in Congress on a bill to introduce federal censorship. In that same year, the U.S. Supreme Court in its *Mutual Film Corp. v Industrial Commission of Ohio* decision ruled that film was not entitled to legal protection as being free speech. "Movies are business, plain and simple" said the Court, and like other businesses are subject to regulation. Movies were "not to be regarded as part of the press, or as organs of public opinion." Beginning in 1907, states and localities had begun passing their own censorship ordinances. Chicago was the first city to do so, and it would become one of the most notorious. Pennsylvania was the first state to follow suit in 1911.

In March 1909 the National Board of Censorship was established at the behest of New York City movie theater owners. It later morphed into the National Board of Review of Motion Pictures. This was no doubt a move undertaken to forestall worse problems, and possibly the owners thought they could control the Board. One goal was to avoid censorship being a tool of the police which is "an attribute of autocratic and paternalistic societies." Film producers called for any censorship to be done with their input because "censorship in itself is essentially destructive and coercive."

Given the questionable, often downright murderous, morality of many Theda Bara characters, and the costumes—or lack of them—that she wore, it was inevitable that censorship would be a factor. To the many critics of her portrayals including state and local censorship boards, religious bodies, women's groups, etc., she would often insist that she was providing the moral lesson: "Don't sin or you will end up like me."

The Fox studio, and occasionally Bara herself, would strike back with legal action. Nevertheless, censorship of Theda Bara films continued for almost the entirety of her career. It was the release of her fourth and seventh 1915 films, *The Devil's Daughter* and *Sin*, that really unleashed the tide of censorship. For instance, under the headline "Kansas Would Not Sin," the *Moving Picture World* of October 30, 1915, reported the uproar in that state over *Sin*. The reactions of city and state censors, and the appeals against their decisions, would be reported in detail. Such detail often included a listing of the specific cuts demanded.

Chicago's censorship apparatus certainly did have police involvement in the person of Bara bane-to-be Metellus Lucullus Cicero Funkhouser, always known as The Major. He had risen to be Second Deputy Superintendent of the Chicago Police Force in 1913. Among the duties of that position was "the supervision of the strict enforcement of all laws and ordinances pertaining to all matters affecting public morals." With that broad mandate and under his puritanical leadership, the Chicago Board of Censors proved to be one of the toughest on Theda Bara films.

Ironically, on the assumption that he would be appointed to his police position, he had averred in a March 21, 1913, interview with the *Chicago Tribune*: "I am going to mind my own business and let the other fellow mind his." The easily shockable Funkhouser quickly decided not to take his own advice and, often overriding the majority of his own censorship board, became more and more dictatorial.

It was said that he ordered the removal of a statue from the Chicago Art Institute. When it was deemed too heavy to move, it had to be draped. Finally, after much litigation against him, including by Fox Pictures, the Major was fired by the mayor in mid-1918. Funkhouser's decisions were so often challenged in court that he had cost Chicago a great deal of money, not to mention ridicule.

Other state censorship boards came into being—presumably coincidentally—about the time of Theda Bara's ascension. Some of the censorship demands on her films were so drastic, at least initially, that all of her scenes were literally ordered pared down or eliminated. Ordered deletions that were not quite that harsh would nevertheless in some cases render plots incomprehensible. For its own survival, the Fox studio was aggressive in using the courts to fight back with injunctions.

From 1914 to 1916, the states of Pennsylvania, Kansas, Ohio, and Maryland added their censorious voices to those of many localities within their states. In Massachusetts, the State Police acted as the censors in the following ways. There were increasing strictures on theater owners about what could not be shown on Sundays. Among the forbidden Sabbath depictions were dancing, cruelty to animals, commissions of crime, etc. Even though it was the Christian Sabbath, films on the life of Christ were banned if they showed the crucifixion. A film about Abraham Lincoln was banned because of the graphic battle scenes. The tagline "Banned in Boston" ultimately became a humorous trope.

Film censorship would remain a factor for the film industry throughout the era of the Hays Code and the powerful influence of the Catholic Church. A few film censorship boards were active, at least on paper, into the 1980s. More than 100 years after Theda Bara's Fox career ended, film historians would be only too happy to rediscover even heavily censored versions of her films. Even the snippets of film—however brief—removed by censorship would be welcomed. Perhaps Major Funkhouser was a secret film historian himself. It was rumored that he actually kept some of those censored snippets for his private titillation.

Bibliography

This bibliography provides a listing of selected resources. As a totality they should provide all necessary information about Theda Bara for the casual film buff and for the more serious researcher. Numerous encyclopedic works have entries about Bara; only a few of the most comprehensive are listed. A great many of the primary sources were used by the author in researching this book.

Books

Altomara, Rita. *Hollywood on the Palisades: A Filmography of Silent Features Made in Fort Lee, NJ, 1903–1927.* New York: Garland, 1983.
Bauer, Laura L.S. *Hollywood Heroines: The Most Influential Women in Film History.* Santa Barbara: Greenwood, 2019.
Bean, Jennifer. *Flickers of Desire: Movie Stars of the 1910s.* New Brunswick: Rutgers University Press, 2011.
Blue Book of the Screen. Hollywood: Blue Book of the Screen, 1924.
Blum, Daniel. *A Pictorial History of the Silent Screen.* New York: Putnam, 1953.
Bodeen, DeWitt. *From Hollywood: The Careers of 15 Great American Stars.* South Brunswick, NJ: Barnes, 1976.
Brode, Douglas, and Leah Deyneka. *Dracula's Daughters: The Female Vampire on Film.* Lanham, MD: Scarecrow Press, 2013.
Browne, Porter Emerson. *A Fool There Was.* New York: Grosset & Dunlap, 1911.
Brownlow, Kevin. *The Parade's Gone By.* New York: Knopf, 1968.
Craig, Joan, with Beverly Stout. *Theda Bara, My Mentor: Under the Wing of Hollywood's First Femme Fatale.* Jefferson, NC: McFarland, 2016.
Davis, Lon. *Silent Lives: 100 Biographies of the Silent Film Era.* Albany, GA: BearManor Media, 2008.
DeMille, William. *Hollywood Saga.* New York: Dutton, 1939.
Dye, Phillip. *Lost Cleopatra: A Tale of Ancient Hollywood.* Orlando: BearManor Media, 2020.
Eyman, Scott. *20th Century Fox: Darryl F. Zanuck and the Creation of the Modern Film Studio.* Philadelphia: Running Press, 2021.
Fox Film Corporation. *Catalogue of the Stories and Plays Owned by Fox Film Corporation.* Los Angeles: Times-Mirror Press, 1931.
Franklin, Joe. *Classics of the Silent Screen.* New York: Citadel, 1960.
Geltzer, Jeremy. *Dirty Words and Filthy Pictures: Film and the First Amendment.* Austin: University of Texas Press, 2015.
Genini, Ronald. *Theda Bara: A Biography of the Silent Film Vamp, with a Filmography.* Jefferson, NC: McFarland, 1996.
Golden, Eve. *Vamp: The Rise and Fall of Theda Bara.* Lanham, MD: Vestal Press, 1996.
Graham, Tomas. *Silent Films in St. Augustine.* Gainesville: University Press of Florida, 2017.
Griffith, Richard. *The Movie Stars.* New York: Doubleday, 1970.
Grossman, Julie. *The Femme Fatale.* New Brunswick: Rutgers University Press, 2021.
Halliwell, Leslie. *The Filmgoer's Companion.* New York: Hill & Wang; Scribner's, 1966.
Halsey, Forrest. *The Stain.* Chicago: F.G. Browne and Co., 1913.
Higashi, Sumiko. *Virgins, Vamps and Flappers: The American Silent Movie Heroine.* Montreal: Eden Press Women's Publications, 1978.
Hoberman, J., and Jeffrey Shandler. *Entertaining America: Jews, Movies, and Broadcasting.* Princeton: Princeton University Press, 2003.
Hopper, Hedda. *From Under My Hat.* New York: Doubleday, 1952.
International Dictionary of Films and Filmmakers. Chicago: St. James, 1986.

Katz, Ephraim. *The Film Encyclopedia*. New York: Crowell; Harper, 1979.
Keesey, Pam. *Vamps: An Illustrated History of the Femme Fatale*. San Francisco: Cleis, 1997.
Krefft, Vanda. *The Man Who Made the Movies: The Meteoric Rise and Tragic Fall of William Fox*. New York: Harper, 2017.
Liebman, Roy. *Silent Film Performers: An Annotated Bibliography of Published, Unpublished and Archival Sources for Over 350 Actors and Actresses*. Jefferson, NC: McFarland, 1996.
MacCann, Richard D. *The Stars Appear*. Metuchen, NJ: Scarecrow, 1992.
Mainon, Dominique, and James Ursini. *Femme Fatale: Cinema's Most Lethal Ladies*. New York: Limelight, 2009.
Manvell, Roger. *Love Goddesses of the Movies*. New York: Crescent Books, 1976.
Medoff, Rafael, editor. *Great Lives from History: Jewish Americans*. Pasadena, CA: Salem Press, 2011.
Menefee, David. *The First Female Stars: Women of the Silent Era*. Santa Barbara: ABC-CLIO, 2004.
Molnar, Ferenc. *The Devil: A Tragedy of the Heart and Conscience*. Novelized by Joseph O'Brien. New York: Grosset & Dunlap, 1908.
Mordden, Ethan. *Movie Star: A Look at the Women Who Made Hollywood*. New York: St. Martin's, 1983.
Motion Picture Studio Directory and Trade Annual. New York: Motion Picture News.
Parish, James R. *The Fox Girls*. New Rochelle, NY: Arlington House, 1972.
Parish, James Robert. *The Hollywood Death Book: From Theda Bara to Rudolph Valentino*. Las Vegas: Pioneer Books, 1992.
_____. *Hollywood Divas: The Good, the Bad, and the Fabulous*. Chicago: Contemporary Books, 2003.
Parsons, Louella. *The Gay Illiterate*. New York: Doubleday, Doran, 1944.
Quinlan, David. *Wicked Women of the Screen*. New York: St. Martin's, 1988.
Ragan, David. *Who's Who in Hollywood*. New York: Facts on File, 1992.
Ramsaye, Terry. *A Million and One Nights: A History of the Motion Picture*. New York: Simon & Schuster, 1926.
Robson, E.E., and M.M. Robson. The *Film Answers Back: An Historical Appreciation of the Cinema*. London: J. Lane, 1939.
Schickel, Richard, and Allen Hurlburt. *The Stars*. New York: Bonanza Books, 1962.
Slide, Anthony. *The Idols of Silence*. South Brunswick, NJ: Barnes, 1976.
Smith, Michael Glover, and Adam Selzer. *Flickering Empire: How Chicago Invented the U.S. Film Industry*. New York: Wallflower Press, 2015.
Solomon, Aubrey. *The Fox Film Corporation, 1915–1935: A History*. Jefferson, NC: McFarland, 2011.
Stuart, Ray. *Immortals of the Screen*. Los Angeles: Sherbourne, 1965.
Taylor, Deems, Marcelene Peterson, and Bryant Hale. *A Pictorial History of the Movies*. New York: Simon & Schuster, 1943.
Thomson, David. *A Biographical Dictionary of Film*. New York: William Morrow; Knopf, 1976–1994.
_____. *The New Biographical Dictionary of Film*. New York: Knopf, 2002.
Truitt, Evelyn Mack. *Who Was Who on Screen*. New York: Bowker, 1974–1983.
Van Wyck, Caroline. *Photoplay's Cook Book: 150 Favorite Recipes of the Stars*. Chicago: Photoplay Publishing Co., W.F. Hall, 1929.
Webb, Graham. *Encyclopedia of American Short Films, 1926–1954*. Jefferson, NC: McFarland, 2020.
Zierold, Norman. *Sex Goddesses of the Silent Screen*. Chicago: Regnery, 1973.

Theses

Hain, Mark Andrew. *Revamped: Theda Bara, Cultural Memory, and the Repurposing of Star Image*. Ph.D, Indiana University, 2015.
Hamilton, Gayla Jamison. *Theda Bara and the Vamp Phenomenon, 1915–1920*. M.A., University of Georgia, 1972.
Raines, Carmelina. *The Ultimate Cleopatra: American Film's Conceptualization of Cleopatra*. M.A, University of Wyoming, 1994.

Manuscript

Bara, Theda. [Memoir: *What Women Never Tell*]. Unpublished typescript, early 1920s?

Periodicals/Newspapers

American Magazine
Anglo-Indian Fortnightly
Atlanta Constitution
Atlanta Georgian
Boxoffice
Broadcasting-Telecasting

Bibliography

Brooklyn Eagle
Camera!
Chicago Daily News
Chicago Post
Chicago Tribune/Chicago Daily Tribune
Cincinnati Post
Cinema (Beverly Hills)
Classic Film Collector
Classic Images
Cleveland Leader
Cleveland Plain Dealer
Close Up
Columbus Journal
Corsicana Sun
Cue
Daily Beast
Detroit Free Press
Detroit Journal
Detroit News
Exhibitors Herald
Exhibitors Trade Review
Film Daily
Film Fun
Film Mercury
Films in Review
Forum
Green Book
Harper's Bazaar
Hollywood
Hollywood Filmograph
Hollywood Reporter
Horizon
Houston Chronicle
Independent Exhibitors Film Bulletin
Journal of the Society of Motion Picture Engineers
Life
Los Angeles Examiner
Los Angeles Record
Los Angeles Times/Los Angeles Daily Times
Los Angeles Tribune
Louisville Post
Modern Screen
Motion Picture Classic
Motion Picture Herald
Motion Picture Magazine
Motion Picture Mail
Motion Picture News
Motion Picture Review
Motion Picture Story Magazine
Motography
Moving Picture World
Nassau Daily Review
National Board of Review Magazine
New Movie Magazine
New York Clipper
New York Mail
New York Mirror
New York Review
New York Telegraph
New York Times
New York Tribune
New Yorker
Newsweek
Philadelphia Public Ledger
Philadelphia Telegraph
Photo-Play Journal
Photo-Play World
Photodramatist
Photoplay
Picture and the Picturegoer
Picture-Play Magazine
Picture Show
Reel Life
San Francisco Chronicle
Screen Weekly
Screenland
Shadowland
Silver Screen
Spectator
Sponsor
Theatre
Time
TV Radio Mirror
Universal Weekly
Variety
Washington News
Wheeling News
Wid's Daily
Wid's Weekly
Wired
World Film and Television Progress
Writer's Monthly

Online Resources

CB: Cinephilia and Beyond
Digiguide.tv
Filmthreat.com
ibdb.com
imdb.com
kamera.co.uk.
Letterboxd.com
Lostcleopatra.com
silentsaregolden.com
University Press Scholarship Online
Videolibrarian.com
Youtube.com

Blogs

The Dead Ladies Show
Messy Nessy Chic
You Must Remember This

Index

Acord, Art 104
Allison, May 34
Anger, Kenneth 179
Arbuckle, Roscoe "Fatty" 131
Arena (series) 184

Bara, Bernard *see* Goodman, Bernard
Bara, Esther (Lori) *see* Goodman, Esther
Bara, Marque *see* Goodman, Marque
Bara, Pauline *see* Goodman, Pauline
Bayne, Beverly 82
Belasco, David 155
Bella Donna 24, 192–193
Belle Russe 155–158
Bergen, Thurlow 30, 158
Blackton, J. Stuart 172
Blue Flame 19, 23, 187–191
Brabin, Charles 5, 20, 22, 26, 150
Bracken, Bertram 70
Brenon, Herbert 37, 39, 49, 51
Breuil, Betta 134
Browne, Porter Emerson 31
Burne-Jones, Philip 31
Bushman, Francis X. 82

Camille 98–101
Campbell, Bartley 58
Carmen 53–58
Casting Couch 180–181
Chadwick Pictures 161
Chaplin, Charles 26, 55
Claxton, Kate 50
Clemenceau Case 40–43
Cleopatra 101–110
Cook 131
Creel, George 113

D'Annunzio, Gabriele 44
Darling of Paris 88–90
Daughter of Salome 22
Davidson, William B. 147
Davis, Will S. 61
Day with Theda Bara 20
Dead Ladies Show 197
Decoppet, Pauline *see* Goodman, Pauline
Destruction 60–62
Devil 9, 186–187
Devil's Daughter 43–45
Director's Cut 200
Du Barry 114–117
Dumas fils, Alexandre 41

East Lynne 1, 4, 73–76
Edwards, J. Gordon 19, 58, 147

Empire of the Censors 181–182
Eternal Sapho 69–73

Farnum, Marshall 46
Farrar, Geraldine 54, 56–57, 107
Fata Morgana 24, 192
Film Parade 171–172
Flicker Flashbacks, Series 5, no. 2 174–175
Fool There Was 30–37
For Men Only 196
Forbidden Path 117–120
Ford 50th Anniversary Show 175–176
Forty-Five Minutes from Broadway 170–171
Fragments 183–184
Funkhouser, "Major" 105, 113, 125, 204

Galley Slave 58–60
Gardner, Helen 9, 107
Gold and the Woman 66–69
Goldfrap, John 10, 11
Goodman, Bernard 8, 24
Goodman, Esther (Lori) 7, 13, 19, 20, 26
Goodman, Marque 7, 25
Goodman, Pauline 8, 26
Great Vampire 25

Haggard, H. Rider 96
Hall, Thurston 104
Halsey, William Forrest 28
Heart and Soul 95–98
Her Double Life 79–81
Her Greatest Love 93–95
Hilliard, Harry 66, 82
Hollywood 179–180
Hollywood and the Stars 177–178
Hollywood Babylon 178–179
Hollywood Sex Symbols 180
Hollywood: The Golden Years 176–177
Hollywood Walk of Fame 5
Hopkins, George James "Neje" 104, 137, 147
Horror Heroes 197

In Theda Bara's Tent 200

Johnson, Adrian 82
Jose, Edward 10, 30, 34
Just Like John 187

Kaelred, Katherine 31
Kathleen Mavourneen 150–155
Keaton, Buster 131
Kipling, Rudyard 31, 147
Kreutzer Sonata 37–40

Index

Lady Audley's Secret 46–48
LaRue, Fontine 19
Laurel and Hardy 167, 170
Lawrence, Edmund 158
Lee Jane 41, 59, 79, 82
Lee, Katherine 41, 79, 82
Leiber, Fritz 104
Light 139–141
Linden, Einar 71, 82
Lost Cleopatra 2, 102, 185
Love Goddesses 178
Lure of Ambition 158–160

Madam Satan 22
Madame Du Barry see Du Barry
Madame Mystery 166–169
Many Faces of Cleopatra 183
McConville, Bernard 111
Meeting Theda Bara 194–195
Mix, Tom 138
Movies March On (March of Time) 174
Murillo, Mary 66, 86

Nazimova, Alla 138

Oland, Warner 51
O'Neil, Nance 38–39
O'Neil, Sally 151
Ordynski, Richard 111
Ouida (Marie Louise de la Ramee) 76, 93

Parsons, Louella 14, 121
Pearson, Virginia 30
Pickford, Mary 26
Powell, Frank 1, 10, 28, 31, 43

Quaker Girl 187

Red Devil 192
Restless Wives 22
Romeo and Juliet 81–86
Roscoe, Albert (Alan) 98
Rose of Blood 110–114
Russia Not Today 185
Ryan, Sam 30

Salome 2, 3, 127–134
Scarborough, George 124
Screen Snapshots, Series 3, no. 19 165–166
Screen Snapshots, Series 16, no. 11 172–173
Screen Snapshots, Series 17, no. 1 173
Selig, Al 10, 19
Selznick, David O. 20

Serpent 62–66
Serpent of the Neva 24, 192
Sex, Censorship and the Silver Screen 183
She-Devil 136–139
Sheldon, E. Lloyd 117
Sin 51–53
Siren's Song 141–146
Sothern, Jean 49
Soul of Buddha 120–124
Stain 9, 28–30
Starr 91
Stars of Yesterday 171

Texaco Star Theater 196
Theda 195
Theda Bara and the Frontier Rabbi 197
Theda Bara and the Vamp Phenomenon 1
Theda Bara and William Fox 196
Theda Bara Productions 22
Thirteen Moons 200
Tiger Woman 90–93
"Tinee, Mae" 93
Two Orphans 48–51

Unchastened Woman 23, 160–164
Under the Yoke 124–127
Under Two Flags 76–79

Vamp (musical) 25, 196
Vamp (play) 2
Vampire 31, 43
Vixen 86–88

Walk of Fame Wednesdays 198
Wallace, Richard 166
Walsh, George 62–63, 66
Walsh, Raoul 54
What Women Never Tell 6, 27, 162
When a Woman Sins 134–136
When Men Desire 141–144
Why Be Good 182–183
Wilde, Oscar 128
Woman There Was 146–150
Woman with the Hungry Eyes 2, 182
Wood, Mrs. Henry 73
Woodruff, Eleanor 30
Woods, Al H. 187

You Must Remember This 197
Young, James 160

Zola, Emile 61

www.ingramcontent.com/pod-product-compliance
Lightning Source LLC
Chambersburg PA
CBHW060343010526
44117CB00017B/2943